CW01431686

# NORRŒNA

## ANGLO-SAXON CLASSICS

...for the indestructibleness of its fame.

...WELL, M.A., F.S.A.

...SON, LL.D., Ph.D.

...OHL, Ph.D.

## VOL. I

PUBLISHED BY THE

## ...RRŒNA SOCIETY

...AGEN STOCKHOLM BERLIN NEW YORK

# THE NINE BOOKS

OF

## THE DANISH HISTORY

OF

# Saxo Grammaticus

IN TWO VOLUMES

TRANSLATED BY

## OLIVER ELTON, B.A.

SOMETIME SCHOLAR OF CORPUS CHRISTI COLLEGE, OXFORD, AND LECTURER
ON ENGLISH LITERATURE AT THE OWENS COLLEGE (VICTORIA
UNIVERSITY), MANCHESTER

*WITH SOME CONSIDERATIONS ON SAXO'S SOURCES,*
*HISTORICAL METHODS, AND FOLK-LORE*

BY

### FREDERICK YORK POWELL, M.A., F.S.A.

STUDENT OF CHRIST CHURCH, OXFORD

---

HON. RASMUS B. ANDERSON, LL.D., Ph.D.
EDITOR IN CHIEF

J. W. BUEL, Ph.D.
MANAGING EDITOR

VOL. I

PUBLISHED BY THE

## NORRŒNA SOCIETY

LONDON  COPENHAGEN  STOCKHOLM  BERLIN  NEW YORK

# TABLE OF CONTENTS.

## SAXO GRAMMATICUS.

## VOL. I.

General Introduction to Norrœna Library, by
Hon. Rasmus B. Anderson.

Introduction to Saxo Grammaticus, by Frederick Y. Powell.

# LIST OF PHOTOGRAVURES.

## VOL. I.

# Services Rendered by the
# Scandinavians to the World and to America.

By RASMUS B. ANDERSON, LL.D.,

Ex-United States Minister to Denmark.

Author of "Norse Mythology," "America Not Discovered
by Columbus," and other Works.

SCANDINAVIANS is a term used to designate the inhabitants of Norway, Sweden, Denmark and Iceland. In the early centuries, that is, during the so-called Viking age, they are usually treated as one people under the name of Northmen or Norsemen, but as we proceed into the full daylight of history, it gradually becomes customary to discuss the Scandinavians separately, as Norwegians, Swedes, Danes and Icelanders. Thus, while we designate the old asa-faith of the Scandinavians as Norse mythology, we are expected to know to which of the four countries a modern celebrity or institution belongs. It is necessary to say the Swedish singer Jenny Lind, the Norwegian violinist Ole Bull, the Danish story-teller Hans Christian Andersen, and the Icelandic lexicographer Gudbrand Vigfusson.

The total number of Scandinavians, including those who have emigrated during this century, is probably less than eleven millions: 4,775,000 in Sweden, 2,300,000 (including 70,000 Icelanders) in Denmark, 2,300,000 in Norway, and, say, 2,000,000 in America, the British colonies and in other countries.

But though they be few in number, they inherit considerable renown. Though confined to the more or less inhospita-

ble northwest corner of Europe, they have rendered the world some services the memory of which will not willingly be allowed to perish. In Iceland they have preserved and still speak one of the oldest of the Teutonic languages, a monument of the Viking age, which still furnishes the means of illustrating many of the social features of those remote times, and is held in deserved veneration by all the great philologists of our day. In the Icelandic tongue we have a group of sagas, a literature which in many respects is unique, and which sheds a flood of light upon the customs and manners of the dark centuries of the middle age. The Icelandic sagas tell us not only of what happened in Scandinavia, but they also describe conditions and events in England, France, Russia and elsewhere. We are indebted to the Scandinavians for the Eddas, for Saxo Grammaticus and for various other sources of information in regard to the grand and beautiful mythology of our ancestors. Our knowledge of the old Teutonic religion would have been very scanty indeed, had not the faithful old Norsemen given us a record of it on parchment. The grand mythological system conceived and developed by the poetic and imaginative childhood of the Scandinavians commands the attention of the scholars of all lands, and as we enter the solemn halls and palaces of the old Norse gods and goddesses, where all is cordiality and purity, we find there perfectly reflected the wild and tumultuous conflict of the robust northern climate and scenery, strong, rustic pictures, full of earnest and deep thought, awe-inspiring and wonderful. We find in the Eddas of Iceland that simple and martial religion which inspired the early Scandinavians and developed them like a tree full of vigor extending long branches over all Europe. We find that simple and martial religion, which gave the Scandinavians that restless, unconquerable spirit, apt to take fire at the very mention of subjection or restraint, that religion by which instruments were forged to break the fetters forged by the Roman Cæsars, to destroy tyrants and slaves, and to teach the world that nature, having made all men and women free and equal, no other reason but their mutual happiness could be assigned for their government. We will find that

simple and martial religion, which was cherished by those vast multitudes, which, as Milton says, the populous North

"* * * poured from her frozen loins to pass
Rhene or the Danaw, when her barbarous sons
Came like a deluge on the South and spread
Beneath Gibraltar and the Libyan sands."

During the viking age we find the Scandinavians everywhere. They came in large swarms to France, England and Spain. During the crusades they led the van of the chivalry of Europe in rescuing the Holy Sepulchre; they passed between the pillars of Hercules, devastated the classic fields of Greece and penetrated the walls of Constantinople. Straying far into the East, we find them laying the foundations of the Russian Empire, and swinging their two-edged battle-axes in the streets of Constantinople, where they served as captains of the Greek Emperor's body-guard, and the chief support of his tottering throne. They ventured out upon the surging main and discovered Iceland, Greenland and North America, thus becoming the discoverers, not only of America, but also of pelagic navigation. The Vikings were the first navigators to venture out of sight of land. And everywhere they scattered the seeds of liberty, independence and culture. They brought to France that germ of liberty that was planted in the soil of Normandy, where the Normans adopted the French tongue and were the first to produce and spread abroad a vernacular literature, that germ of liberty which, when brought to England, budded in the Magna Charta and Bill of Rights, and which in course of time was carried in the Mayflower to America, where it developed full-blown flowers in our Declaration of Independence and the ripest fruit in the Constitution of the United States.

The Scandinavians in Denmark, Sweden, Norway and Iceland gave a hearty reception to the Gospel and preserved its teaching for many centuries free from pagan influence. In the Swedish ruler Gustavus Adolphus, protestantism found one of its most efficient and valiant defenders. The Scandinavians are still faithful to the banner of pro-

iii

testantism. They are distinguished for the earnestness of
their religious worship, for their ardent advocacy of the
cause of civil and religious liberty and for the well-nigh total
absence of great crimes. Wherever they settle in the world,
we find them associated with the most loyal and law-abiding
citizens, giving their best energies to culture, law and order.
Proofs of this statement are abundant both in Russia, Normandy and England, and in their more recent settlements in
the various western states of America.

As stated, they have enriched the world with a whole class
of literature, which is held in deserved respect. Is not
Beowulf, the most important surviving monument of Anglo-
Saxon poetry, a Swedish and Danish poem, and was it not
first published from the British Museum manuscript by the
great Danish scholar, G. J. Thorkelin? And does not the
world owe to Denmark and her traditions Hamlet, the
greatest drama of the immortal Shakespeare? In Saxo
Hamlet is found as the son of the viceroy Horvendel, in
Jutland, and of Gerude, who was the daughter of Rerek,
King at Leire in Seland, Denmark.

The Scandinavians present to all oppressed nationalities
the gratifying example of a people who, being true to their
countries and to the traditions handed down from the mists
of ages in the far past, have vindicated for themselves
against many opposing and oppressing powers and in the
midst of many obstacles and vicissitudes, their distinctive
rights and liberties. A mere glance at the history of Scandinavia is sufficient to reveal to the student many events and
the names of many individuals of far-reaching importance.

I have already enumerated a few of the many services rendered to the world by the Scandinavians of antiquity, and in
this connection I may be permitted to mention a few Scandinavians who in more recent times have achieved world-
wide fame. I do this with a view of demonstrating that the
Scandinavians, though comparatively few in number, easily
rank with the most prominent nations in the domains of
science, art and literature. There is the great Danish as-
tronomer Tycho Brahe, one of the most marked individuals
of the 16th century. From his Uranienborg observatory his

fame spread throughout Europe and the little island near Elsinore became the trysting place of savants from all lands. Even kings and princes did not think it beneath their dignity to make pilgrimages to the Isle of Hveen. Brahe made his name immortal through his services to astronomy. For thirty years he made regular and careful observations in regard to the movements of the planets, and it was only on the foundation of his vast preliminary labors, which in accuracy surpassed all that practical astronomy had previously achieved, that Keppler was able to produce his celebrated theories and laws. With perfect justice, it has been said, that Tycho Brahe made the observations, that Keppler discovered the law, and that Newton conceived the nature of the law.

Geology is at the present time a most highly developed science, but its devotees should not forget that the world's first geologist was the Dane Niels Stensen, who was born in 1638. He was not only the most celebrated anatomist of his time, but he also laid the foundation of the science of geognosy and geology by studying the mountain formations and examining the fossils of Italy, and the result of his investigations were embodied in his *"De Solido intra solidum naturaliter contento dissertationis prodromus,"* a work which may rightly be regarded as the corner stone of geological science.

Archæology serves as a magnificent telescope by which we are able to contemplate social conditions far beyond the ken of ordinary historical knowledge and this valuable science was born and cradled in Denmark, where the renowned Christian Thomsen laid the foundation of the systematic study of all the weapons, implements and ornaments gathered from pre-historic times.

Then we have the science called comparative philology. Where did it begin? Who unravelled its first complicated threads? The answer comes from every philologist in the world. It shed its first rays in Denmark, and there Rasmus Rask discovered those laws and principles upon which the comparative study of languages is built. Rask found the laws and they were used as the corner stone of that beautiful

v

and symmetrical pyramid which has since been constructed by the brothers Grimm, by Max Müller, by our own W. D. Whitney and many other famous linguists, to take the place of that tower of Babel, which the old linguistic students had built with their clumsy hands and poor materials. In this connection I may also mention the Dane J. N. Madvig, the greatest Latin scholar of the last century, a scholar who created a new epoch in the study of the old texts. The scholars of all lands accept his views as final.

He who would write the history of electricity must study the life of the great Dane, H. C. Oersted. His discovery in 1820 of electro-magnetism—the identity of electricity and magnetism— which he not only discovered, but demonstrated incontestably, placed him at once in the highest rank of physical philosophers and has led the way to all the wonders of this subtle force. He supplied the knowledge by which Morse was enabled to build the first telegraph line, and he is in fact the predecessor of Morse, Edison, Tesla, Marconi and of that brilliant galaxy of men, who have astonished the world by all their wonderful inventions in the domain of electricity.

Suppose we cross the sound and enter the territory of Sweden. There we at once discover the polar star in the science of botany in the name of Carl von Linné. In his twenty-fourth year he established the celebrated sexual system in plants, whereby the chaos of the botanical world was reduced to order and a faithful study of it was made possible. His extensive investigations rightly secured for him the title of the king of botanists. As Linné became the father of botany, so another Swede, Carl Scheele, might be called the founder of the present system of chemistry. He is one of the greatest ornaments of science and the world is indebted to him for the discovery of many new elementary principles· and valuable chemical combinations now in general use.

Hardly less conspicuous is J. J. Berzelius, the contemporary of Scheele. Like the latter Berzelius published a number of works, the most of which contained capital discoveries, either the explanation of a phenomenon or reaction pre-

viously misunderstood, or the description of some new element or compound. The discoveries made by Scheele and Berzelius in the domain of chemistry are most important, but too numerous to mention in this paper. Berzelius also devoted himself to mineralogy and published his "Treatise on the Blow Pipe," and he set up for himself a regularly graduated system of minerals, the value of which was felt to be so great that the Royal Society of London voted him its gold medal for it. Scheele unfortunately died at only 54 years of age, but his works, many of which are regarded as the most important in the whole field of chemical literature, appeared after his death in French, German and Latin editions. In Linné, Scheele, Berzelius and in the naturalist and archæologist, Sven Nilsson, Sweden touched the zenith of scientific fame.

Before leaving Sweden, we may be permitted to mention N. A. E. Nordenskjold, who is famous for his various Arctic expeditions, and who, with his Vega accomplished the work so often attempted by many brave explorers, the discovery and navigation of a northeast passage by sea from North Cape, the extreme northwest point of Europe, to the extreme notheastern point of Asia,—that is a passage by sea from the north Atlantic ocean eastward to the north Pacific ocean. Nordenskjold has the honor of being the first man to double Cape Cheljuskin, the northern point of the continent, and by his voyage he made many new and valuable additions to our geographical knowledge of the Arctic regions. His signal triumph well deserves the most distinguished marks of honor showered upon him during his homeward journey.

Entering the domain of Norway, we at once meet the brilliant name of the immortal mathemetician, Henrik Abel. I have observed that the great mathemeticians of our time can scarcely open their mouths wide enough when they want to say *A*—bel. He unfortunately died too young, but his great fame keeps on increasing. He is justly designated as one of the greatest geniuses ever born in the domain of exact science, and the solution of problems made by the

youthful Norwegian everywhere provokes the greatest wonder and admiration. In some of his problems there is incor-
porated work for a lifetime. Though but twenty-seven
years old at his death, he had gained wide distinction by his
discoveries in the theory of elliptic functions and was highly
eulogized by Legendre.

Norway has also produced the distinguished Arctic explorer, Frithiof Nansen, who in 1888, with three other brave
Norwegians and two Lapps, crossed Greenland from the east
to the west on about the 65th degree north latitude. This
crossing was done on skees, a kind of long snow shoes, and
with small sleds, on which they carried their provisions. An
account of this first and only crossing of Greenland was
published by the explorer, and it is universally conceded that
he not only performed a feat of the greatest courage and
bravery, but that he also made important contributions to
our fund of geographical and scientific knowledge. Nansen
has also presented a new plan for reaching the great goal of
all Artic explorers, the North pole, by following the current
supposed to flow from the New Siberian islands across or
near the North pole to the sea between Spitzbergen and east
Greenland. On his memorable voyage he did not quite reach
the goal of his ambition, but he touched the North Pole of
Norse courage and adventure.

Ask the Icelanders whether they have produced any name
of world-wide reputation, and that whole little island will
unite in shouting Albert Thorwaldsen, and the mountains
of Iceland will re-echo "Thorwaldsen." He was descended
from Snorre Thorfinson, who was born in America (Vinland) in the year 1008, and though born of humble parents,
he succeeded in developing his talents and became the greatest sculptor of modern times.

I have enumerated only a few of the many services ren-
dered to the world by the Scandinavians. I could easily
have added a discussion of such brilliant names as Hans
Christian Andersen, Grundtvig, Tegnér, Bellman, Rydberg,
Holberg Wergeland, Bjornson, Ibsen, Snorre Sturleson,
Gudbrand Vigfusson, Gade, Hartmann, Grieg, Svendson,

Sinding, Ole Bull, Jenny Lind, and many others, but enough has been said on this point to demonstrate the fact that the Scandinavians are the peers of any other race in every field of intellectual effort. Considering their numerical strength, they have contributed their full share toward the enlightenment and progress of the world.

The brilliant services which I have cited, and which are universally admitted, have been rendered to the world generally, but I shall now demonstrate by indisputable facts, that the Scandinavians have an honorable place in the annals of America. America is indebted to them for special services. The civilized history of America begins with the Norsemen. Look at your map and you will find that Greenland and a part of Iceland belongs to the western hemisphere. Iceland became the hinge upon which the door swings which opened America to Europe. It was the occupation of Iceland by the Norsemen in the year 874, and the frequent voyages between this island and Norway that led to the discovery and settlement, first of Greenland and then of America, and it is due to the culture and fine historical taste of the old Icelanders that carefully prepared records of the Norse voyages were kept, first to teach pelagic navigation to Columbus and afterwards to solve for us the mysteries concerning the first discovery of this continent. In this connection I want to repeat that the old republican vikings fully understood the importance of studying the art of ship-building and navigation. They knew how to measure time by the stars and how to calculate the course of the sun and moon. They were themselves pioneers in venturing out upon the high seas, and taught the rest of the world to navigate the ocean. Every scrap of written history sustains me, when I say with all the emphasis I can put into so many words, that the other peoples of Europe were limited in their nautical knowledge to coast navigation. The Norse vikings, who crossed the stormy North Sea and found their way to Great Britain, to the Orkneys, the Fareys and to Iceland, and all those heroes who found their way to Greenland and Vinland taught the world pelagic navigation. They demonstrated the possibility of venturing out of sight of land and in this sense, if in

no other, we may with perfect propriety assert that the Norsemen taught Columbus how to cross the Atlantic ocean. Into every history of the world I would put this sentence: The navigation of the ocean was discovered by the old Norsemen.

A most admirable introduction of the honorable place held by the Scandinavians in the annals of America is the brilliant fact in the world's history and the lustrous page in the annals of the Scandinavians, that the Norsemen anticipated by five centuries Christopher Columbus, and Amerigo Vespucci, and that the New World was discovered by Leif Erikson in the year 1000; for the finding of America is the most prominent fact in the history of maritime discovery and has been fraught with the most important consequences to the world at large from that time to the present. About the year 860 the Norsemen discovered Iceland and soon afterwards (in 874) they established upon this island a republic which flourished for 400 years. Greenland was seen for the first time in 876 by Gunnbjörn Ulfsson from Norway. About a century later, in the year 984, Erik the Red resolved to go in search of the land in the West, which Gunnbjörn, as well as others later, had seen. He sailed from Iceland and found the land as he had expected and remained there exploring the country for two years. At the end of this period he returned to Iceland, giving the newly-discovered country the name of Greenland, in order as he said, to attract settlers, who would be favorably impressed with so pleasing a name. Thus, as Greenland belongs geographically wholly to America, it will be seen that Erik the Red was the first white man to boom American real estate. And he did it successfully. Many Norsemen emigrated to Greenland, and a flourishing colony, with Gardar for its capital, and Erik the Red as its first ruler, was established, which in the year 1261 became subject to the crown of Norway. We have a list of seventeen bishops who served in Greenland. This is the first settlement of Europeans in the New World. Erik the Red and his followers were not Christians when they settled in Greenland, but worshippers of Odin and Thor, though they relied chiefly on their own might and strength.

Christianity was introduced among them about the year 1000, though Erik the Red continued to adhere to the religion of his fathers to his dying day.

The first white man whose eyes beheld any part of the American continent was the Norseman Bjarne Herjulfson in the year 986. The first white man who, to our certain knowledge, planted his feet on the soil of the American continent, was Leif Erikson, the son of Erik the Red, in the year 1000. The first white man and the first Christian, who was buried beneath American sod, was Leif's brother Thorwald in the year 1002. The first white man, who founded a settlement within the limits of the present United States, was Thorfin Karlsefne in the year 1007. The first white woman, who came to Vinland, was Thorfin's talented and enterprising wife, Gudrid. In the year 1008 she gave birth to a son in Vinland. The boy was called Snorre, and he was the first person of European descent to see the light of day in the new world. From the accounts of these voyages and settlements we get our first knowledge and descriptions of the aborigines of America. In 1012 Helge and Finnboge, with the woman Freydis, made a voyage to Vinland. In 1112 Erik Upse settled as bishop in Greenland, and in 1121 this same bishop went on a missionary journey from Greenland to Vinland. This is the first visit of a Christian minister to the American continent. The last of these interesting voyages before the re-discovery of America by Columbus was in the year 1347, when a Greenland ship with a crew of eighteen men came from Nova Scotia (Markland) to Stromfjord in Iceland. Thus it appears that the Vinland voyages extended over a period of about 450 years and to within 144 years of the re-discovery in 1492.

While Leif Erikson was the first white man who planted his feet on the eastern shores of the American continent, it was left to another plucky Scandinavian to become the discoverer of the narrow body of water which separates America from Asia. Vitus Bering was a Dane, born in Jutland, in Denmark, in 1680. He entered the service of Russia and in 1725 he was made chief commander of one of the greatest geographical expeditions ever undertaken. He ex-

plored the Sea of Kamtchatka and during this voyage he discovered Bering Strait in 1728, and ascertained that Asia was not joined to America. Thus, as the Norwegian Leif Erikson is the first white man who sets foot on the extreme eastern part of this continent, so the Dane, Vitus Bering, becomes the discoverer of its extreme western boundary line. They stand at the rising and setting sun and clasp what is now the territory of the United States in their strong Scandinavian arms, and we might here fittingly add a Swede to complete the trio. Did not Sweden give us John Ericson, who with his little cheese-box, the famous "Monitor" gave most valuable help to this beloved land in the hour of its greatest danger?

Who will deny that the Scandinavians have rendered important services to this country? But we must hurry on.

The first visit of Scandinavians to America proper in post-Columbian times, is in the year 1619, one year before the landing of the Pilgrims at Plymouth. In the spring of that year King Christian IV fitted out two ships for the purpose of finding a northwest passage to Asia. The commander of this expedition was the Norwegian, Jens Munk, born at Berby in Southern Norway in 1579. He sailed from Copenhagen with his two ships and 66 men May 9, 1619. He explored Hudson Bay and took possession of the surrounding country in the name of his sovereign, and gave it the name of Nova Dania. All the members of this expedition perished except Jens Munk and two of his crew, who returned to Norway September 25, 1620, the undertaking having proved a complete failure. The ship chaplain on this expedition was the Danish Lutheran minister Rasmus Jensen Aarhus, and my friend Rev. Adolph Bredesen, of Stoughton, Wis., has called attention to the fact that he was the first minister of the Lutheran church in the New World. Mr. Bredesen speaks thus touchingly of this minister and his ministry among all those who perished from disease and exposure during that terrible winter of 1620 in the Hudson Bay country: "Rasmus Jensen Aarhus, a Danish Lutheran pastor, ministered faithfully to these unlucky men, almost to his dying breath. He died February 20, 1620, on the south-

western shore of Hudson Bay, near the mouth of the
Churchill River. His last sermon was a funeral sermon,
preached from his own death bed." It is strange that Jens
Munk is not mentioned in our English and American cyclo-
pedias.

Norwegians and Danes certainly arrived in New Amsterdam, now New York, at a very early period. The Rev.
Rasmus Andersen of Brooklyn, N. Y., has given this matter
much attention and he claims that he can find traces of Scandinavians in New York as early as 1617. He states that several Danes (more probably Norwegians) were settled on
Manhattan Island in 1617. In 1704 he says they built a
handsome stone church on the corner of Broadway and
Rector streets. Here regular services were held in the Danish language until the property was sold to Trinity Church,
the present churchyard occupying the site of the early building. He adds that "an examination of the first directory
published in New York shows many names of unquestion-
ably Danish origin." I have taken the liberty of assuming
that these people were Norwegians rather than Danes, and
my reason for so doing is that the descendants of those people, whom I have met or with whom I have corresponded,
invariably claim to be of Norwegian descent. A very large
number belong to the Bergen family and their family history
was published some years ago in a substantial volume. From
this volume I gather the salient fact, that Hans Hansen
Bergen, the common ancestor of the Bergen family of Long
Island, New Jersey, and their vincinity, was a native of
Bergen in Norway, a ship carpenter by trade, and had removed thence to Holland. From Holland he emigrated in
1633 to New Amsterdam, now New York. In the early
colonial records, his name appears in various forms, among
which may be found that of "Hans Hansen van Bergen in
Noorwegan," "Hans Hansen Noorman," "Hans Noorman,"
"Hans Hansen de Noorman," "Hans Hansz," "Hans Hansen," and others. The term "Noorman," meaning North-
man, clearly refers to Norway, like "in Noorwegan," and
was applied to natives of that place. Another very clear
instance of this sort is that of Claes Carstensen, who was

xiii

married in New Amsterdam in 1646. In the marriage entry, this Claes Carstensen is said to be from Norway, and he was subsequently called the "Noorman."

Finding a baronial family in Europe by the name of *Bergen,* some people of that name in this country have flattered themselves that they were scions of that stock, and thus link themselves by imagnination with the aristocracy of the old world. But, as Mr. Teunis Bergen suggests, they may as well descend from this imaginary eminence and make up their minds that they belong to the commonality and not to the nobility. The Bergens and the Carstensens, like the great mass of the original immigrants to this country, belonged to the humble class of society and came to America to better their prospects and fortunes. It must be sufficient for their descendants to know that their Norwegian ancestors came from a country where the feudal system was never known, where the land was held under no superior, not even the king. They are scions of those vikings who laid the foundations of Russia, founded a kingdom in France, and another in Italy, and who conquered and carried their institutions into England. They may point with pride to the fact that their ancestors discovered America five centuries before Columbus, but they need not boast of aristocratic blood.

We next come to the Swedish settlement on the Delaware, founded in 1638. This is well known to most readers and I will only add that the Swedish language was used in a Philadelphia church as late as 1823. But I will here call attention to a fact probably not so well known, that John Morton, one of the signers of the Declaration of Independence and an active member of the Continental Congress, born at Ridley, Pa., in 1724, was a descendant of the Swedes on the Delaware. Robert Anderson, the gallant defender of Fort Sumpter, against which the first gun of the civil war was fired, was also a scion of the Swedes on the Delaware. In the language of W. W. Thomas, Jr., "love of freedom and patriotism and state-craft and valor came over to America not only in the *Mayflower,* but also in that Swedish ship the *Kalmar Nyckel.*" The first Swedish settlers on the Delaware came in the ship *Kalmar Nyckel* and the yacht *Vogel Grip* in 1638.

xiv

Among the distinguished representatives of our Swedish American group we may also mention the famous rear admiral of the United States navy, John A. Dahlgren, who was born in Philadelphia in 1809. During the late war he silenced Fort Sumter and received a safe anchorage for the Monitor inside the bar of Charleston, and in this manner effectually put a stop to the blockade running, which had been before so successfully practiced. His name is thus linked with that of the world-renowned John Ericsson, the inventor of the Monitor, and our navy is largely indebted to Dahlgren for the great improvements in its ordnance, which have been made since 1840. Thomas F. Bayard, late secretary of state, and afterwards ambassador to England, was proud of the fact that he was descended on his mother's side from the Swedes on the Delaware.

Passing now to the war of the revolution, many Scandinavians are found serving in the American navy, and doubtless too in the army. While investigating this and similar matters my attention was called to the somewhat remarkable case of Thomas Johnson. In vol. 28 (1874), of the New England Historical and Genealogical Register, I find this interesting account of him: "Johnson was the son of a pilot in Mandal, a seaport on the coast of Norway, where he was born in 1758. In the absence of his father, he towed the first American vessel, the Ranger, commanded by Paul Jones, into the harbor of Mandal. After their arrival, Jones sent for the young pilot, and presenting him with a piece of gold, expressed his pleasure at his expert seamanship, which he had minutely watched during the towing of his ship into harbor. He (Jones) had made the port of Mandal for the purpose of recruiting the crew of the Ranger and satisfactory arrangements being made with his father, Johnson was received on board as a seaman. On assuming command of the *Bon Homme Richard,* Jones transferred some thirty volunteers from the Ranger, among whom was Thomas Johnson who, following the fortunes of his leader, went with him to the *Serapis* and *Alliance,* and finally arrived with him in the *Ariel* in Philadelphia, February 18, 1781, when 23 years of age—the first time he had seen the land of his adoption. At

this time congress was sitting in Philadelphia and several members were removing their families to that city. Application having been made to Capt. Jones to furnish a man to take charge of a sloop to Boston to convey the furniture of John Adams to Philadelphia, he appointed Johnson, who performed the service. This circumstance often brought Johnson in contact with Mr. Adams, who knew that he was one of the crew of Captain Jones, and consequently must have been in the conflict of the Serapis and Bon Homme Richard, which having occurred so recently, was a subject of general conversation. Many of the sailors frequented the hall of congress, and Johnson became so interested in listening and observing what was so new to him, that he was a daily visitor. When the members found that the sailors were part of the crew of Captain Jones, they frequently left their seats and came over to them to inquire the particulars of the recent engagement. Mr. Adams particularly engaged the attention of Johnson. To use the veteran's (Mr. Johnson's) own words, he says 'a nervous sensation seemed to pervade the patriot, as he listened to the description of the battle given by the sailors; fire flashed from his eyes, and his hair seemed perfectly erect; he would clasp his hands and exclaim "What a scene!" During the time they remained in Philadelphia, General Washington arrived and was presented to Congress. Johnson was present and listened to the introduction by President Hancock and the reply by the general. Some days after, when the sailors were in the hall, Mr. Adams brought General Washington to them, who kindly shook each by the hand, calling them our gallant tars. and asking them questions relative to the many successful adventures they had recently achieved. Johnson soon after left the navy and engaged in the merchant service for some years, but eventually returned to it again, where he remained till near the end of his "life's voyage." This Thomas Johnson assisted Jones in lashing the *Bon Homme Richard* to the *Serapis*, and was probably the last survivor of this celebrated combat. He died at the United States Naval Asylum, Philadelphia, on the 12th of July, 1851, ninety-three years old, where he had been for many years a pensioner and was known by the soub-

riquet "Paul Jones." Miss Stafford, who was still living in
1873, had been a frequent visitor to Thomas Johnson while
living, and after his death she annually visited his grave,
"a tribute," adds the writer, "the humble sailor does not
often receive, whatever his services."

This account of Thomas Johnson led me to investigate
further into the history of John Paul Jones, and in his biog-
raphy written by John Henry Sherburne, Register of the
Navy of the United States, in 1825, published at Washington
I found the roll of officers, seamen, marines and volunteers
who served on board the *Bon Homme Richard* in her cruise
made in 1779. In this roll the native country of every man
is given, and in it I found two seamen, born in Norway, viz:
Lewis Brown and George Johnson; and no less than seven
born in Sweden, viz: Peter Nolde, Charles Peterson, Daniel
Emblon (m), Peter Biorkman, Benjamin Gartineau, Peter
Molin and Oliver Gustaff. Thomas Johnson is not mentioned, but he is doubtless given incorrectly as George Johnson and is in the list of the wounded. Suffice it here to say
that these were Scandinavians who fought and bled for this
country in the war of the revolution, as there were thousands,
who died likewise in our recent sectional conflict when
brother fought against brother.

The brilliant Swede, Colonel (afterwards field marshal)
Axel Fersen, who in 1779 went to France where he was appointed colonel of the royal regiment of Swedes, must not
be forgotten. At the head of his regiment he served with
distinction in the latter campaigns of the American war, distinguished himself on various occasions, particularly in 1781,
during the siege of Yorktown, where he was aide-de-camp
to General Rochambeau. He afterwards became marshal of
the kingdom of Sweden.

I have myself known Norwegians who served under Gen.
Scott in the Mexican War. I have mentioned John Morton
and Captain John Ericsson, and I could have gone on and
mentioned many others of Scandinavian birth or descent
who have acquired a lasting reputation in the annals of
America. To enumerate them all would exceed the limits
of this preface, and I might be charged with partiality, if I

xvii

should attempt to make a selection. Anyone interested may easily find them among our state officials, members of congress, among the officers of our army and navy, among our authors, artists, lawyers, professors, preachers, journalists, and among our leading merchants and manufacturers, for many of them have played no unimportant part in the history of our country. This much is at least clear, that a complete history of America cannot be written without some account of what the Scandinavians have contributed in connection with the discovery and development of this country.

In the above rapid sketch of the Scandinavians in European and American history, I have made a few bold and emphatic assertions, and as some of these may be regarded by certain of my readers, who have not had the time or opportunity to search the records for themselves, and find out whether or not these things are so, as wild, unfounded and unsustained by the highest authority, I take the liberty of closing this introduction with a few quotations from authors, who cannot be suspected of being biased by national prejudice.

In discussing the story of Sigurd, the Volsung, as portrayed in the old Norse eddas and sagas, H. A. Taine, the great Frenchman, who was himself a disciple of Guizot, the historian of civilization, says: "This is the conception of a hero as engendered by the Teutonic race in its infancy. Is it not strange to see them put their happiness in battle, their beauty in death? Is there any people, Hindoo, Persian, Greek of Gallic, which has founded so tragic a conception of life? Is there any which has peopled its infantine mind with such gloomy dreams? Is there any which has so entirely banished the sweetness from enjoyment and the softness from pleasure? Energy, tenacious and mournful energy, an ecstacy of energy, such was their chosen condition. In the somber obstinacy of an English laborer still survives the tacit rage of the Norse warrior. Strife for strife's sake. Such is their pleasure. With what sadness, madness, such a disposition breaks its bonds we see in Shakespeare and Byron. With what completeness, in what duties it can employ and entrench itself under moral ideas, we see in the case of the Puritans." In thus tracing American and English greatness

back to the hardy Norsemen, no one will accuse Taine of being influenced by a desire to eulogize his own kith and kin.

In his history of the United States, our American historian, Benson John Lossing uses these pregnant words: "It is back to the Norwegian Vikings we must look for the hardiest elements of progress in the United States."

The eminent American scholar, B. F. De Costa, says: "Let us remember that in vindicating the Norsemen we honor those who not only give us the first knowledge possessed of the American continent, but to whom we are indebted for much beside that we esteem valuable. For we fable in a great measure when we speak of our Saxon inheritance. It is rather from the Northmen that we have derived our vital energy, our freedom of thought, and in a measure that we do not yet suspect our strength of speech."

Let us take a look into the works of the French historian, Paul Henri Mallet: "History has not recorded," he says, "the annals of a people, who have occasioned greater, more sudden, or more numerous revolutions in Europe than the Scandinavians, or whose antiquities at the same time are so little known. Had, indeed, their emigrations been only like those sudden torrents of which all traces and remembrance are soon effaced, the indifference that has been shown to them would have been sufficiently justified by the barbarism they have been reproached with. But during those general inundations the face of Europe underwent so total a change, and during the confusion they occasioned, such different establishments took place; new societies were formed, animated so entirely with a new spirit, that the history of our own manners and institutions ought necessarily to ascend back and even dwell a considerable time upon a period which discovers to us their chief origin and source."

After giving a brief description of Scandinavian influence in Europe and the downfall of the Roman empire. Mr. Mallet adds: "It is easy to see from this short sketch how greatly the nations of the North have influenced the different fates of Europe, and if it be worth while to trace its revolutions to their causes, if the illustration of its institutions, of its police, of its customs, of its manners, of its laws, be a subject

of useful and interesting inquiry, it must be allowed that the antiquities of the North, that is to say, everything which tends to make us acquainted with its ancient inhabitants, merits a share in the attention of thinking men. But to render this obvious by a particular example: Is it not well known that the most flourishing and celebrated states of Europe owe orginally to the Northern nations whatever liberty they now enjoy, either in their constitution or in the spirit of their government? For although the Gothic form of government has been almost everywhere altered or abolished, have we not retained, in most things, the opinions, the customs, the manners, which that government had a tendency to produce? Is not this in fact, the principal source of that courage, of that aversion to slavery of that empire of honor, which characterized in general the European nations, and of that moderation, of that easiness of access, and peculiar attention to the rights of humanity, which so happily distinguish our sovereigns from the inaccessible and superb tyrants of Asia? The immense extent of the Roman empire had rendered its constitution so despotic and military, many of its emperors were such ferocious monsters, its senate was become so mean-spirited and vile, that all elevation of sentiment, everything that was noble and manly, seem to have been forever vanished from their hearts and minds, insomuch that if all Europe had received the yoke of Rome, in this her state of debasement, this fine part of the world reduced to the inglorious condition of the rest could not have avoided falling onto that kind of barbarity which is of all others the most incurable, as by making as many slaves as there are men, it degrades them so low as not to leave them even a thought or desire of bettering their condition. But nature had long prepared a remedy for such great evils in that unsubmitting, unconquerable spirit with which she had inspired the people of the North; and thus she made amends to the human race for all the calamities which, in other respects, the inroads of these nations and the overthrow of the Roman empire produced."

We will close the quotations with the following enthusiastic words of the Scotch author and traveler, Samuel Laing:

"All that men hope for of good government and future improvement in their physical and moral condition—all that civilized men enjoy at this day of civil, religious and political liberty—the British constitution, representative legislation, the trial by jury, security of property, freedom of mind and person, the influence of public opinion over the conduct of public affairs, the reformation, the liberty of the press, the spirit of the age—all that is or has been of value to man in modern times as a member of society, either in Europe or the New World, may be traced to the spark left burning upon our shores by these Northern barbarians."

Our western civilization is a protest against autocracy, whether embodied in a man or a class or a nation. It matters not whether the nature of the autocracy be political, ecclesiastical, professional or commercial. It has been developed in France, England and America, but it was born more than a thousand years ago among our Scandinavian ancestors.

And now a word about the volumes to be published in the present Norrœna Library.

Saxo Grammaticus is the most important literary monument from the middle age in Denmark. It was written by its author in Latin, but has been translated into Danish, and the present edition translated by Professor Elton with an introduction by F. York Powell contains all that is of interest to foreign readers. While the matter is treated by Saxo as history, it is in fact mythology, and sheds a flood of light on the ancient religion of the Teutons.

The crown of Icelandic Historiography is the "Heimskringla" which towers above all other historical works of the middle ages like a majestic tree over the low brushwood. The work not only gives a graphic account of events in Scandinavia, but also contains invaluable information in regard to contemporaneous events in England, Russia, France, Germany and other countries; in fact, it is impossible to write an adequate history of England or Russia from the 9th to the 12th century without consulting the Heimskringla.

The story of "Burnt Njal" holds the first rank of the celebrated Sagas describing life in Iceland. It abounds in

characters drawn with masterly skill, and in entertaining descriptions of life and customs. This Saga contains interesting descriptions of feuds and lawsuits, and is exceedingly important to any one interested in the history of civilization, on account of the key which it gives to Icelandic law. It is told in a beautiful, noble language showing that its anonymous author was master of an admirable style.

The "Eddas," that is the elder and the younger Edda are the main sources from which we draw our information concerning the religion of our ancestors. The elder Edda is in poetry and the younger Edda is in prose. The two may be regarded as the old and new testament of the Odinic religion. The age of the elder Edda is not known, but it was put in writing by Sæmund in the 12th century, and for that reason it is also known as Sæmund's Edda. The younger Edda which retells in prose form the contents of the elder Edda is written by Snorre Sturlason the author of "Heimskringla." The word "Edda" means great grandmother, and occurs in this sense in one of the poems of the elder Edda. The venerable age of the collection of poems doubtless suggested this name for them. There are in all in the elder Edda 39 poems or lays, the second half of which are based on the same traditions as the old Norse Volsunga Saga, and middle high German "Niebelungen Lied." While the "Niebelungen Lied" has been materially modified, both as to form and contents by the later christian culture whereby its poetical merit has been greatly damaged, the story as told in the Edda version preserves all its original grandeur and heathen spirit. There is no other Teutonic work which sits in divine tranquility of unapproachable nobility like a King of Kings amongst all other books which can be compared in all its elements of greatness with the Elder Edda. There is a loftiness of stature and a growth of muscle about it which commands the admiration of all lovers of literature. The obscurity which hangs over some parts of the Eddas, like the deep shadows crouching amidst the ruins of the past, is probably the result of dilapidation; but amidst this stands forth the boldest masses of intellectual masonry.

We are astonished at the wisdom which is shaped into maxims and at the tempestous strength of passions to which all modern emotions appear puny and constrained. In the bright sunlight of the far away past, surrounded by the densest shadows of forgotten ages, we come at once into the presence of Gods and Heroes, Goddesses and fair women, Giants and Dwarfs moving about in a world of wonderful imagery, unlike any other world or creation which God has founded or man has imagined, but still beautiful beyond conception.

In Rydberg's Teutonic Mythology we have a profound and at the same time most fascinating systematic presentation of the pre-Christian religion of our fathers as found in the Eddas. Victor Rydberg was one of Sweden's greatest scholars, and he devoted the ripest years of his master mind to a research into the antiquities of the North and as F. York Powell of Oxford, in his review of this work puts it: It is the most important addition to our knowledge of early Teutonic myths since Grimm, that is to say, during the past 70 years. The work is of the greatest interest both to the scholar and to the general reader.

In the Eddas, but more directly in the Volsunga Saga and in the Epics and Romances given by Dr. W. Wagner and W. M. MacDowall, we find the material which inspired the great musical composer Richard Wagner, and out of which he created his wonderfully brilliant operas. These Romances are of absorbing interest, but they become doubly interesting, if possible, by the interpretation they afford of the new musical school founded by Wagner.

This set of books also contains a volume of Norse-Folklore. Folk-lore stories are of interest not only to children, but the greatest scholars find in them much help in solving riddles in our old Mythology, Tradition and Romances. When the heathen religion passed into decay and was superceded by Christianity, the myths were not entirely forgotten, but re-appeared in new form in an endless number of charming tales for the fireside. Younger people are charmed by these wonderful stories, while the scholar is aided by them in interpreting some of the most difficult passages in the Elder

Edda. England, Germany, Hungary and Russia have all gathered from the lips of the people a vast number of Folk-lore tales, but in the opinion of the most competent authorities, Norwegian Folk-lore represents the high water-mark in this department of literature.

The book on Vinland contains all the Norse Sagas or documents relating to the discovery and colonization of America by the Norsemen in the 10th, 11th and following centuries. The editor discusses the probable location of Vinland on our coast in one chapter. In a second chapter he summarizes the contents of the Saga narrative, and in a third chapter he demonstrates conclusively that Christopher Columbus had full knowledge of the Norse voyages before he set sail for the new world.

Thus it will be seen that this set of 15 volumes covers in a very satisfactory manner the Mythology, the Romances and the History of Scandinavia, and it will be found that the Norsemen, the bold Norse Vikings, were not barbarians, but the possessors of a high degree of culture. They were lovers of freedom and independence, and as has already been shown, the institutions of England and America have their origin in Scandinavia. Scandinavian poetry, tradition and romance are a fountain of delight, which no man can drain dry.

# INTRODUCTION.

SAXO "GRAMMATICUS," or "The Lettered," one of the
notable historians of the Middle Ages, may fairly be called
not only the earliest chronicler of Denmark, but her earliest
writer. In the latter half of the twelfth century, when Iceland was in the flush of literary production, Denmark lin-
gered behind. No literature in her vernacular, save a few
Runic inscriptions, has survived. Monkish annals, devotional
works, and lives were written in Latin; but the chronicle of
Roskild, the necrology of Lund, the register of gifts to the
cloister of Sora, are not literature. Neither are the half-
mythological genealogies of kings; and besides, the mass of
these, though doubtless based on older verses that are lost,
are not proved to be, as they stand, prior to Saxo. One
man only, Saxo's elder contemporary, Sueno Aggonis, or
Sweyn (Svend) Aageson, who wrote about 1185, shares or
anticipates the credit of attempting a connected record. His
brief draft of annals is written in rough mediocre Latin. It
names but a few of the kings recorded by Saxo, and tells
little that Saxo does not. Yet there is a certain link between the two writers. Sweyn speaks of Saxo with respect;
he not obscurely leaves him the task of filling up his omis-
sions. Both writers, servants of the brilliant Bishop Absalon,
and probably set by him upon their task, proceed, like
Geoffrey of Monmouth, by gathering and editing mythical

5

matter. This they more or less embroider, and arrive in due course insensibly at actual history. Both, again, thread their stories upon a genealogy of kings in part legendary. Both write at the spur of patriotism, both to let Denmark linger in the race for light and learning, and desirous to save her glories, as other nations have saved theirs, by a record. But while Sweyn only made a skeleton chronicle, Saxo leaves a memorial in which historian and philologist find their account. His seven later books are the chief Danish authority for the times which they relate; his first nine, here translated, are a treasure of myth and folk-lore. Of the songs and stories which Denmark possessed from the common Scandinavian stock, often her only native record is in Saxo's Latin. Thus, as a chronicler both of truth and fiction, he had in his own land no predecessor, nor had he any literary tradition behind him. Single-handed, therefore, he may be said to have lifted the dead-weight against him, and given Denmark a writer. The nature of his work will be discussed presently.

### Life of Saxo.

Of Saxo little is known but what he himself indicates, though much doubtful supposition has gathered round his name.

That he was born a Dane his whole language implies; it is full of a glow of aggressive patriotism. He also often praises the Zealanders at the expense of other Danes, and Zealand as the centre of Denmark; but that is the whole contemporary evidence for the statement that he was a Zealander. This statement is freely taken for granted three centuries afterwards by Urne in the first edition of the book (1514), but is not traced further back than an epito-

mator, who wrote more than 200 years after Saxo's death. Saxo tells us that his father and grandfather fought for Waldemar the First of Denmark, who reigned from 1157 to 1182. Of these men we know nothing further, unless the Saxo whom he names as one of Waldemar's admirals be his grandfather, in which case his family was one of some distinction and his father and grandfather probably "King's men." But Saxo was a very common name, and we shall see the licence of hypothesis to which this fact has given rise. The notice, however, helps us approximately towards Saxo's birth-year. His grandfather, if he fought for Waldemar, who began to reign in 1157, can hardly have been born before 1100, nor can Saxo himself have been born before 1145 or 1150. But he was undoubtedly born before 1158, since he speaks of the death of Bishop Asker, which took place in that year, as occurring "in our time." His life therefore covers and overlaps the last half of the twelfth century.

His calling and station in life are debated. Except by the anonymous Zealand chronicler, who calls him Saxo "the Long," thus giving us the one personal detail we have, he has been universally known as Saxo *Grammaticus* ever since the epitomator of 1431 headed his compilation with the words, "A certain notable man of letters (*grammaticus*), a Zealander by birth, named Saxo, wrote," etc. It is almost certain that this general term, given only to men of signal gifts and learning, became thus for the first time, and for good, attached to Saxo's name. Such a title, in the Middle Ages, usually implied that its owner was a churchman, and Saxo's whole tone is devout, though not conspicuously professional.

But a number of Saxos present themselves in the same surroundings with whom he has been from time to time

3          7

identified. All he tells us himself is, that Absalon, Archbishop of Lund from 1179 to 1201, pressed him, who was "the least of his companions, since all the rest refused the task," to write the history of Denmark, so that it might record its glories like other nations. Absalon was previously, and also after his promotion, Bishop of Roskild, and this is the first circumstance giving colour to the theory—which lacks real evidence—that Saxo the historian was the same as a certain Saxo, Provost of the Chapter of Roskild, whose death is chronicled in a contemporary hand without any mark of distinction. It is unlikely that so eminent a man would be thus barely named; and the appended eulogy and verses identifying the Provost and the historian are of later date. Moreover, the Provost Saxo went on a mission to Paris in 1165, and was thus much too old for the theory. Nevertheless, the good Bishop of Roskild, Lave Urne, took this identity for granted in the first edition, and fostered the assumption. Saxo was a cleric; and could such a man be of less than canonical rank? He was (it was assumed) a Zealander; he was known to be a friend of Absalon, Bishop of Roskild. What more natural than that he should have been the Provost Saxo? Accordingly this latter worthy had an inscription in gold letters, written by Lave Urne himself, affixed to the wall opposite his tomb.

Even less evidence exists for identifying our Saxo with the scribe of that name—a comparative menial—who is named in the will of Bishop Absalon; and hardly more warranted is the theory that he was a member, perhaps a subdeacon, of the monastery of St. Laurence, whose secular canons formed part of the Chapter of Lund. It is true that Sweyn Aageson, Saxo's senior by about twenty years, speaks (writing about 1185) of Saxo as his *contubernalis*. Sweyn Aageson is known to have had strong family connections

8

with the monastery of St. Laurence; but there is only a tolerably strong probability that he, and therefore that Saxo, was actually a member of it. (*Contubernalis* may only imply comradeship in military service.) Equally doubtful is the consequence that since Saxo calls himself "one of the least" of Absalon's "followers" (*comitum*), he was probably, if not the inferior officer, who is called an *acolitus,* at most a sub-deacon, who also did the work of a superior *acolitus.* This is too poor a place for the chief writer of Denmark, high in Absalon's favor, nor is there any direct testimony that Saxo held it.

His education is unknown, but must have been careful. Of his training and culture we only know what his book betrays. Possibly, like other learned Danes, then and afterwards, he acquired his training and knowledge at some foreign University. Perhaps, like his contemporary Anders Suneson, he went to Paris; but we cannot tell. It is not even certain that he had a degree; for there is really little to identify him with the "M(agister) Saxo" who witnessed the deed of Absalon founding the monastery at Sora.

## The History.

How he was induced to write his book has been mentioned. The expressions of modesty Saxo uses, saying that he was "the least" of Absalon's "followers," and that "all the rest refused the task," are not to be taken to the letter. A man of his parts would hardly be either the least in rank, or the last to be solicited. The words, however, enable us to guess an upward limit for the date of the inception of the work. Absalon became Archbishop in 1179, and the language of the Preface (written, as we shall see, last) implies that he was already Archbishop when he suggested the His-

tory to Saxo. But about 1185 we find Sweyn Aageson complimenting Saxo, and saying that Saxo "had *determined* to set forth all the deeds" of Sweyn Estridson, in his eleventh book, "at greater length in a more elegant style." The exact bearing of this notice on the date of Saxo's History is doubtful. It certainly need not imply that Saxo had already written ten books, or indeed that he had written any, of his History. All we can say is, that by 1185 a portion of the History was planned. The order in which its several parts were composed, and the date of its completion, are not certainly known, as Absalon died in 1201. But the work was not then finished; for, at the end of Bk. xi, one Birger, who died in 1202, is mentioned as still alive.

We have, however, a yet later notice. In the Preface, which, as its whole language implies, was written last, Saxo speaks of Waldemar II having "encompassed (*complexus*) the ebbing and flowing waves of Elbe." This language, though a little vague, can hardly refer to anything but an expedition of Waldemar to Bremen in 1208. The whole History was in that case probably finished by about 1208. As to the order in which its parts were composed, it is likely that Absalon's original instruction was to write a history of Absalon's own doings. The fourteenth and succeeding books deal with these at disproportionate length, and Absalon, at the expense even of Waldemar, is the protagonist. Now Saxo states in his Preface that he "has taken care to follow the statements (*asserta*) of Absalon, and with obedient mind and pen to include both his own doings and other men's doings of which he learnt."

The latter books are, therefore, to a great extent, Absalon's personally communicated memoirs. But we have seen that Absalon died in 1201, and that Bk. xi, at any rate, was not written after 1202. It almost certainly follows that the

latter books were written in Absalon's life; but the Preface, written after them, refers to events in 1208. Therefore, unless we suppose that the issue was for some reason delayed, or that Saxo spent seven years in polishing—which is not impossible—there is some reason to surmise that he began with that portion of his work which was nearest to his own time, and added the previous (especially the first nine, or mythical) books, as a completion, and possibly as an afterthought. But this is a point which there is no real means of settling. We do not know how late the Preface was written, except that it must have been some time between 1208 and 1223, when Anders Suneson ceased to be Archbishop; nor do we know when Saxo died.

## History of the Work.

Nothing is stranger than that a work of such force and genius, unique in Danish letters, should have been forgotten for three hundred years, and have survived only in an epitome and in exceedingly few manuscripts. The history of the book is worth recording. Doubtless its very merits, its "marvellous vocabulary, thickly-studded maxims, and excellent variety of images," which Erasmus admired long afterwards, sealed it to the vulgar. A man needed some Latin to appreciate it, and Erasmus' natural wonder "how a Dane at that day could have such a force of eloquence" is a measure of the rarity both of the gift and of a public that could appraise it. The epitome (made about 1430) shows that Saxo was felt to be difficult, its author saying: "Since Saxo's work is in many places diffuse, and many things are said more for ornament than for historical truth, and moreover his style is too obscure on account of the number of terms (*plurima vocabula*) and sundry poems, which are unfamiliar

to modern times, this opuscle puts in clear words the more notable of the deeds there related, with the addition of some that happened after Saxo's death." A Low-German version of this epitome, which appeared in 1485, had a considerable vogue, and the two together "helped to drive the history out of our libraries, and explains why the annalists and geographers of the Middle Ages so seldom quoted it." This neglect appears to have been greatest of all in Denmark, and to have lasted until the appearance of the *First Edition* in 1514.

The first impulse towards this work by which Saxo was saved, is found in a letter from the Bishop of Roskild, Lave Urne, dated May 1512, to Christian Pederson, Canon of Lund, whom he compliments as a lover of letters, antiquary, and patriot, and urges to edit and publish *tam divinum latinae eruditionis culmen et splendorem Saxonem nostrum.* Nearly two years afterwards Christian Pederson sent Lave Urne a copy of the first edition, now all printed, with an account of its history. "I do not think that any mortal was more inclined and ready for" the task. "When living at Paris, and paying heed to good literature, I twice sent a messenger at my own charges to buy a faithful copy at any cost, and bring it back to me. Effecting nothing thus, I went back to my country for this purpose; I visited and turned over all the libraries, but still could not pull out a Saxo, even covered with beetles, bookworms, mould, and dust. So stubbornly had all the owners locked it away." A worthy prior, in compassion offered to get a copy and transcribe it with his own hand, but Christian, in respect for the prior's rank, absurdly declined. At last Birger, the Archbishop of Lund, by some strategy, got a copy, which King Christian the Second allowed to be taken to Paris on condition of its being wrought at "by an instructed and skilled graver (printer)." Such a person was found in Jodocus

Badius Ascensius, who adds a third letter written by himself
to Bishop Urne, vindicating his application to Saxo of the
title *Grammaticus,* which he well defines as "one who knows
how to speak or write with diligence, acuteness, or knowledge." The beautiful book he produced was worthy of the
zeal, and unsparing, unwcariable pains, which had been
spent on it by the band of enthusiasts, and it was truly a
little triumph of humanism. Further editions were reprinted
during the sixteenth century at Basle and at Frankfort-on-
Main, but they did not improve in any way upon the first;
and the next epoch in the study of Saxo was made by the
edition and notes of Stephanus Johansen Stephanius, published at Copenhagen in the middle of the seventeenth century (1644). Stephanius, the first commentator on Saxo,
still remains the best upon his language. Immense knowledge of Latin, both good and bad (especially of the authors
Saxo imitated), infinite and prolix industry, a sharp eye for
the text, and continence in emendation, are not his only
virtues. His very bulkiness and leisureliness are charming;
he writes like a man who had eternity to write in, and who
knew enough to fill it, and who expected readers of an equal
leisure. He also prints some valuable notes signed with the
famous name of Bishop Bryniolf of Skalholt, a man of force
and talent, and others by Casper Barth, *corculum Musarum,*
as Stephanius calls him, whose textual and other comments
are sometimes of use, and who worked with a MS. of Saxo.
The edition of Klotz, 1771, based on that of Stephanius, I
have but seen; however, the first standard commentary is
that begun by P. E. Müller, Bishop of Zealand, and finished
after his death by Johan Velschow, Professor of History at
Copenhagen, where the first part of the work, containing
text and notes, was published in 1839; the second, with pro-
legomena and fuller notes, appearing in 1858. The standard

13

edition, containing bibliography, critical apparatus based on
all the editions and MS. fragments, text, and index, is the
admirable one of that indefatigable veteran, Alfred Holder,
Strasburg, 1886.
Hitherto the translations of Saxo have been into Danish.
The first that survives, by Anders Soffrinson Vedel, dates
from 1575, some sixty years after the first edition.  In such
passages as I have examined it is vigorous, but very free, and
more like a paraphrase than a translation, Saxo's verses being put into loose prose.  Yet it has had a long life, having
been modified by Vedel's grandson, John Laverentzen, in
1715, and reissued in 1851.  The present version has been
much helped by the translation of Seier Schousbölle, published at Copenhagen in 1752.  It is true that the verses,
often the hardest part, are put into periphrastic verse (by
Laurentius Thura, *c.* 1721), and Schousbölle often does not
face a difficulty; but he gives the sense of Saxo simply and
concisely.  The lusty paraphrase by the enthusiastic Nik.
Fred. Sev. Grundtvig, of which there have been several editions, has also been of occasional use.  No other translations,
save of a scrap here and there into German, seem to be
extant.

## The MSS.

It will be understood, from what has been said, that no
complete MS. of Saxo's History is known.  The epitomator
in the fourteenth century, and Krantz in the seventeenth,
had MSS. before them; and there was that one which Christian Pedersen found and made the basis of the first edition,
but which has disappeared.  Barth had two manuscripts,
which are said to have been burnt in 1636.  Another, possessed by a Swedish parish priest, Aschaneus, in 1630, which

Stephenius unluckily did not know of, disappeared in the
Royal Archives of Stockholm after his death. These are
practically the only MSS. of which we have sure information, excepting the four fragments that are now preserved.
Of these by far the most interesting is the "Angers Fragment."

This was first noticed in 1863, in the Angers Library,
where it was found degraded into the binding of a number of
devotional works and a treatise on metric, dated 1459, and
once the property of a priest at Alençon. In 1877 M. Gaston
Paris called the attention of the learned to it, and the result
was that the Danish Government received it next year in
exchange for a valuable French manuscript which was in the
Royal Library at Copenhagen. This little national treasure,
the only piece of contemporary writing of the History, has
been carefully photographed and edited by that enthusiastic
and urbane scholar, Christian Bruun. In the opinion both of
Dr. Vigfússon and M. Paris, the writing dates from about
1200; and this date, though difficult to determine, owing to
the paucity of Danish MSS. of the 12th and early 13th centuries, is confirmed by the character of the contents. For
there is little doubt that the Fragment shows us Saxo in the
labour of composition. The MSS. looks as if expressly written for interlineation. Besides a marginal gloss by a later,
fourteenth century hand, there are two distinct sets of variants, in different writings, interlined and running over into
the margin. These variants are much more numerous in the
prose than in the verse. The first set are in the same hand
as the text, the second in another hand: but both of them
have the character, not of variants from some other MSS.,
but of alternative expressions put down tentatively. If either
hand is Saxo's it is probably the second. He may conceiv-
ably have dictated both at different times to different scribes.

No other man would tinker the style in this fashion. A complete translation of all these changes has been deemed unnecessary in these volumes; there is a full collation in Holder's *Apparatus Criticus.* The verdict of the Angers-Fragment, which, for the very reason mentioned, must not be taken as the final form of the text, nor therefore, despite its antiquity, as conclusive against the First Edition where the two differ, is to confirm, so far as it goes, the editing of Ascensius and Pederson. There are no vital differences, and the care of the first editors, as well as the authority of their source, is thus far amply vindicated.

A sufficient account of the other fragments will be found in Holder's list. In 1855 M. Kall-Rasmussen found in the private archives at Kronborg a scrap of fourteenth century MS., containing a short passage from Bk. vii. Five years later G. F. Lassen found, at Copenhagen, a fragment of Bk. vi, believed to be written in North Zealand, and in the opinion of Bruun belonging to the same codex as Kall-Rasmussen's fragment. Of another longish piece, found in Copenhagen at the end of the seventeenth century by Johannes Laverentzen, and belonging to a codex burnt in the fire of 1728, a copy still extant in the Copenhagen Museum, was made by Otto Sperling. For fragments, either extant or alluded to, of the later books. the student should consult the carefully collated text of Holder. The whole MS. material, therefore, covers but a little of Saxo's work, which was practically saved for Europe by the perseverance and fervour for culture of a single man, Bishop Urne.

## SAXO AS A WRITER.

Saxo's countrymen have praised without stint his remarkable style, for he has a style. It is often very bad; but he

16

*writes,* he is not in vain called *Grammaticus,* the man of letters. His style is not merely remarkable considering its author's difficulties; it is capable at need of pungency and of high expressiveness. His Latin is not that of the Golden Age, but neither is it the common Latin of the Middle Ages. There are traces of his having read Virgil and Cicero. But two writers in particular left their mark on him. The first and most influential is Valerius Maximus, the mannered author of the *Memorabilia,* who lived in the first half of the first century, and was much relished in the Middle Ages. From him Saxo borrowed a multitude of phrases, sometimes apt but often crabbed and deformed, as well as an exemplary and homiletic turn of narrative. Other idioms, and perhaps the practice of interspersing verses amid prose (though this also was a twelfth century Icelandic practice), Saxo found in a fifth-century writer, Martianus Capella, the pedantic author of the *De Nuptiis Philologiae et Mercurii.* Such models may have saved him from a base mediæval vocabulary; but they were not worthy of him, and they must answer for some of his falsities of style. These are apparent. His accumulation of empty and motley phrase, like a garish bunch of coloured bladders; his joy in platitude and pomposity, his proneness to say a little thing in great words, are only too easy to translate. We shall be well content if our version also gives some inkling of his qualities; not only of what Erasmus called his "wonderful vocabulary, his many pithy sayings, and the excellent variety of his images;" but also of his feeling for grouping, his barbaric sense of colour, and his stateliness. For he moves with resource and strength both in prose and verse, and is often only hindered by his own wealth. With no kind of critical tradition to chasten him, his force is often misguided and his work shapeless; but he stumbles into many splendours.

FOLK-LORE INDEX.

The mass of archaic incidents, beliefs, and practices recorded by the 12th-century writer seemed to need some other classification than a bare alphabetic index. The present plan, a subject-index practically, has been adopted with a view to the needs of the anthropologist and folk-lorist. Its details have been largely determined by the bulk and character of the entries themselves. No attempt has been made to supply full parallels from any save the more striking and obvious old Scandinavian sources, the end being to classify material rather than to point out its significance of geographic distribution. With regard to the first three heads, the reader who wishes to see how Saxo compares with the Old Northern poems may be referred to the Grimm Centenary papers, Oxford, 1886, and the Corpus Poeticum Boreale, Oxford, 1883.

POLITICAL INSTITUTIONS.

*King.*—As portrayed by Saxo, the ideal king should be (as in Beowulf's Lay) generous, brave and just. He should be a man of accomplishments, of unblemished body, presumably of royal kin (peasant-birth is considered a bar to the kingship), usually a son or a nephew, or brother of his foregoer (though no strict rule of succession seems to appear in Saxo), and duly chosen and acknowledged at the proper place of election. In Denmark this was at a stone circle, and the stability of these stones was taken as an omen for the king's reign. There are exceptional instances noted, as the serf-king Eormenric (cf. Guthred-Canute of Northumberland), whose noble birth washed out this blot of his captivity,

and there is a curious tradition of a conqueror setting his hound as king over a conquered province in mockery.

The king was of age at twelve. A king of seven years of age has twelve Regents chosen in the Moot, in one case by lot, to bring him up and rule for him till his majority. Regents are all appointed in Denmark, in one case for lack of royal blood, one to Scania, one to Zealand, one to Funen, two to Jutland. Underkings and Earls are appointed by kings, and though the Earl's office is distinctly official, succession is sometimes given to the sons of faithful fathers. The absence of a settled succession law leads (as in Muslim States) to rebellions and plots.

Kings sometimes abdicated, giving up the crown perforce to a rival, or in high age to a kinsman. In heathen times, kings, as Thiodwulf tells us in the case of Domwald and Yngwere, were sometimes sacrificed for better seasons (African fashion), and Wicar of Norway perishes, like Iphigeneia, to procure fair winds. Kings having to lead in war, and sometimes being willing to fight wagers of battle, are short-lived as a rule, and assassination is a continual peril, whether by fire at a time of feast, of which there are numerous examples, besides the classic one on which Biarca-mal is founded and the not less famous one of Hamlet's vengeance, or whether by steel, as with Hiartuar, or by trick, as in Wicar's case above cited. The reward for slaying a king is in one case 120 gold lbs.; 12 "talents" of gold from each ringleader, 1 oz. of gold from each commoner, in the story of Godfred, known as Ref's gild, *i. e., Fox tax*. In the case of a great king, Frode, his death is concealed for three years to avoid disturbance within and danger from without. Captive kings were not as a rule well treated. A Slavonic king, Daxo, offers Ragnar's son Whitesark his daughter and half his realm, or death, and the captive strangely desires death

by fire. A captive king is exposed, chained to wild beasts, thrown into a serpent-pit, wherein Ragnar is given the fate of the elder Gunnar in the Eddic Lays, Atlakvida. The king is treated with great respect by his people, he is finely clad, and his commands are carried out, however abhorrent or absurd, as long as they do not upset customary or statute law. The king has slaves in his household, men and women, besides his guard of housecarles and his bearsark champions. A king's daughter has thirty slaves with her, and the foot-maiden existed exactly as in the stories of the *Wicked Waiting Maid*. He is not to be awakened in his slumbers (cf. St. Olaf's Life, where the naming of King Magnus is the result of adherence to this etiquette). A champion weds the king's leman.

His *thanes* are created by the delivery of a sword, which the king holds by the blade and the thane takes by the hilt. (English earls were created by the girding with a sword. "Taking treasure, and weapons and horses, and feasting in a hall with the king" is synonymous with thane-hood or gesith-ship in Beowulf's Lay). A king's thanes must avenge him if he falls, and owe him allegiance. (This was paid in the old English monarchies by kneeling and laying the head down at the lord's knee.)

The trick by which the Mock-king, or King of the Beggars (parallel to our Boy-bishop, and perhaps to that enigmatic churls' King of the *O. E. Chronicle*, s. a. 1017, Eadwi ceorla-kyning) gets allegiance paid to him, and so secures himself in his attack on the real king, is cleverly devised. The king, besides being a counsel giver himself, and speaking the law, has *counsellors*, old and wise men, *sapientes* (like the O. E. Thyle). The aged warrior counsellor, as Starcad here and Master Hildebrand in the *Nibelungenlied*, is one type of these persons, another is the false counsellor,

20

as Woden in guise of Bruni, another the braggart, as Hún-
ferth in Beowulf's Lay. At *moots* where laws are made,
kings and regents chosen, cases judged, resolutions taken of
national importance, there are discussions, as in that armed
most the host.

The king has, beside his estates up and down the country,
sometimes (like Hrothgar with his palace Heorot in Beowulf's Lay) a great fort and treasure house, as Eormenric,
whose palace may well have really existed. There is often
a primitive and negroid character about dwellings of formidable personages, heads placed on stakes adorn their ex-
terior, or shields are ranged round the walls.

The *provinces* are ruled by removable earls appointed by
the king, often his own kinsmen, sometimes the heads of old
ruling families. The *hundreds* make up the province or sub-
kingdom. They may be granted to king's thanes, who became *hundred-elders*. Twelve hundreds are in one case bestowed upon a man.

The *yeoman's* estate is not only honourable but useful,
as Starcad generously and truly acknowledges. Agriculture
should be fostered and protected by the king, even at the
cost of his life.

But gentle birth and birth royal place certain families
above the common body of freemen (landed or not); and for
a commoner to pretend to a king's daughter is an act of pre-
sumption, and generally rigorously resented.

The *smith* was the object of a curious prejudice, probably
akin to that expressed in St. Patrick's Lorica, and derived
from the smith's having inherited the functions of the savage
weapon-maker with his poisons and charms. The curious
attempt to distinguish smiths into good and useful sword-
smiths and base and bad goldsmiths seems a merely modern
explanation: Weland could both forge swords and make

21

ornaments of metal. Starcad's loathing for a smith recalls the mockery with which the Homeric gods treat Hephaistos.

*Slavery.*—As noble birth is manifest by fine eyes and personal beauty, courage and endurance, and delicate behaviour, so the slave nature is manifested by cowardice, treachery, unbridled lust, bad manners, falsehood, and low physical traits. Slaves had, of course, no right either of honour, or life, or limb. Captive ladies are sent to a brothel; captive kings cruelly put to death. Born slaves were naturally still less considered, they were flogged; it was disgraceful to kill them with honourable steel; to accept a slight service from a slave-woman was beneath old Starcad's dignity. A man who loved another man's slave-woman, and did base service to her master to obtain her as his consort, was looked down on. Slaves frequently ran away to escape punishment for carelessness, or fault, or to gain liberty.

### CUSTOMARY LAW.

The evidence of Saxo to archaic law and customary institutions is pretty much (as we should expect) that to be drawn from the Icelandic Sagas, and even from the later Icelandic rímur and Scandinavian kæmpe-viser. But it helps to complete the picture of the older stage of North Teutonic Law, which we are able to piece together out of our various sources, English, Icelandic, and Scandinavian. In the twilight of Yore every glowworm is a helper to the searcher.

There are a few MAXIMS of various times, but all seemingly drawn from custom cited or implied by Saxo as authoritative:—

*It is disgraceful to be ruled by a woman.*—The great men of Teutonic nations held to this maxim. There is no Boudi-

22

cea or Maidhbh in our own annals till after the accession of the Tudors, when Great Eliza rivals her elder kins-women's glories. Though Tacitus expressly notices one tribe or confederacy, the Sitones, within the compass of his Germania, ruled by a woman, as an exceptional case, it was contrary to the feeling of mediæval Christendom for a woman to be emperor; it was not till late in the Middle Ages that Spain saw a queen regnant, and France has never yet allowed such rule. It was not till long after Saxo that the great queen of the North, Margaret, wielded a wider sway than that rejected by Gustavus' wayward daughter.

*The suitor ought to urge his own suit.*—This, an axiom of the most archaic law, gets evaded bit by bit till the professional advocate takes the place of the plaintiff. Njal's Saga, in its legal scenes, shows the transition period, when, as at Rome, a great and skilled chief was sought by his client as the supporter of his cause at the Moot. In England, the idea of representation at law is, as is well known, late and largely derived from canon law practice.

*To exact the blood-fine was as honourable as to take vengeance.*—This maxim, begotten by Interest upon Legality, established itself both in Scandinavia and Arabia. It marks the first stage in a progress which, if carried out wholly, substitutes law for feud. In the society of the heathen Danes the maxim was a novelty; even in Christian Denmark men sometimes preferred blood to fees.

MARRIAGE.—There are many reminiscences of *archaic marriage customs in Saxo.* The capture marriage has left traces in the guarded king's daughters, the challenging of kings to fight or hand over their daughters, in the promises to give a daughter or sister as a reward to a hero who shall accomplish some feat. The existence of polygamy is attested, and it went on till the days of Charles the Great and Harold

4                    23

Fairhair in singular instances, in the case of great kings, and finally disappeared before the strict ecclesiastic regulations.

But there are evidences also of later customs, such as *marriage by purchase*, already looked on as archaic in Saxo's day; and the free women in Denmark had clearly long had a veto or refusal of a husband for some time back, and sometimes even free choice. "Go-betweens" negotiate marriages.

Betrothal was of course the usage. For the groom to defile an espoused woman is a foul reproach. Gifts made to father-in-law after bridal by bridegroom seem to denote the old bride-price. Taking the bride home in her car was an important ceremony, and a bride is taken to her future husband's by her father. The wedding-feast, as in France in Rabelais' time, was a noisy and drunken and tumultuous rejoicing, when bone-throwing was in favor, with other rough sports and jokes. The three days after the bridal and their observance in "sword-bed" are noticed below.

A commoner or one of slave-blood could not pretend to wed a high-born lady. A woman would sometimes require some proof of power or courage at her suitor's hands; thus Gywritha, like the famous lady who weds Harold Fairhair, required her husband Siwar to be over-king of the whole land. But in most instances the father or brother betrothed the girl, and she consented to their choice. Unwelcome suitors perish.

The prohibited degrees were, of course, different from those established by the mediæval church, and brother weds brother's widow in good archaic fashion. Foster-sister and foster-brother may marry, as Saxo notices carefully. The Wolsung incest is not noticed by Saxo. He only knew, apparently, the North-German form of the Niflung story. But the reproachfulness of incest is apparent.

Birth and beauty were looked for in a bride by Saxo's

heroes, and chastity was required. The modesty of maidens in old days is eulogised by Saxo, and the penalty for its infraction was severe: sale abroad into slavery to grind the quern in the mud of the yard. One of the tests of virtue is noticed, *lac in ubere*.

That favourite *motif*, the *Patient Grizzle*, occurs, rather, however, in the Border ballad than the Petrarcan form.

*Good wives* die with their husbands as they have vowed, or of grief for their loss, and are wholly devoted to their interests. Among *bad wives* are those that wed their husband's slayer, run away from their husbands, plot against their husbands' lives. The penalty for adultery is death to both, at husband's option—disfigurement by cutting off the nose of the guilty woman, an archaic practice widely spread. In one case the adulterous lady is left the choice of her own death. Married women's Homeric duties are shown.

There is a curious story, which may rest upon fact, and not be merely typical, where a mother who had suffered wrong forced her daughter to suffer the same wrong.

Captive women are reduced to degrading slavery as *harlots* in one case, according to the eleventh century English practice of Gytha.

THE FAMILY AND BLOOD REVENGE.—This duty, one of the strongest links of the family in archaic Teutonic society, has left deep traces in Saxo.

To slay those most close in blood, even by accident, is to incur the guilt of parricide, or kin-killing, a bootless crime, which can only be purged by religious ceremonies ; and which involves exile, lest the gods' wrath fall on the land, and brings the curse of childlessness on the offender until he is forgiven.

BOOTLESS CRIMES.—As among the ancient Teutons, bótes and were-gilds satisfy the injured who seek redress at law

rather than by the steel. But there are certain bootless crimes, or rather sins, that imply *sacratio,* devotion to the gods, for the clearing of the community. Such are *treason,* which is punishable by hanging; by drowning in sea.

*Rebellion* is still more harshly treated by death and forfeiture; the rebels' heels are bored and thonged under the sinew, as Hector's feet were, and they are then fastened by the thongs to wild bulls, hunted by hounds, till they are dashed to pieces (for which there are classic parallels), or their feet are fastened with thongs to horses driven apart, so that they are torn asunder.

For *parricide, i. e.,* killing within near degrees, the criminal is hung up, apparently by the heels, with a live wolf (he having acted as a wolf which will slay its fellows). Cunning avoidance of the guilt by trick is shown.

For *arson* the appropriate punishment is the fire.

For *incestuous adultery* of stepson with his stepmother, hanging is awarded to the man. In the same case Swanwhite, the woman, is punished by treading to death with horses. A woman accomplice in adultery is treated to what Homer calls a "stone coat." Incestuous adultery is a foul slur.

For *witchcraft,* the horror of heathens, hanging was the penalty.

*Private revenge* sometimes deliberately inflicts a cruel death for atrocious wrong or insult, as when a king, enraged at the slaying of his son and seduction of his daughter, has the offender hanged, an instance famous in Nathan's story, so that Hagbard's hanging and hempen necklace were proverbial.

For the slayer by a cruel death of their captive father, Ragnar's sons act the blood-eagle on Ella, and salt his flesh. There is an undoubted instance of this act of vengeance (the

26

symbolic meaning of which is not clear as yet) in the Orkney Saga.

But the story of Daxo and of Ref's gild show that for such wrongs were-gilds were sometimes exacted, and that they were considered highly honourable to the exactor.

Among OFFENCES NOT BOOTLESS, and left to individual pursuit, are:—

*Highway robbery.*—There are several stories of a type such as that of Ingemund and Iokul (see Landnámabóc) told by Saxo of highwaymen; and an incident of the kind that occurs in the Theseus story (the Bent-tree, which sprung back and slew the wretch bound to it) is given. The romantic trick of the mechanic bed, by which a steel-shod beam is let fall on the sleeping traveller, also occurs. Slain highwaymen are gibbeted as in Christian days.

*Assassination*, as distinct from manslaughter in vengeance for a wrong, is not very common. A hidden mail-coat foils a treacherous javelin-cast (cf. the Story of Olaf the Stout and the Blind King, Hrorec); murderers lurk spear-armed at the threshold sides, as in the Icelandic Sagas; a queen hides a spear-head in her gown, and murders her husband (cf. Olaf Tryggwason's Life). Godfred was murdered by his servant (and *Ynglingatal*).

*Burglary.*—The crafty discovery of the robber of the treasury by Hadding is a variant of the world-old Rhampsinitos tale, but less elaborate, possibly abridged and cut down by Saxo, and reduced to a mere moral example in favour of the goldenness of silence and the danger of letting the tongue feed the gallows.

Among other disgraceful acts, that make the offender infamous, but do not necessarily involve public action:—

*Manslaughter in Breach of Hospitality.*—Probably any gross breach of hospitality was disreputable and highly ab-

horred, but *guest-slaughter* is especially mentioned. The ethical question as to whether a man should slay his guest or forego his just vengeance was often a *problème du jour* in the archaic times to which these traditions witness. Ingeld prefers his vengeance, but Thuriswend, in the Lay cited by Paul the Deacon, chooses to protect his guest. Heremod slew his messmates in his wrath, and went forth alone into exile. (Beowulf's Lay.)

*Suicide.*—This was more honourable than what Earl Siward of Northumberland called a "cow-death." Hadding resolves to commit suicide at his friend's death. Wermund resolves to commit suicide if his son be slain (in hopelessness of being able to avenge him, cf. Njal's Saga, where the hero, a Christian, prefers to perish in his burning house than live dishonoured, "for I am an old man and little fitted to avenge my sons, but I will not live in shame"). Persons commit suicide by slaying each other in time of famine; while in England (so Bæda tells) they "decliffed" themselves in companies, and, as in the comic little Icelandic tale of Gautrec's birth, a Tarpeian death is noted as the customary method of relieving folks from the hateful starvation-death. It is probable that the violent death relieved the ghost or the survivors of some inconveniences which a "straw death" would have brought about.

*Procedure by Wager of Battle.*—This archaic process pervades Saxo's whole narrative. It is the main incident of many of the sagas from which he drew. It is one of the chief characteristics of early Teutonic custom-law, and along with Cormac's Saga, Landnámabóc, and the Walter Saga, our author has furnished us with most of the information we have upon its principles and practice.

Steps in the process are the Challenge. the Acceptance and Settlement of Conditions, the Engagement, the Treat-

ment of the vanquished, the Reward of the conqueror, and
there are rules touching each of these, enough almost to
furnish a kind of "Galway code."

A challenge could not, either to war or wager of battle,
be refused with honor, though a superior was not bound to
fight an inferior in rank. An ally might accept for his principal, or a father for a son, but it was not honourable for a
man unless helpless to send a champion instead of himself.

Men were bound to fight one to one, and one man might
decline to fight two at once. Great champions sometimes
fought against odds.

The challenged man chose the place of battle, and possibly
fixed the time. This was usually an island in the river.

The regular weapons were swords and shields for men of
gentle blood. They fought by alternate separate strokes;
the senior had the first blow. The fight must go on face to
face without change of place; for the ground was marked
out for the combatants, as in our prize ring, though one can
hardly help fancying that the fighting ground so carefully
described in Cormac's Saga, ch. 10, may have been Saxo's
authority. The combatants change places accidentally in
the struggle in one story.

The combat might last, like Cuchullin's with Ferdia, several days; a nine days' fight occurs; but usually a few blows
settled the matter. Endurance was important, and we are
told of a hero keeping himself in constant training by walking in a mail coat.

The conqueror ought not to slay his man if he were a
stripling, or maimed, and had better take his were-gild for
his life, the holmslausn or ransom of Cormac's Saga (three
marks in Iceland); but this was a mere concession to natural
pity, and he might without loss of honor finish his man, and

cut off his head, though it was proper, if the slain adversary has been a man of honor, to bury him afterward.

The stakes are sometimes a kingdom or a kingdom's tribute, often a lady, or the combatants fought for "love" or the point of honor. Giants and noted champions challenge kings for their daughters (as in the fictitious parts of the Icelandic family sagas) in true archaic fashion, and in true archaic fashion the prince rescues the lady from a disgusting and evil fate by his prowess.

The champion's fee or reward when he was fighting for his principal and came off successful was heavy—many lands and sixty slaves. Bracelets are given him; a wound is compensated for at ten gold pieces; a fee for killing a king is 120 of the same.

Of the incidents of the combat, beside fair sleight of fence, there is the continual occurrence of the sword-blunting spell, often cast by the eye of the sinister champion, and foiled by the good hero, sometimes by covering his blade with thin skin, sometimes by changing the blade, sometimes by using a mace or club.

The strength of this tradition sufficiently explains the necessity of the great oath against magic taken by both parties in a wager of battle in Christian England.

The chief combats mentioned by Saxo are:—

Sciold *v.* Attila.

" *v.* Scate, for the hand of Alfhild.

Gram *v.* Swarin and eight more, for the crown of the Swedes.

Hadding *v.* Toste, by challenge.

Frode *v.* Hunding, on challenge.

" *v.* Hacon, " "

Helge *v.* Hunding, by challenge at Stad.

Agnar *v.* Bearce, by challenge.

Wizard *v.* Danish champions, for truage of the Slavs.
"       *v.* Ubbe,               "          "
Coll *v.* Horwendill, on challenge.
Athisl *v.* Frowine, meeting in battle.
"       *v.* Ket and Wig, on challenge.
Uffe *v.* Prince of Saxony and Champion, by challenge.
Frode *v.* Froger, on challenge.
Eric *v.* Grep's brethren, on challenge, twelve a side.
Eric *v.* Alrec, by challenge.
Hedin *v.* Hogni, the mythic everlasting battle.
Arngrim *v.* Scalc, by challenge.
"       *v.* Egtheow, for truage of Permland.
Arrow-Odd and Hialmar *v.* twelve sons of Arngrim
Samsey fight.
Ane Bow-swayer *v.* Beorn, by challenge.
Starkad *v.* Wisin,              "
"       *v.* Tanne,              "
"       *v.* Wasce—Wilzce.       "
"       *v.* Hame,               "
"       *v.* Angantheow and eight of his brethren, on
            challenge.
Halfdan *v.* Hardbone and six champions, on challenge.
"       *v.* Egtheow, by challenge.
"       *v.* Grim, on challenge.
"       *v.* Ebbe,       "       by moonlight.
"       *v.* Twelve champions, on challenge.
"       *v.* Hildeger, on challenge.
Ole *v.* Skate and Hiale,       "
Homod and Thole *v.* Beorn and Thore, by challenge.
Ref. *v.* Gaut, on challenge.
Ragnar and three sons *v.* Starcad of Sweden and seven
sons, on challenge.
CIVIL PROCEDURE.—*Oaths* are an important part of early

procedure, and noticed by Saxo; one calling the gods to witness and therefor, it is understood, to avenge perjury if he spake not truth.

*Testification,* or calling witnesses to prove the steps of a legal action, was known, Glum's Saga and Landn, and when a manslayer proceeded (in order to clear himself of murder) to announce the manslaughter as his act, he brings the dead man's head as his proof, exactly as the hero in the folk-tales brings the dragon's head or tongue as his voucher.

A *will* is spoken of. This seems to be the solemn declaration of a childless man to his kinsfolk, recommending some person as his successor. Nothing more was possible before written wills were introduced by the Christian clergy after the Roman fashion.

## STATUTE LAWS.

*Lawgivers.*—The realm of Custom had already long been curtailed by the conquests of Law when Saxo wrote, and some epochs of the invasion were well remembered, such as Canute's laws. But the beginnings were dim, and there were simply traditions of good and bad *lawyers* of the past; such were *Sciold* first of all the arch-king, *Frode* the model law-giver, *Helge* the tyrant, *Ragnar* the shrewd conqueror.

*Sciold,* the patriarch, is made by tradition to fulfil, by abolishing evil customs and making good laws, the ideal of the Saxon and Frankish Coronation oath formula (which may well go back with its two first clauses to heathen days). His fame is as widely spread. However, the only law Saxo gives to him has a story to it that he does not plainly tell. Sciold had a freedman who repaid his master's manumission

32

of him by the ingratitude of attempting his life. Sciold thereupon decrees the unlawfulness of manumissions, *or* (as Saxo puts it), revoked all manumissions, thus ordaining perpetual slavery on all that were or might become slaves. The heathen lack of pity noticed in Alfred's preface to Gregory's Handbook is illustrated here by contrast with the philosophic humanity of the Civil Law, and the sympathy of the mediæval Church.

But FRODE (known also to the compiler of Beowulf's Lay, 2025) had, in the Dane's eyes, almost eclipsed Sciold as conqueror and lawgiver. His name Frode almost looks as if his epithet *Sapiens* had become his popular appellation, and it befits him well. Of him were told many stories, and notably the one related of our Edwin by Bede (and as it has been told by many men of many rulers since Bede wrote, and before). Frode was able to hang up an arm-ring of gold in three parts of his kingdom that no thief for many years dared touch. How this incident (according to our version preserved by Saxo), brought the just king to his end is an archaic and interesting story. Was this ring the Brosinga men?

Saxo has even recorded the *Laws of Frode* in four separate bits, which we give as A, B, C, D.

A. is mainly a civil and military code of archaic kind:

(*a*) The division of spoil shall be—gold to captains, silver to privates, arms to champions, ships to be shared by all. Cf. Jomswickinga S. on the division of spoil by the law of the pirate community of Jom.

(*b*) No house stuff to be locked; if a man used a lock he must pay a gold mark.

(*c*) He who spares a thief must bear his punishment.

(*d*) The coward in battle is to forfeit all rights (cf. Beowulf, 2885).

(*e*) Women to have free choice (or, at least, veto) in taking husbands.

(*f*) A free woman that weds a slave loses rank and freedom (cf. Roman Law).

(*g*) A man must marry a girl he has seduced.

(*h*) An adulterer to be mutilated at pleasure of injured husband.

(*i*) Where Dane robbed Dane, the thief to pay double and peace-breach.

(*k*) Receivers of stolen goods suffer forfeiture and flogging at most.

(*l*) Deserter bearing shield against his countrymen to lose life and property.

(*m*) Contempt of fyrd-summons *or* call to military service involves outlawry and exile.

(*n*) Bravery in battle to bring about increase in rank (cf. the old English "Ranks of Men").

(*o*) No suit to lie on promise and pledge; fine of ½ gold lb. for asking pledge.

(*p*) Wager of battle is to be the universal mode of proof.

(*q*) If an alien kill a Dane two aliens must suffer. (This is practically the same principle as appears in the half were-gild of the Welsh in West Saxon Law.)

B. An illustration of the more capricious of the old enactments and the jealousy of antique kings.

(*a*) Loss of gifts sent to the king involves the official responsible; he shall be hanged. (This is introduced as illustration of the cleverness of Eric and the folly of Coll.)

C. Saxo associates another set of enactments with the completion of a successful campaign of conquest over the Ruthenians, and shows Frode chiefly as a wise and civilising statesman, making conquest mean progress.

(*a*) Every free householder that fell in war was to be set

34

in his barrow with horse and arms (cf. Vatzdæla Saga, ch. 2).

The body-snatcher was to be punished by death and the lack of sepulture.

Earl or king to be burned in his own ship.

Ten sailors may be burnt on one ship.

(*b*) Ruthenians to have the same *law of war* as Danes.

(*c*) Ruthenians must adopt Danish sale-marriage. (This involves the abolition of the Baltic custom of capture-marriage. That capture-marriage was a bar to social progress appears in the legislation of Richard II, directed against the custom as carried out on the borders of the Palatine county of Chester, while cases such as the famous one of Rob Roy's sons speak to its late continuance in Scotland. In Ireland it survived in a stray instance or two into this century, and songs like "William Riley" attest the sympathy of the peasant with the eloping couple.)

(*e*) A veteran, one of the Doughty, must be such a man as will attack one foe, will stand two, face three without withdrawing more than a little, and be content to retire only before four. (One of the traditional folk-sayings respecting the picked men, the Doughty or Old Guard, as distinguished from the Youth or Young Guard, the new-comers in the king's Company of House-carles. In Harald Hardrede's Life the Norwegians dread those English house-carles, "each of whom is a match for four," who formed the famous guard that won Stamford Bridge and fell about their lord, a sadly shrunken band, at Senlake.)

(*f*) The house-carles to have winter-pay. The house-carle three pieces of silver, a hired soldier two pieces, a soldier who had finished his service one piece.

(The treatment of the house-carles gave Harald Harefoot a reputation long remembered for generosity, and several old

Northern kings have won their nicknames by their good or ill feeding and rewarding their comitatus.)

D. Again a civil code, dealing chiefly with the rights of travellers.

(*a*) Seafarers may use what gear they find (the "remis" of the text may include boat or tackle).

(*b*) No house is to be locked, nor coffer, but all thefts to be compensated threefold. (This, like A, *b*, which it resembles, seems a popular tradition intended to show the absolute security of Frode's reign of seven or three hundred years. It is probably a gloss wrongly repeated.)

(*c*) A traveller may claim a single supper; if he take more he is a thief (the mark of a præ-tabernal era when hospitality was waxing cold through misuse).

(*d*) Thief and accomplices are to be punished alike, being hung up by a line through the sinews and a wolf fastened beside. (This, which contradicts A, *i*, *k*, and allots to theft the punishment proper for parricide, seems a mere distorted tradition.)

But beside just Frode, tradition spoke of the unjust Kinge HELGE, whose laws represent ill-judged harshness. They were made for conquered races, (*a*) the Saxons and (*b*) the Swedes.

(*a*) Noble and freedmen to have the same were-gild (the lower, of course, the intent being to degrade all the conquered to one level, and to allow only the lowest were-gild of a freedman, fifty pieces, probably, in the tradition).

(*b*) No remedy for wrong done to a Swede by a Dane to be legally recoverable. (This is the traditional interpretation of the conqueror's haughty dealing; we may compare it with the Middle-English legends of the pride of the Dane towards the conquered English. The Tradition sums up the position in such concrete forms as this Law of Helge's.)

36

Two statutes of RAGNAR are mentioned:—

(*a*) That any householder should give up to his service in war the worst of his children, or the laziest of his slaves (a curious tradition, and used by Saxo as an opportunity for patriotic exaltation).

(*b*) That all suits shall be absolutely referred to the judgment of twelve chosen elders (Lodbroc here appearing in the strange character of originator of trial by jury).

*Tributes.*—Akin to laws are the tributes decreed and imposed by kings and conquerors of old. Tribute infers subjection in archaic law. The poll-tax in the fourteenth century in England was unpopular, because of its seeming to degrade Englishmen to the level of Frenchmen, who paid tribute like vanquished men to their absolute lord, as well as for other reasons connected with the collection of the tax.

The old fur tax (mentioned in Egil's Saga) is here ascribed to FRODE, who makes the Finns pay him, every three years, a car full *or* sledge full of skins for every ten heads; and extorts one skin per head from the Perms. It is Frode, too (though Saxo has carved a number of Frodes out of one or two kings of gigantic personality), that made the Saxons pay a poll-tax, a piece of money per head, using, like William the Conqueror, his extraordinary revenue to reward his soldiers, whom he first regaled with double pay. But on the conquered folks rebelling, he marked their reduction by a tax of a piece of money on every limb a cubit long, a "limb-geld" still more hateful than the "neb-geld."

HOTHERUS (Hodr) had set a tribute on the Kurlanders and Swedes, and HROLF laid a tribute on the conquered Swedes.

GODEFRIDUS-GOTRIC is credited with a third Saxon tribute, a heriot of 100 snow-white horses payable to each Danish king at his succession, and by each Saxon chief on his acces-

sion: a statement that, recalling sacred snow-white horses
kept in North Germany of yore makes one wish for fuller
information. But Godefridus also exacted from the Swedes
the *Ref-gild,* or Fox-money; for the slaying of his henchman Ref, twelve pieces of gold from each man of rank, one
from every commoner. And his Friesland tribute is stranger
still, nor is it easy to understand from Saxo's account. There
was a long hall built, 240 feet, and divided up into twelve
"chases" of 20 feet each (probably square). There was a
shield set up at one end, and the taxpayers hurled their
money at it; if it struck so as to sound, it was good; if not,
it was forfeit, but not reckoned in the receipt. This (a popular version, it may be, of some early system of treasury
test) was abolished, so the story goes, by Charles the Great.

RAGNAR'S exaction from Daxo, his son's slayer, was a
yearly tribute brought by himself and twelve of his elders
barefoot, resembling in part such submissions as occur in
the Angevin family history, the case of the Calais burgesses,
and of such criminals as the Corporation of Oxford, whose
penance was only finally renounced by the local patriots in
our own day.

WAR.

*Weapons.*—The *sword* is the weapon *par excellence* in
Saxo's narrative, and he names several by name, famous old
blades like our royal Curtana, which some believed was once
Tristrem's, and that sword of Carlus, whose fortunes are
recorded in Irish annals. Such are *Snyrtir,* Bearce's sword;
*Hothing,* Agnar's blade; *Lauf,* or *Leaf,* Bearce's sword;
*Screp,* Wermund's sword, long buried and much rust-eaten,
but sharp and trusty, and known by its whistle; Miming's

38

sword (Mistletoe), which slew Balder. Wainhead's curved blade seems to be a halbert; *Lyusing* and *Hwíting*, Ragnald of Norway's swords; *Lögthe,* the sword of Ole Siward's son.

The *war-club* occurs pretty frequently. But it is usually introduced as a special weapon of a special hero, who fashions a gold-headed club to slay one that steel cannot touch, or who tears up a tree, like the Spanish knight in the ballad, or who uses a club to counteract spells that blunt steel. The bat-shapen archaic rudder of a ship is used as a club in the story of the Sons of Arngrim.

The *spear* plays no particular part in Saxo: even Woden's spear Gungne is not prominent.

*Bows* and *arrows* are not often spoken of, but archer heroes, such as Toki, Ane Bow-swayer, and Orwar-Odd, are known. *Slings* and *stones* are used.

The *shield,* of all defensive armour, is far the most prominent. They were often painted with devices, such as Hamlet's shield, Hildiger's Swedish shield. Dr. Vigfússon has shown the importance of these painted shields in the poetic history of the Scandinavians.

A red shield is a signal of peace. Shields are set round ramparts on land as round ships at sea.

*Mail-coats* are worn. Frode has one charmed against steel. Hother has another; a mail-coat of proof is mentioned and their iron meshes are spoken of.

*Helmets* are used, but not so carefully described as in Beowulf's Lay; crested helmets and a gilded helmet occur in Bearca-mal and in another poem.

*Banners* serve as rallying points in the battle and on the march. The Huns' banners are spoken of in the classic passage for the description of a huge host invading a country. Bearca-mal talks of golden banners.

6          39

*Horns** were blown up at the beginning of the engagement and for signalling. The gathering of the host was made by delivery of a *wooden arrow* painted to look like iron.

*Tactics.*—The hand-to-hand fight of the wager of battle with sword and shield, and the fighting in ranks and the wedge-column at close quarters, show that the close infantry combat was the main event of the battle. The preliminary hurling of stones, and shooting of arrows, and slinging of pebbles, were harassing and annoying, but seldom sufficiently important to affect the result of the main engagement.

Men ride to battle, but fight on foot; occasionally an aged king is car-borne to the fray, and once the car, whether by Saxo's adorning hand, or by tradition, is scythe-armed.

The gathered host is numbered, once, where, as with Xerxes, counting was too difficult, by making each man as he passed put a pebble in a pile (which piles survive to mark the huge size of Frode's army). This is, of course, a folk-tale, explaining the pebble-hills and illustrating the belief in Frode's power; but armies were mustered by such expedients of old. Burton tells of an African army each man of whom presented an egg, as a token of his presence and a means of taking the number of the host.

We hear of men marching in light order without even scabbards, and getting over the ice in socks.

The war equipment and habits of the Irish, light armoured, clipped at back of head, hurling the javelin backwards in their feigned flight; of the Slavs, small blue targets and long swords; of the Finns, with their darts and skees, are given.

Watches are kept, and it is noted that "uht," the early watch after midnight, is the worst to be attacked in (the

---

*A horn and a tusk of great size are described as things of price, and great uroch's horns are mentioned in Thorkill's Second Journey. Horns were used for feast as well as fray.

duke's two-o'clock-in-the-morning courage being needed, and the darkness and cold helping the enemy).

Spies were, of course, slain if discovered. But we have instances of kings and heroes getting into foeman's camps in disguise (cf. stories of Alfred and Anlaf).

The order of battle of Bravalla fight is given, and the ideal array of a host. To Woden is ascribed the device of the boar's head, hamalt fylking (the swine-head array of Manu's Indian kings), the terrible column with wedge head which could cleave the stoutest line.

The host of Ring has men from Wener, Wermland, Gota-elf, Thotn, Wick, Thelemark, Throndham, Sogn, Firths, Fialer, Iceland; Sweden, Gislamark, Sigtun, Upsala, Pannonia.

The host of Harold had men from Iceland, the Danish provinces, Frisia, Lifland; Slavs, and men from Jom, Aland, and Sleswick.

The battle of Bravalla is said to have been won by the Gotland archers and the men of Throndham, and the Dales. The death of Harald by treachery completed the defeat, which began when Ubbe fell (after he had broken the enemy's van) riddled with arrows.

The defeated, unless they could fly, got little quarter. One-fifth only of the population of a province are said to have survived an invasion. After sea-battles (always necessarily more deadly) the corpses choke the harbours. Seventy sea-kings are swept away in one sea-fight. Heads seem to have been taken in some cases, but not as a regular Teutonic usage, and the practice, from its being attributed to ghosts and aliens, must have already been considered savage by Saxo, and probably by his informants and authorities.

Prisoners were slaves; they might be killed, put to cruel death, outraged, used as slaves, but the feeling in favour of

mercy was growing, and the cruelty of Eormenric, who used tortures to his prisoners, of Rothe, who stripped his captives, and of Fro, who sent captive ladies to a brothel in insult, is regarded with dislike.

Wounds were looked on as honourable, but they must be in front or honourably got. A man who was shot through the buttocks, or wounded in the back, was laughed at and disgraced. We hear of a mother helping her wounded son out of battle.

That much of human interest centered round war is evident by the mass of tradition that surrounds the subject in Saxo, both in its public and private aspects. Quaint is the analysis of the four kinds of warriors: (*a*) The Veterans, or Doughty, who kill foes and spare flyers; (*b*) the Young men who kill foes and flyers too; (*c*) the well-to-do, landed, and propertied men of the main levy, who neither fight for fear nor fly for shame; (*d*) the worthless, last to fight and first to fly; and curious are the remarks about married and unmarried troops, a matter which Chaka pondered over in later days. Homeric speeches precede the fight.

*Stratagems of War* greatly interested Saxo (probably because Valerius Maximus, one of his most esteemed models, was much occupied with such matters), so that he diligently records the military traditions of the notably skillful expedients of famous commanders of old.

There is the device for taking a town by means of the *pretended death* of the besieging general, a device ascribed to Hastings and many more commanders (see Steenstrup Normannerne); the plan of *firing* a besieged town by *fire-bearing birds,* ascribed here to Fridlev, in the case of Dublin to Hadding against Duna (where it was foiled by all tame birds being chased out of the place).

There is the *Birnam Wood* stratagem, by which men

advanced behind a screen of boughs, which is even used for
the concealment of ships, and the curious legend (occurring
in Irish tradition also, and recalling Capt. B. Hall's "quaker
gun" story) by which a commander bluffs off his enemy by
*binding his dead to stakes* in rows, as if they were living
men.

Less easy to understand are the *brazen horses* or *machines*
driven into the close lines of the enemy to crush and open
them, an invention of Gewar. The use of *hooked weapons*
to pull down the foes' shields and helmets was also taught to
Hother by Gewar.

The use of *black tents* to conceal encampment; the defence of a pass by *hurling rocks* from the heights; the *bridge
of boats* across the Elbe; and the employment of *spies,* and
the bold venture, ascribed in our chronicles to Alfred and
Anlaf, of visiting in disguise the enemy's camp, is here attributed to Frode, who even assumed women's clothes for
the purpose.

Frode is throughout the typical general, as he is the typical
statesman and law-giver of archaic Denmark.

There are certain heathen usages connected with war, as
the hurling of a javelin or shooting of an arrow over the
enemy's ranks as a *sacratio* to Woden of the foe at the beginning of a battle. This is recorded in the older vernacular
authorities also, in exact accordance with the Homeric usage,
*Od.* xxiv, 516-525.

The dedication of part of the spoils to the god who gave
good omens for the war is told of the heathen Baltic peoples;
but though, as Sidonius records, it had once prevailed among
the Saxons, and, as other witnesses add, among the Scandinavian people, the tradition is not clearly preserved by Saxo.

*Sea and Sea Warfare.*—As might be expected, there is
much mention of Wicking adventure and of maritime warfare in Saxo.

Saxo tells of Asmund's huge ship (Gnod), built high that he might shoot down on the enemy's craft; he speaks of a ship (such as Godwin gave as a gift to the king his master), and the monk of St. Bertin and the court-poets have lovingly described a ship with gold-broidered sails, gilt masts, and red-dyed rigging. One of his ships has, like the ships in the Chansons de Geste, a carbuncle for a lantern at the mast-head. Hedin signals to Frode by a shield at the masthead. A red shield was a peace signal, as noted above. The practice of "strand-hewing," a great feature in Wicking-life (which, so far as the victualling of raw meat by the fishing fleets, and its use raw, as Mr. P. H. Emerson informs me, still survives), is spoken of. There was great fear of monsters attacking them, a fear probably justified by such occasional attacks of angry whales as Melville (founding his narrative on repeated facts) has immortalised. The whales, like Moby Dick, were uncanny, and inspired by troll-women or witches (cf. Frithiof Saga and the older Lay of Atle and Rimegerd). The clever sailing of Hadding, by which he eludes pursuit, is tantalising, for one gathers that Saxo knows the details that he for some reason omits. Big fleets of 150 and a monster armada of 3,000 vessels are recorded.

The ships were moved by oars and sails; they had rudders, no doubt such as the Gokstad ship, for the hero Arrow-Odd used a rudder as a weapon.

*Champions.*—Professed fighting men were often kept by kings and earls about their court as useful in feud and fray. Harald Fairhair's champions are admirably described in the contemporary Raven Song by Hornclofe—

> "Wolf-coats they call them that in battle
> Bellow into bloody shields.
> They wear wolves' hides when they come into the fight,
> And clash their weapons together."

and Saxo's sources adhere closely to this pattern.

These *bear-sarks*, or wolf-coats of Harald give rise to an O. N. term, "bear-sarks' way," to describe the frenzy of fight and fury which such champions indulged in, barking and howling, and biting their shield-rims (like the ferocious "rook" in the narwhale ivory chessmen in the British Museum) till a kind of state was produced akin to that of the Malay when he has worked himself up to "run a-muck." There seems to have been in the 10th century a number of such fellows about unemployed, who became nuisances to their neighbours by reason of their bullying and highhandedness. Stories are told in the Icelandic sagas of the way such persons were entrapped and put to death by the chiefs they served when they became too troublesome. A favourite (and fictitious) episode in an "edited" Icelandic saga is for the hero to rescue a lady promised to such a champion (who has bullied her father into consent) by slaying the ruffian. It is the same *motif* as Guy of Warwick and the Saracen lady, and one of the regular Giant and Knight stories.

Beside men-warriors there were *women-warriors* in the North, as Saxo explains. He describes shield-maidens, as Alfhild, Sela, Rusila (the Ingean Ruadh, or Red Maid of the Irish Annals, as Steenstrup so ingeniously conjectures) ; and the three she-captains, Wigbiorg, who fell on the field, Hetha, who was made queen of Zealand, and Wisna, whose hand Starcad cut off, all three fighting manfully at Bravalla fight.

### SOCIAL LIFE AND MANNERS.

*Feasts.*—The hall-dinner was an important feature in the old Teutonic court-life. Many a fine scene in a saga takes place in the hall while the king and his men are sitting over their ale. The hall decked with hangings, with its fires,

lights, plate and provisions, appears in Saxo just as in the Eddic Lays, especially Rígsmál, and the Lives of the Norwegian Kings and Orkney Earls.

The order of seats is a great point of archiac manners. Behaviour at table was a matter of careful observance. The service, especially that of the cup-bearer, was minutely regulated by etiquette. An honoured guest was welcomed by the host rising to receive him and giving him a seat near himself, but less distinguished visitors were often victims to the rough horseplay of the baser sort, and of the wanton young gentleman at court. The food was simple, boiled beef and pork, and mutton without sauce, ale served in horns from the butt. Roast meat, game, sauces, mead, and flagons set on the table, are looked on by Starcad as foreign luxuries, and Germany was credited with luxurious cookery.

*Mimes and jugglers,* who went through the country or were attached to the lord's court to amuse the company, were a despised race because of their ribaldry, obscenity, cowardice, and unabashed self-debasement; and their new-fangled dances and piping were loathsome to the old court-poets, who accepted the harp alone as an instrument of music.

The story that once a king went to war with his jugglers and they ran away, would represent the point of view of the old house-carle, who was neglected, though "a first-class fighting man," for these debauched foreign buffoons.

### SUPERNATURAL BEINGS.

GODS AND GODDESSES.—The gods spring, according to Saxo's belief, from a race of sorcerers, some of whom rose to pre-eminence and expelled and crushed the rest, ending the

*wizard-age,* as the wizards had ended the monster or *giant-age.* That they were identic with the classic gods he is inclined to believe, but his difficulty is that in the week-days we have Jove : Thor :: Mercury : Woden; whereas it is perfectly well known that Mercury is Jove's son, and also that Woden is the father of Thor—a comic *embarras.* That the persons the heathens worshipped as gods existed, and that they were men and women false and powerful, Saxo plainly believes. He has not Snorre's appreciation of the humorous side of the mythology. He is ironic and scornful, but without the kindly, naive fun of the Icelander.

The most active god, the Dane's chief god (as Frey is the Swede's god, and patriarch), is *Woden.* He appears in heroic life as patron of great heroes and kings. Cf. Hyndla-Lay, where it is said of Woden :—

> "Let us pray the Father of Hosts to be gracious to us!
> He granteth and giveth gold to his servants,
> He gave Heremod a helm and mail-coat,
> And Sigmund a sword to take.
> He giveth victory to his sons, to his followers wealth,
> Ready speech to his children and wisdom to men,
> Fair wind to captains, and song to poets;
> He giveth luck in love to many a hero."

He appears under various disguises and names, but usually as a one-eyed old man, cowled and hooded; sometimes with another, bald and ragged, as before the battle Hadding won; once as *Hróptr,* a huge man skilled in leechcraft, to Ragnar's son Sigfrid.

Often he is a helper in battle or doomer of feymen. As *Lysir,* a rover of the sea, he helps Hadding. As veteran slinger and archer he helps his favourite Hadding; as charioteer, *Brune,* he drives Harald to his death in battle. He teaches Hadding how to array his troops. As *Yggr* the

47

prophet he advises the hero and the gods. As *Wecha* (Wacr) the leech he woos Wrinda. He invented the wedge array. He can grant charmed lives to his favourites against steel. He prophesies their victories and death. He snatches up one of his disciples, sets him on his magic horse that rides over seas in the air, as in Skída-ríma the god takes the beggar over the North Sea. His image (like that of Frey in the Swedish story of Ogmund dytt and Gunnar helming, Flatey book, i, 335) could speak by magic power.

Of his life and career Saxo gives several episodes.

Woden himself dwelt at Upsala and Byzantium (Asgard) ; and the northern kings sent him a golden image ringbedecked, which he made to speak oracles. His wife Frigga stole the bracelets and played him false with a servant, who advised her to destroy and rob the image.

When Woden was away (hiding the disgrace brought on him by Frigga his wife), an imposter, Mid Odin, possibly Loke in disguise, usurped his place at Upsala, instituted special drink-offerings, fled to Finland on Woden's return, and was slain by the Fins and laid in barrow. But the barrow smote all that approached it with death, till the body was unearthed, beheaded, and impaled, a well-known process for stopping the haunting of an obnoxious or dangerous ghost.

Woden had a son Balder, rival of Hother for the love of Nanna, daughter of King Gewar. Woden and Thor his son fought for him against Hother, but in vain, for Hother won the lady and put Balder to shameful flight ; however, Balder, half-frenzied by his dreams of Nanna, in turn drove him into exile (winning the lady) ; finally Hother, befriended by luck and the Wood Maidens, to whom he owed his early successes and his magic coat, belt, and girdle (there is obvious confusion here in the text), at last met Balder and stabbed him in the side. Of this wound Balder died in three days, as was

48

foretold by the awful dream in which Proserpina (Hela) appeared to him. Balder's grand burial, his barrow, and the magic flood which burst from it when one Harald tried to break into it, and terrified the robbers, are described. The death of Balder led Woden to seek revenge. Hross-thiof the wizard, whom he consulted, told him he must beget a son by *Wrinda* (Rinda, daughter of the King of the Ruthenians), who should avenge his half-brother.

Woden's wooing is the best part of this story, half spoilt, however, by euhemeristic tone and lack of epic dignity. He woos as a victorious warrior, and receives a cuff; as a generous goldsmith, and gets a buffet; as a handsome soldier, earning a heavy knock-down blow; but in the garb of a women as Wecha (Wákr), skilled in leechcraft, he won his way by trickery; and (*Wale*) *Bous* was born, who, after some years, slew Hother in battle, and died himself of his wounds. Bous' barrow in Bohusland, Balder's haven, Balder's well, are named as local attestations of the legend, which is in a late form, as it seems.

The story of Woden's being banished for misbehaviour, and especially for sorcery and for having worn woman's attire to trick Wrinda, his replacement by *Wuldor* (*Oller*), a high priest who assumed Woden's name and flourished for ten years, but was ultimately expelled by the returning Woden, and killed by the Danes in Sweden, is in the same style. But Wuldor's bone vessel is an old bit of genuine tradition mangled. It would cross the sea as well as a ship could, by virtue of certain spells marked on it.

Of *Frey*, who appears as *satrapa* of the gods at Upsala, and as the originator of human sacrifice, and as appeased by black victims, at a sacrifice called Fröblod (Freys-blót) instituted by Hadding, who began it as an atonement for having slain a sea-monster, a deed for which he had incurred a

49

curse. The priapic and generative influences of Frey are only indicated by a curious tradition mentioned. It almost looks as if there had once been such an institution at Upsala as adorned the Phœnician temples, under Frey's patronage and for a symbolic means of worship.

*Thunder,* or *Thor,* is Woden's son, strongest of gods or men, patron of Starcad, whom he turned, by pulling off four arms, from a monster to a man.

He fights by Woden's side and Balder's against Hother, by whose magic wand his club (hammer) was lopped off part of its shaft, a wholly different and, a much later version than the one Snorre gives in the prose Edda. Saxo knows of Thor's journey to the haunt of giant Garfred (Geirrod) and his three daughters, and of the hurling of the iron "bloom," and of the crushing of the giantesses, though he does not seem to have known of the river-feats of either the ladies or Thor, if we may judge (never a safe thing wholly) by his silence.

Whether *Tew* is meant by the Mars of the Song of the Voice is not evident. Saxo may only be imitating the repeated catch-word "war" of the original.

*Loke* appears as Utgard-Loke, Loke of the skirts of the World, as it were; is treated as a venomous giant bound in agony under a serpent-haunted cavern (no mention is made of *Sigyn* or her pious ministry).

*Hela* seems to be meant by Saxo's Proserpina.

*Nanna* is the daughter of Gewar, and Balder sees her bathing and falls in love with her, as madly as Frey with Gertha in Skirnismal.

*Freya,* the mistress of Od, the patroness of Othere the homely, the sister of Frey-Frode, and daughter of Niord-Fridlaf, appears as Gunwara Eric's love and Syritha Ottar's love and the hair-clogged maiden, as Dr. Rydberg has shown.

cases. The people and ... ...
only indicated by a ... ...
looks as if there had ... ... ...
as adorned the ... ...
and for a ... ...

Thunder, or ... ... ...
men, patron of ... ...
arms, from ... ...

He fights ... ...
whose image ... ...
in chief, a ... ...
the ... ...

Thor's journey ... ...
his three daughters

THE custom long obtained among Scandinavians of trying both civil and criminal cases before juries at what was called the Thing, which met in the open air within a space enclosed by a ring of stones set upright in the ground. The ... at the Danish Thing was beside the ... stones upon which Runish inscriptions were engraved ... Before him any free man might plead his own case as before a judge of our own time and verdicts were rendered by a jury ... twelve, sometimes eighteen, peers

The gods can disguise their form, change their shape, are often met in a mist, which shrouds them save from the right person; they appear and disappear at will. For the rest they have the mental and physical characteristics of the kings and queens they protect or persecute so capriciously. They can be seen by making a magic sign and looking through a witch's arm held akimbo. They are no good co-mates for men or women, and to meddle with a goddess or nymph or giantess was to ensure evil or death for a man. The god's loves were apparently not always so fatal, though there seems to be some tradition to that effect. Most of the god-sprung heroes are motherless or unborn (*i. e.*, born like Macduff by the Cæsarean operation)—Sigfred, in the Eddic Lays for instance.

Besides the gods, possibly older than they are, and presumably mightier, are the *Fates* (Norns), three Ladies who are met with together, who fulfil the parts of the gift-fairies of our Sleeping Beauty tales, and bestow endowments on the new-born child, as in the beautiful Helge Lay, a point of the story which survives in Ogier of the Chansons de Geste, wherein Eadgar (Otkerus or Otgerus) gets what belonged to Holger (Holge), the Helga of Beowulf's Lay. The caprices of the Fates, where one corrects or spoils the others' endowments, are seen in Saxo, when beauty, bounty, and meanness are given together. They sometimes meet heroes, as they met Helgi in the Eddic Lay (Helgi and Sigrun Lay), and help or begift them; they prepare the magic broth for Balder, are charmed with Hother's lute-playing, and bestow on him a belt of victory and a girdle of splendour, and prophesy things to come.

The verse in Biarca-mal, where "Pluto weaves the dooms of the mighty and fills Phlegethon with noble shapes," recalls Darrada-lióð, and points to Woden as death-doomer of the warrior. 51

*Giants.*—These are stupid, mischievous, evil and cunning in Saxo's eyes. Oldest of beings, with chaotic force and exuberance, monstrous in extravagant vitality.

The giant nature of the older troll-kind is abhorrent to man and woman. But a giantess is enamoured of a youth she had fostered, and giants carry off king's daughters, and a three-bodied giant captures young children.

Giants live in ·caves by the sea, where they keep their treasure. One giant, Unfoot (Ofóti), is a shepherd, like Polyphemus, and has a famous dog which passed into the charge of Biorn, and won a battle; a giantess is keeping goats in the wilds. A giant's fury is so great that it takes twelve champions to control him, when the rage is on him. The troll (like our Puss-in-Boots Ogre) can take any shape.

Monstrous apparitions are mentioned, a giant hand (like that in one story of Finn) searching for its prey among the inmates of a booth in the wilds. But this Grendel-like arm is torn off by a giantess, Hardgrip, daughter of Wainhead and niece possibly of Hafle.

The voice heard at night prophesying is that of some god or monster, possibly Woden himself.

*Dwarves.*—These Saxo calls Satyrs, and but rarely mentions. The dwarf Miming, who lives in the desert, has a precious sword of sharpness (Mistletoe?) that could even pierce skin-hard Balder, and a ring (Draupnir) that multiplied itself for its possessor. He is trapped by the hero and robbed of his treasures.

### FUNERAL RITES AND MAN'S FUTURE STATE.

*Barrow-burials.*—The obsequies of great men (such as the classic funeral of Beowulf's Lay, 3138-80) are much noticed by Saxo, and we might expect that he knew such a poem

(one similar to Ynglingatal, but not it) which, like the Books of the Kings of Israel and Judah, recorded the deaths and burials, as well as the pedigrees and deeds, of the Danish kings.

The various stages of the *obsequy by fire* are noted; the pyre sometimes formed out of a ship; the *sati;* the devoted bower-maidens choosing to die with their mistress, the dead man's beloved (cf. the Eddic funerals of Balder, Sigfred, and Brunhild, in the Long Brunhild's Lay, Tregrof Gudrunar and the lost poem of Balder's death paraphrased in the prose Edda); the last message given to the corpse on the pyre (Woden's last words to Balder are famous); the riding round the pyre; the eulogium; the piling of the barrow, which sometimes took whole days, as the size of many existing grass mounds assure us; the funeral feast, where an immense vat of ale or mead is drunk in honor of the dead; the epitaph, like an ogham, set up on a stone over the barrow.

The inclusion of a live man with the dead in a barrow, with the live or fresh-slain beasts (horse and hound) of the dead man, seems to point to a time or district when burning was not used. Apparently, at one time, judging from Frode's law, only chiefs and warriors were burnt.

Not to bury was, as in Hellas, an insult to the dead, reserved for the bodies of hated foes. Conquerors sometimes show their magnanimity (like Harald Godwineson) by offering to bury their dead foes.

The buried *barrow-ghost* was formidable; he could rise and slay and eat, vampire-like, as in the tale of Asmund and Aswit. He must in such case be mastered and prevented doing further harm by decapitation and thigh-forking, or by staking and burning. So criminals' bodies were often burnt to stop possible haunting.

53

Witches and wizards could *raise corpses* by spells to make them prophesy. The dead also appeared in visions, usually foretelling death to the person they visited.

OTHER WORLDS.—The *Land of Undeath* is spoken of as a place reached by an exiled hero in his wanderings. We know it from Eric the traveller's S., Helge Thoreson's S., Herraud and Bose S., Herwon S., Thorstan Bæarmagn S., and other Icelandic sources. But the voyage to the Other Worlds are some of the most remarkable of the narratives Saxo has preserved for us.

*Hadding's Voyage Underground.*—(*a*) A woman bearing in her lap angelica fresh and green, though it was deep winter, appears to the hero at supper, raising her head beside the brazier. Hadding wishes to know where such plants grow.

(*b*) She takes him with her, under cover of her mantle, underground.

(*c*) They pierce a mist, get on a road worn by long use, pass nobly-clad men, and reach the sunny fields that bear the angelica:—

"Through griesly shadowes by a beaten path,
Into a garden goodly garnished."
F. Q. ii. 7, 51.

(*d*) Next they cross, by a bridge, the *River of Blades*, and see *two armies fighting*, ghosts of slain soldiers.

(*e*) Last they came to a high wall, which surrounds the land of Life, for a cock the woman brought with her, whose neck she wrung and tossed over this wall, came to life and crowed merrily.

Here the story breaks off. It is unfinished, we are only told that Hadding got back. Why he was taken to this under-world? who took him? what followed therefrom? Saxo does not tell. It is left to us to make out.

That it is an archaic story of the kind in the Thomas of

Ercildoune and so many more fairy-tales, *e. g.*, Kate Crack-a-Nuts, is certain. The *River of Blades* and *The Fighting Warriors* are known from the Eddic Poems. The angelica is like the green birk of that superb fragment, the ballad of the Wife of Usher's Well—a little more frankly heathen, of course—

> "It fell about the Martinmas, when nights are long and mirk,
> The carline wife's three sons cam hame, and their hats were
>    o' the birk.
> It neither grew in syke nor dyke, nor yet in ony sheugh,
> But at the gates o' Paradise that birk grew fair eneuch."

The *mantel* is that of Woden when he bears the hero over seas; the *cock* is a bird of sorcery the world over; the black fowl is the proper gift to the Underground powers—a heriot really, for did not the Culture god steal all the useful beasts out of the underground world for men's use?

Dr. Rydberg has shown that the *Seven Sleepers* story is an old Northern myth, alluded to here in its early pre-Christian form, and that with this is mixed other incidents from voyages of Swipdag, the Teutonic Odusseus.

*Thorkill's Second Voyage to Outgarth-Loke to get Knowledge.*—(*a*) Guthrum is troubled as to the immortality and fate of the soul, and the reward of piety after death. To spite Thorkill, his enviers advised the king to send him to consult Outgarth-Loke. He required of the king that his enemies should be sent with him.

(*b*) In one well-stored and hide-defended ship they set out, reached a sunless, starless land, without fuel; ate raw food and suffered. At last, after many days, a fire was seen ashore. Thorkill, setting a jewel at the mast-head to be able to regain his vessel easily, rows ashore to get fire.

(*c*) In a filthy, snake-paved, stinking cavern he sees two

horny-nebbed giants,* making a fire. One of the giants offers to direct him to Loke if he will say three true things in three phrases, and this done, tells him to row four days and then he would reach a Dark and Grassless Land. For three more true sayings he obtains fire, and gets back to his vessel.

(*d*) With good wind they make Grassless Land, go ashore, find a huge, rocky cavern, strike a flint to kindle a fire at the entrance as a safeguard against demons, and a torch to light them as they explored the cavern.

(*e*) First appears iron seats set amid crawling snakes.

(*f*) Next is sluggish water flowing over sand.

(*g*) Last a steep, sloping cavern is reached, in a chamber of which lay Outgarth-Loke chained, huge and foul.

(*h*) Thorkill plucks a hair of his beard "as big as a cornelwood spear." The stench that arose was fearful; the demons and snakes fell upon the invaders at once; only Thorkill and five of the crew, who had sheltered themselves with hides against the virulent poison the demons and snakes cast, which would take a head off at the neck if it fell upon it, got back to their ship.

(*i*) By vow to the "God that made the world," and offerings, a good voyage was made back, and Germany reached, where Thorkill became a Christian. Only two of his men survived the effects of the poison and stench, and he himself was scarred and spoilt in the face.

(*k*) When he reached the king, Guthrum would not listen to his tale, because it was prophesied to him that he would die suddenly if he heard it; nay, he even sent men to smite him as he lay in bed, but, by the device of laying a log

---

*Such bird-beaked, bird-legged figures occur on the Cross at Papil, Burra Island, Shetland. Cf. Abbey Morne Cross, and an Onchan Cross, I. of Man.

in his place, he escaped, and going to the king as he sat at
meat, reproached him for his treachery.

(*l*) Guthrum bade him tell his story, but died of horror
at hearing his god Loke foully spoken of, while the stench of
the hair that Thorkill produced, as Othere did his horn for
a voucher of his speech, slew many bystanders.

This is the regular myth of Loke, punished by the gods,
lying bound with his own sons' entrails on three sharp stones
and a sword-blade (this latter an addition, when the myth
was made stones were the only blades), with snakes' venom
dripping on to him, so that when it falls on him he shakes
with pain and makes earthquakes—a Titan myth in answer
to the question, "Why does the earth quake?" The vitriolic
power of the poison is excellently expressed in the story.
The plucking of the hair as a token is like the plucking of a
horn off the giant or devil that occurs in some folk-tale.

### MAGIC AND FOLK-SCIENCE.

There is a belief in magic throughout Saxo's work, showing how fresh heathendom still was in men's minds and
memories. His explanations, when he euhemerizes, are
those of his day.

By means of *spells* all kinds of wonders could be effected,
and the powers of nature forced to work for the magician or
his favourite.

*Skin-changing* (so common in Landnámabóc) was as well
known as in the classic world of Lucian and Apuleius; and,
where Frode perishes of the attacks of a witch metamor-
phosed into a walrus.

*Mist* is induced by spells to cover and hide persons, as in
Homer, and *glamour* is produced by spells to dazzle foemen's
sight. To cast glamour and put confusion into a besieged

57

place a witch is employed by the beleaguerer, just as William the Conqueror used the witch in the Fens against Hereward's fortalice. A soothsayer warns Charles the Great of the coming of a Danish fleet to the Seine's mouth.

*Rain and bad weather* may be brought on, as in a battle against the enemy, but in this, as in other instances, the spell may be counteracted.

*Panic Terror* may be induced by the spell worked with a dead horse's head set up on a pole facing the antagonist, but the spell may be met and combatted by silence and a counter-curse.

*Magic help* may be got by calling on the friendly magician's name. The magician has also the power of summoning to him anyone, however unwilling, to appear.

Of spells and magic power to blunt steel there are several instances; they may be counteracted (as in the Icelandic Sagas) by using the hilt, or a club, or covering the blade with fine skin. In another case the champion can only be overcome by one that will take up some of the dust from under his feet. This is effected by the combatants shifting their ground and exchanging places. In another case the foeman can only be slain by gold, whereupon the hero has a gold-headed mace made and batters the life out of him therewith. The brothers of Swanhild cannot be cut by steel, for their mail was charmed by the witch Gudrun, but Woden taught Eormenric, the Gothic king, how to overcome them with stones (which apparently cannot, as archaic weapons, be charmed against at all, resisting magic like wood and water and fire). Jordanis tells the true history of Ermanaric, that great Gothic emperor whose rule from the Dnieper to the Baltic and Rhine and Danube, and long reign of prosperity, were broken by the coming of the Huns. With him vanished the first great Teutonic empire.

Magic was powerful enough even to raise the dead, as was practised by the Perms, who thus renewed their forces after a battle. In the Everlasting battle the combatants were by some strange trick of fate obliged to fulfil a perennial weird (like the unhappy Vanderdecken). Spells to wake the dead were written on wood and put under the corpses' tongue. Spells (written on bark) induce frenzy.

*Charms* would secure a man against claw or tooth.

*Love philtres* (as in the long Lay of Gudrun) appear as everywhere in savage and archaic society.

*Food,* porridge mixed with the slaver of tortured snakes, gives magic strength or endues the eater with eloquence and knowledge of beast and bird speech (as Finn's broiled fish and Sigfred's broiled dragon-heart do).

*Poison* like these hell-broths are part of the Witch or Obi stock-in-trade, and Frode uses powdered gold as an antidote.

*Omens* are observed; tripping as one lands is lucky (as with our William the Norman). Portents, such as a sudden reddening of the sea where the hero is drowned, are noticed and interpreted.

*Dreams* (cf. Eddic Lays of Attila, and the Border ballads) are prophetic (as nine-tenths of Europeans firmly believe still); thus the visionary flame-spouting dragon is interpreted exactly as Hogne's and Attila's dreams. The dreams of the three first bridals nights (which were kept hallowed by a curious superstition, either because the dreams would then hold good, or as is more likely, for fear of some Asmodeus) were fateful. Animals and birds in dreams are read as persons, as nowadays.

A *curse* is powerful unless it can be turned back, when it will harm its utterer, for harm someone it must. The *curse* of a dying man on his slayer, and its lack of effect, is noted.

Sometimes *magic messengers* are sent, like the swans that bore a token and uttered warning songs to the hero.

*Witches* and *wizards* (as belonging to the older layer of archaic beliefs) are hateful to the gods, and Woden casts them out as accursed, though he himself was the mightiest of wizards. Heathen Teutonic life was a long terror by reason of witchcraft, as is the heathen African life to-day, continual precautions being needful to escape the magic of enemies. The Icelandic Sagas, such as Gretter's, are full of magic and witchcraft. It is by witchcraft that Gretter is first lamed and finally slain; one can see that Glam's curse, the Beowulf *motif*, was not really in the original Gretter story.

*Folk-medicine* is really a branch of magic in old days, even to such pioneers of science as Paracelsus.

Saxo's traditions note drinking of a lion's blood that eats men as a means of gaining might and strength; the drinking of bear's blood is also declared to give great bodily power.

The tests for *madness* are of a primitive character, such as those applied to Odusseus, who, however, was not able, like Hamlet, to evade them.

The *test for death* is the red-hot iron or hot brand (used by the Abyssinians of to-day, as it was supposed in the thirteenth century to have been used by Grimhild. "And now Grimhild goes and takes a great brand, where the house had burnt, and goes to Gernot her brother, and thrusts the burning brand in his mouth, and will know whether he is dead or living. But Gernot was clearly dead. And now she goes to Gislher and thrusts the firebrand in his mouth. He was not dead before, but Gislher died of that. Now King Thidrec of Bern saw what Grimhild is doing, and speaks to King Attila. 'See how that devil Grimhild, thy wife, is

killing her brothers, the good warriors, and how many men have lost their lives for her sake, and how many good men she has destroyed, Huns and Amalungs and Niflungs; and in the same way would she bring thee and me to hell, if she could do it !' Then spake King Attila, 'Surely she is a devil, and slay thou her, and that were a good work if thou had done it seven nights ago! Then many a gallant fellow were whole that is now dead.' Now King Thidrec springs at Grimhild and swings up his sword Eckisax, and hews her asunder at the middle").

It was believed (as in Polynesia, where *Captain Cook's path* was shown in the grass) that the heat of the hero's body might blast the grass; so Starcad's entrails withered the grass.

It was believed that a severed head might bite the ground in rage, and there were certainly plenty of opportunities for observation of such cases.

It was believed that a *dumb man* might be so wrought on by passion that he would speak, and wholly acquire speech-power.

Little is told of *surgery*, but in one case of intestines protruding owing to wounds, withies were employed to bind round the trunk and keep the bowels from risk till the patient could be taken to a house and his wounds examined and dressed. It was considered heroic to pay little heed to wounds that were not dangerous, but just to leave them to nature.

Personal *cleanliness* was not higher than among savages now. A lover is loused by his lady after the mediæval fashion.

CHRISTIANITY.—In the first nine books of Saxo, which are devoted to heathendom, there is not much save the author's own Christian point of view that smacks of the New Faith.

The apostleships of Ansgarius in Denmark, the conversion
of King Eric, the Christianity of several later Danish Kings,
one of whom was (like Olaf Tryggwason) baptised in Britain are also noticed.

Of *Christian legends* and beliefs, besides the euhemerist
theory, widely held, of the heathen gods there are few hints,
save the idea that Christ was born in the reign of Frode,
Frode having been somehow synchronised with Augustus,
in whose reign also there was a world-peace.

Of course the christening of Scandinavia is history, and
the mythic books are little concerned with it. The episode
in Adam of Bremen, where the king offers the people, if they
want a new god, to deify Eric, one of their hero-kings, is
eminently characteristic and true.

## FOLK-TALES.

There might be a classification of Saxo's stories akin to
that of the Irish poets, Battles, Sieges, Voyages, Rapes, Cattle Forays, etc.; and quite apart from the historic element,
however faint and legendary, there are a set of stories
ascribed by him, or rather his authorities, to definite persons,
which had, even in his day, probably long been the property
of Tis, their original owners not being known owing to lapse
of time and the wear of memory, and the natural and acci-
dental catastrophies that impair the human record. Such are
the *Dragon-Slayer* stories. In one type of these the hero
(Frithlaf) is cast on a desolate island, and warned by a
dream to attack and slay a dragon guarding treasure. He
wakes, sees the dragon arise out of the waves, apparently,
to come ashore and go back to the cavern or mound wherein
the treasure lay. His scales are too hard to pierce; he is
terribly strong, lashing trees down with his tail, and wear-

ing a deep path through the wood and over the stones with his huge and perpetual bulk; but the hero, covered with hide-wrapped shield against the poison, gets down into the hollow path, and pierces the monster from below, afterward rifling its underground store and carrying off its treasure.

Again the story is repeated; the hero (Frode Haddingsson) is warned by a countryman of the island-dragon and its hoard, is told to cover his shield and body with bulls' hides against the poison, and smite the monster's belly. The dragon goes to drink, and, as it is coming back, it is attacked, slain, and its treasure lifted precisely as before. The analogies with the Beowulf and Sigfred stories are evident; but no great poet has arisen to weave the dragon-slaying intimately into the lives of Frode and Frithlaf as they have been woven into the tragedy of Sigfred the wooer of Brunhild and, if Dr. Vigfússon be right the conqueror of Varus, or into the story of Beowulf, whose real engagements were with sea-monsters, not fiery dragons.

Another type is that of the *Loathly Worm*. A king out hunting (Herod *or* Herraud, King of Sweden), for some unexplained reason brings home two small snakes as presents for his daughter. They wax wonderfully, have to be fed a whole ox a day, and proceed to poison and waste the countryside. The wretched king is forced to offer his daughter (Thora) to anyone who will slay them. The hero (Ragnar) devises a dress of a peculiar kind (by help of his nurse, apparently), in this case, woolly mantle and hairy breeches all frozen and ice-covered to resist the venom, then strapping his spear to his hand, he encounters them boldly alone. The courtiers hide "like frightened little girls," and the king betakes him to a "narrow shelter," an euphemism evidently of Saxo's, for the scene is comic. The king comes forth when the hero is victorious, and laughing at his hairy legs, nick-

names him Shaggy-breech, and bids him to the feast. Ragnar fetches up his comrades, and apparently seeks out the frightened courtiers (no doubt with appropriate quip, omitted by Saxo, who hurries on), feasts, marries the king's daughter, and begets on her two fine sons.

Of somewhat similar type is the proud *Maiden guarded by Beasts.* Here the scene is laid in Gaulardale in Norway. The lady is Ladgerda, the hero Ragnar. Enamoured of the maiden by seeing her prowess in war, he accepts no rebuffs, but leaving his followers, enters the house, slays the guardian Bear and Dog, thrusting one through with a spear and throttling the other with his hand. The lady is won and wed, and two daughters and a son (Frithlaf) duly begotten. The story of Alf and Alfhild combines several types. There are the tame snakes, the baffled suitors' heads staked to terrify other suitors, and the hero using red-hot iron and spear to slay the two reptiles.

The *Proud Lady* (cf. Kudrun and the Niebelungen, and Are's story of the queen that burnt her suitors) appears in Hermintrude, Queen of Scotland, who battles and slays her lovers, but is outwitted by the hero (Hamlet), and, abating her arrogance, agrees to wed him. This seems an obvious accretion in the original Hamlet story, and probably owing not to Saxo, but to his authority.

The *Beggar that stole the Lady* (told of Snio Siwaldson and the daughter of the King of the Goths), with its brisk dialogue, must have been one of the most artful of the folk-tales worked on by Saxo or his informants; but it is only half told, unfortunately.

The *Crafty Soaker* is another excellent comic folk-tale. A terrible famine made the king (Snio) forbid brewing to save the barley for bread, and abolished all needless toping. The Soaker baffled the king by sipping, never taking a full

draught. Rebuked, he declared that he never drank, but only sucked a drop. This was forbidden him for the future, so he sopped his bread in ale, and in that inconvenient manner continued to get drunk, excusing himself with the plea that though it was forbidden to drink or sip beer, it was not forbidden to eat it. When this was in turn prohibited, the Soaker gave up any pretence, and brewed and drank unabashed, telling the angry king that he was celebrating his approaching funeral with due respect, which excuse led to the repeal of the obnoxious decree. A good Rabelaisian tale, that must not have been wide-spread among the Danish topers, whose powers both Saxo and Shakespeare have celebrated, from actual experience no doubt.

The *Magician's tricks to elude pursuit*, so common an incident in our fairy tales, *e. g.*, Michael Scot's flight, is ascribed here to the wonder-working and uncanny Finns, who, when pursued, cast behind them successively three pebbles, which become to their enemies' eyes mountains, then snow, which appeared like a roaring torrent. But they could not cast the glamour on Arngrim a third time, and were forced to submit. The glamour here and in the case of the breaking of Balder's barrow is akin to that which the Druid puts on the sons of Uisnach.

The tale of the king who shuts up his daughter in an "earth-house" or underground chamber with treasures (weapons and gold and silver), in fear of invasion, looks like a bit of folk-tale, such as the *Hind in the Wood*, but it may have a traditional base of some kind here.

A folk-tale, very imperfectly narrated, is the *Clever King's Daughter*, who evidently in the original story had to choose her suitor by his feet (as the giantess in the prose Edda chooses her husband), and was able to do so by the device she had practised of sewing up her ring in his leg sometime

65

before, so that when she touched the flesh she could feel the hardness of the ring beneath the scar.

Bits of folk-tales are the *Device for escaping threatened death by putting a log in one's bed* (as in our Jack the Giant-Killer). The device, as old as David's wife, of dressing up a dummy (here a basket with a dog inside, covered outside with clothes), while the hero escapes, is told of Eormenric, the mighty Gothic King of kings, who, like Walter of Aquitaine, Theodoric of Varona, Ecgberht, and Arminius, was an exile in his youth. This traditional escape of the two lads from the Scyths should be compared with the true story in Paul the Deacon of his little ancestor's captivity and bold and successful stroke for freedom.

*Disguise* plays a great part in the folk-tales used by Saxo. Woden disguises himself in a cowl on his earthly travels, and heroes do the same; a king disguises himself as a slave at his rival's court, to try and find occasion of slaying him; a hero wraps himself up in skins, like Alleleirah.

*Escaped recognition* is accordingly a feature in many of these simple but artistic plots. A son is not known by his mother in the story of Hrólf.

Other *Devices* are exemplified, such as the "booby-trap" loaded with a millstone, which slays a hateful and despised tyrant, imposed by a foreign conqueror; evasion by secret passages, and concealment in underground vaults or earth-houses. The feigning of madness to escape death occurs, as well as in the better-known Hamlet story. These stratagems are universal in folk-history.

To Eric, the clever and quick of speech, is ascribed an excellent sailor's smuggling trick to hide slaughtered cattle by sinking them till the search is over.

The *Hero's Mighty Childhood* (like David's) of course occurs when he binds a bear with his girdle. Sciold is full

grown at fifteen, and Hadding is full grown in extreme youth. The hero in his boyhood slays a full-grown man and champion. The cinder-biting, lazy stage of a mighty youth is exemplified.

The *fierce eyes* of the hero or heroine, which can daunt an assassin as could the piercing glance of Marius, are the "falcon eyes" of the Eddic Lays.

The shining, effulgent, *illuminating hair* of the hero, which gives light in the darkness, is noticed here, as it obtains in Cuaran's thirteenth century English legend.

The wide-spread tale of the *City founded on a site marked out by a hide cut into finest thongs*, occurs, told of Hella and Iwarus exactly as our Kentishmen told it of Hengist, and as it is also told of Dido.

The incidents of the *hero sleeping by a rill*, of the *guarded king's daughter*, with her thirty attendants, the *king's son keeping sheep*, are part of the regular stock incidents in European folk-tales. So are the Nausicaa incident of the *king's daughter going a washing*, the *hero* disguising himself as a woman and winding wool (like a second Heracles).

There are a certain number of stories, which only occur in Saxo and in our other Northern sources with attributions, though they are of course legendary; such are:

The *Everlasting Battle* between Hedhin and Hogne, a legend connected with the great Brisinga-men story, and paralleled by the Cordelia-tale among the Britons.

The story of the *Children preserved* is not very clearly told, and Saxo seems to have euhemerized. It is evidently of the same type as the Lionel-Lancelot story in the Arthurian cycle. Two children, ordered to be killed, are saved by the slaying of other children in their place; and afterwards by their being kept and named as dogs; they come to their own and avenge their wrongs.

The *Journey to Hell* story is told of Eric, who goes to a far land to fetch a princess back, and is successful. It is apparently an adventure of Swipdag, if everyone had their rights. It is also told of Thorkill, whose adventures are rather of the *True Thomas* type.

The *Test of Endurance* by sitting between fires, and the relief of the tortured and patient hero by a kindly trick, is a variant of the famous Eddic Lays concerning Agnar.

The *Robbers of the Island,* evidently comes from an Icelandic source (cf. the historic Holmveria Saga and Icelandic folk-tales of later date), the incident of the hero slaying his slave, that the body might be mistaken for his, is archaic in tone; the powerful horse recalls Grani, Bayard, and even Sleipner; the dog which had once belonged to Unfoot (Ofóte), the giant shepherd (cf. its analogues in old Welsh tales), is not quite assimilated or properly used in this story. It seems (as Dr. Rydberg suspects) a mythical story coloured by the Icelandic relater with memory full of the robber-bands of his own land.

The stratagem of *Starcad,* who tried even in death to slay his slayer, seems an integral part of the Starcad story; as much as the doom of three crimes which are to be the price for the threefold life that a triple man or giant should enjoy. The noose story in Starcad (cf. that told of Bicce in the Eormenric story), is also integral.

### SAXO'S MYTHOLOGY.

No one has commented upon Saxo's mythology with such brilliancy, such minute consideration, and such success as the Swedish scholar, Victor Rydberg. More than occasionally he is over-ingenious and over-anxious to reduce chaos to order; sometimes he almost loses his faithful reader in the

68

maze he treads so easily and confidently, and sometimes he stumbles badly. But he has placed the whole subject on a fresh footing, and much that is to follow will be drawn from his *Teutonic Mythology* (cited here from the English version by Rasmus B. Anderson, London, 1889, as *T. M.*).

Let us take first some of the incontestable results of his investigations that affect Saxo.

SCIOLD is the father of Gram in Saxo, and the son of Sceaf in other older authorities. Dr. Rydberg (97-101) forms the following equations for the Sciolding patriarchs:—

    *a.* Scef—Heimdal—Rig.
    *b.* Sciold—Borgar—Jarl.
    *c.* Gram—Halfdan—Konung.

Chief among the mythic tales that concern Saxo are the various portions of the *Swipdag-myth,* which Dr. Rydberg has been able to complete with much success. They may be resumed briefly as follows:—

Swipdag, helped by the incantations of his dead mother, whom he had raised from the dead to teach him spells of protection, sets forth on his quests. He is the Odusseus of the Teutonic mythology. He desires to avenge his father on Halfdan that slew him. To this end he must have a weapon of might against Halfdan's club. The Moon-god tells him of the blade Thiasse has forged. It has been stolen by Mimer, who has gone out into the cold wilderness on the rim of the world. Swipdag achieves the sword, and defeats and slays Halfdan. He now buys a wife, Menglad, of her kinsmen the gods by the gift of the sword, which thus passes into Frey's hands.

How he established a claim upon Frey, and who Menglad was, is explained in Saxo's story of Eric, where the characters may be identified thus:—

| Swipdag—Eric | Wuldor—Roller. |
|---|---|
| Freya—Gunwara | Thor—Brac. |
| Frey—Frode III | Giants—The Greps. |
| Niord—Fridlaf | "   —Coller. |

Frey and Freya had been carried off by the giants, and Swipdag and his faithful friend resolve to get them back for the Anses, who bewail their absence. They journey to Monster-land, win back the lady, who ultimately is to become the hero's wife, and return her to her kindred; but her brother can only be rescued by his father Niord. It is by wit rather than by force that Swipdag is successful here.

The third journey of Swipdag is undertaken on Frey's behalf; he goes under the name of Scirner to woo giant Gymer's daughter Gerth for his brother-in-law, buying her with the sword that he himself had paid to Frey as his sister's bride-price. So the sword gets back to the giants again.

Swipdag's dead foe Halfdan left two young "avengers," Hadding and Guthorm, whom he seeks to slay. But Thor-Brache gives them in charge of two giant brothers. Wainhead took care of Hadding, Hafle of Guthorm. Swipdag made peace with Guthorm, in a way not fully explained to us, but Hadding took up the blood-feud as soon as he was old enough.

Hadding was befriended by a woman, who took him to the Underworld—the story is only half told in Saxo, unluckily—and by Woden, who took him over-sea wrapt in his mantle as they rode Sleipner over the waves; but here again Saxo either had not the whole story before him, or he wished to abridge it for some reason or prejudice, and the only result of this astonishing pilgrimage is that Woden gives the young hero some useful counsels. He falls into captivity, entrapped by Loke (for what reason again we are left to

guess), and is exposed to wild beasts, but he slays the wolf that attacks him, and eating its heart as Woden had bidden him, he gains wisdom and foresight.

Prepared by these adventures, he gets Guthorm to join him (how or why the peace between him and Swipdag was broken, we know not), and they attack their father's slayer, but are defeated, though Woden sunk Asmund Swipdag's son's ship, Gno, at Hlessey, and Wainhead and Hardgrip his daughter fought for Hadding.

Hadding wanders off to the East with his foster-sister and mistress and Hardgrip, who is slain protecting him against an angry ghost raised from the Underworld by her spells. However, helped by Heimdal and Woden (who at this time was an exile), Hadding's ultimate success is assured.

When Woden came back to power, Swipdag, whose violence and pride grew horribly upon him, was exiled, possibly by some device of his foes, and took upon him, whether by will or doom, a sea-monster's shape. His faithful wife follows him over land and sea, but is not able to save him. He is met by Hadding and, after a fierce fight, slain. Swipdag's wife cursed the conqueror, and he was obliged to institute an annual sacrifice to Frey (her brother) at Upsale, who annuls the curse. Loke, in seal's guise, tried to steal the necklace of Freya at the Reef of Treasures, where Swipdag was slain, but Haimdal, also in seal-skin, fought him, and recovered it for the gods.

Other myths having reference to the goddesses appear in Saxo. There is the story of *Heimdall and Sol,* which Dr. Rydberg has recognised in the tale of Alf and Alfhild. The same tale of how the god won the sun for his wife appears in the mediæval German King Ruther (in which title Dr. Rydberg sees Hrútr, a name of the ram-headed god).

The story of *Othar* (Od) and *Syritha* (Sigrid) is obvi-
ously that of Freya and her lover. She has been stolen by
the giants, owing to the wiles of her waiting-maid, Loke's
helper, the evil witch Angrbode. Od seeks her, finds her,
slays the evil giant who keeps her in the cave; but she is still
bewitched, her hair knotted into a hard, horny mass, her eyes
void of brightness. Unable to gain recognition he lets her
go, and she is made by a giantess to herd her flocks. Again
found by Od, and again refusing to recognise him, she is let
go again. But this time she flies to the world of men, and
takes service with Od's mother and father. Here, after a
trial of her love, she and Od are reconciled. Sywald (Sig-
wald), her father, weds Od's sister.

The tale of *the vengeance of Balder* is more clearly given
by the Dane, and with a comic force that recalls the Aristo-
phanic fun of Loka-senna. It appears that the story had a
sequel which only Saxo gives. Woden had the giantess
Angrbode, who stole Freya, punished. Frey, whose mother-
in-law she was, took up her quarrel, and accusing Woden of
sorcery and dressing up like a woman to betray Wrind, got
him banished. While in exile Wuldor takes Woden's place
and name, and Woden lives on earth, part of the time at least,
with Scathe Thiasse's daughter, who had parted from Niord.

The giants now resolved to attack Ansegard; and Woden,
under the name of Yggr. warned the gods, who recall him
after ten years' exile.

But for Saxo this part of the story of the wars of the gods
would be very fragmentary.

The *Hildiger story*, where a father slays his son un-
wittingly, and then falls at his brother's hand, a tale combin-
ing the Rustam and the Balin-Balan types, is one of the
Hilding tragedies, and curiously preserved in the late Saga
of Asmund the Champions' bane. It is an antithesis, as Dr.

Rydberg remarks, to the Hildebrand and Hadubrand story, where father and son must fight and are reconciled.

The *story of Orwandel* (the analogue of Orion the Hunter) must be gathered chiefly from the prose Edda. He was a huntsman, big enough and brave enough to cope with giants. He was the friend of Thor, the husband of Groa, the father of Swipdag, the enemy of giant Coller and the monster Sela. The story of his birth, and of his being blinded, are lost apparently in the Teutonic stories, unless we may suppose that the bleeding of Robin Hood till he could not see by the traitorous prioress is the last remains of the story of the great archer's death.

Great part of the troubles which befell the gods arose from the antagonism of the sons of Iwalde and the brethren Sindre and Brokk (Cinder and Brank), rival artist families; and it was owing to the retirement of their artist foster-parents that Frey and Freya were left among the giants. The Hniflung hoard is also supposed to have consisted of the treasures of one band of primæval artists, the Iwaldings.

Whether we have here the phenomenon of mythological doublets belonging to different tribes, or whether we have already among these early names that descent of story which has led to an adventure of Moses being attributed to Garibaldi, given to Theodoric the king the adventures of Theodoric the god, taken Arthur to Rome, and Charles the Great to Constantinople, it is hard to say.

The skeleton-key of identification, used even as ably as Dr. Rydberg uses it, will not pick every mythologic lock, though it undoubtedly has opened many hitherto closed. The truth is that man is a finite animal; that he has a limited number of types of legend; that these legends, as long as they live and exist, are excessively prehensile; that, like the opossum, they can swing from tree to tree without fall-

73

ing; as one tree dies out of memory they pass on to another. When they are scared away by what is called exact intelligence from the tall forest of great personalities, they contrive to live humbly clinging to such bare plain stocks and poles (Tis and Jack and Cinderella) as enable them to find a precarious perch.

To drop similitudes, we must be prepared, in unravelling our tangled mythology, to go through several processes. We must, of course, note the parallelisms and get back to the earliest attribution-names we can find. But all system is of late creation, it does not begin till a certain political stage, a stage where the myths of coalescing clans come into contact, and an official settlement is attempted by some school of poets or priests. Moreover, systematization is never so complete that it effaces all the earlier state of things. Behind the official systems of Homer and Hesiod lies the actual chaos of local faiths preserved for us by Pausanias and other mythographers. The common factors in the various local faiths are much the majority among the factors they each possess; and many of these common factors are exceedingly primitive, and resolve themselves into answers to the questions that children still ask, still receiving no answer but myth—that is, poetic and subjective hypothesis, containing as much truth as they can receive or their inventors can grasp.

Who were our forbears? How did day and night, sun and moon, earth and water, and fire come? How did the animals come? Why has the bear no tail? Why are fishes dumb, the swallow cleft-tail? How did evil come? Why did men begin to quarrel? How did death arise? What will the end be? Why do dead persons come back? What do the dead do? What is the earth shaped like? Who invented tools and weapons, and musical instruments, and how? When did kings and chiefs first come?

From accepted answers to such questions most of the huge
mass of mythology arises.  Man makes his gods in his own
image, and the doctrines of omen, coincidence, and corres-
pondence helped by incessant and imperfect observation and
logic, bring about a system of religious observance, of magic
and ritual, and all the masses of folly and cruelty, hope and
faith, and even charity, that group about their inventions,
and seem to be the necessary steps in the onward path of
progressive races.

When to these we add the true and exaggerated memories
of actual heroes, the material before the student is pretty
completely comprised.  Though he must be prepared to meet
the difficulties caused in the contact of races, of civilisations,
by the conversion of persons holding one set of mythical
ideas to belief in another set of different, more attractive,
and often more advanced stage.

The task of arriving at the scientific, speculative ethic, and
the actual practice of our remote ancestry (for to that end is
the student of mythology and folk-lore aiming) is not therefore easy.  Nor is the record perfect, though it is not so poor
in most cases as was once believed.  The Brothers Grimm,
patriarchs alike as mythologists and folk-lorists, the Castor
and Pollox of our studies, have proved this as regards the
Teutonic nations, just as they showed us, by many a striking example, that in great part folk-lore was the mythology
of to-day, and mythology the folk-lore of yesterday.

In many cases we are helped by quite modern material to
make out some puzzle that an old tale presents, and there is
little doubt but that the present activity in the field of folk-
lore will not only result in fresh matter but in fresh methods
freshly applied.

The Scandinavian material, at all events, is particularly
rich : there is the extensive Icelandic written literature touch-

ing the ninth and tenth and eleventh centuries; the noble, if fragmentary remains of Old Northern poetry of the Wickingtide; and lastly, the mass of tradition which, surviving in oral form, and changing in colour from generation to generation, was first recorded in part in the seventeenth, and again in part, in the present century; and all these yield a plentiful field for research. But their evidence gains immensely by the existence of Saxo's nine books of traditional and mythic lore, collected and written down in an age when much that was antique and heathen was passing away forever. The gratitude due to the Welshman of the twelfth century, whose garnered hoard has enriched so many poets and romances from his day to now, is no less due to the twelfth-century Dane, whose faithful and eloquent enthusiasm has swept much dust from antique time, and saved us such a story as Shakespeare has not disdained to consecrate to highest use. Not only Celtic and Teutonic lore are the richer for these two men, but the whole Western world of thought and speech. In the history of modern literature, it is but right that by the side of Geoffrey an honourable place should be maintained for Saxo, and

"awake remembrance of these mighty dead."

# SAXO GRAMMATICUS.

## PREFACE.

FORASMUCH as all other nations are wont to vaunt the glory of their achievements, and reap joy from the remembrance of their forefathers: Absalon, Chief Pontiff of the Danes, whose zeal ever burned high for the glorification of our land, and who would not suffer it to be defrauded of like renown and record, cast upon me, the least of his followers—since all the rest refused the task—the work of compiling into a chronicle the history of Denmark, and by the authority of his constant admonition spurred my weak faculty to enter on a labour too heavy for its strength. For who could write a record of the deeds of Denmark? It had but lately been admitted to the common faith: it still languished as strange to Latin as to religion. But now that the holy ritual brought also the command of the Latin tongue, men were as slothful now as they were unskilled before, and their sluggishness proved as faultful as that former neediness. Thus it came about that my lowliness, though perceiving itself too feeble for the aforesaid burden, yet chose rather to strain beyond its strength than to resist his bidding; fear-

ing that while our neighbours rejoiced and transmitted records of their deeds, the repute of our own people might appear not to possess any written chronicle, but rather to be sunk in oblivion and antiquity. Thus I, forced to put my shoulder, which was unused to the task, to a burden unfamiliar to all authors of preceding time, and dreading to slight his command, have obeyed more boldly than effectually, borrowing from the greatness of my admonisher that good heart which the weakness of my own wit denied me.

And since, ere my enterprise reached its goal, his death outran it; I entreat thee chiefly, Andrew, who wast chosen by a most wholesome and accordant vote to be successor in the same office and to headship of spiritual things, to direct and inspire my theme; that I may baulk by the defence of so great an advocate that spiteful detraction which ever reviles what is most conspicuous. For thy breast, very fruitful in knowledge, and dowered with great store of worshipful doctrines, is to be deemed a kind of shrine of heavenly treasures. Thou who hast searched through Gaul and Italy and Britain also in order to gather knowledge of letters and amass them abundantly, didst after thy long wandering obtain a most illustrious post in a foreign school, and proved such a pillar thereof, that thou seemedst to confer more grace on thy degree than it did on thee. Then being made, on account of the height of thy honours and the desert of thy virtues, Secretary to the King, thou didst adorn that employment, in itself bounded and insignificant, with such works of wisdom as to leave it a piece of promotion for men of

78

greatest rank to covet afterwards, when thou wert transferred to that office which now thou holdest. Wherefore
Skaane has been found to leap for joy that she has borrowed a Pontiff from her neighbours rather than chosen
one from her own people; inasmuch as she both elected
nobly and deserved joy of her election. Being a shining
light, therefore, in lineage, in letters, and in parts, and
guiding the people with the most fruitful labours of thy
teaching, thou hast won the deepest love of thy flock, and
by thy boldness in thy famous administration hast conducted the service thou hast undertaken unto the summit of renown. And lest thou shouldst seem to acquire
ownership on the strength of prescription, thou hast,
by a pious and bountiful will, made over a very rich inheritance to Holy Church; choosing rather honourably to
reject riches (which are covered with the rust of cares)
than to be shackled with the greed of them and with
their burden. Likewise thou hast set about an amazing
work upon the reverend tenets of the faith; and in thy
zeal to set the service of public religion before thy private
concerns, hast, by the lesson of thy wholesome admoni-
tions, driven those men who refused payment of the
dues belonging to religion to do to holy things the
homage that they ought; and by thy pious gift of treasure hast atoned for the ancient neglect of sacred buildings.
Further, those who pursued a wanton life, and yielded to
the stress of incontinence above measure, thou hast redeemed from nerveless sloth to a more upright state of
mind, partly by continuing instant in wholesome reproof,
and partly by the noble example of simple living; leaving

it in doubt whether thou hast edified them more by word or deed. Thus thou, by mere counsels of wisdom, hast achieved what it was not granted to any of thy forerunners to obtain.

And I would not have it forgotten that the more ancient of the Danes, when any notable deeds of mettle had been done, were filled with emulation of glory, and imitated the Roman style; not only by relating in a choice kind of composition, which might be called a poetical work, the roll of their lordly deeds; but also by having graven upon rocks and cliffs, in the characters of their own language, the works of their forefathers, which were commonly known in poems in the mother tongue. In the footsteps of these poems, being as it were classic books of antiquity, I have trod; and keeping true step with them as I translated, in the endeavour to preserve their drift, I have taken care to render verses by verses; so that the chronicle of what I shall have to write, being founded upon these, may thus be known, not for a modern fabrication, but for the utterance of antiquity; since this present work promises not a trumpery dazzle of language, but faithful information concerning times past.

Moreover, how many histories must we suppose that men of such genius would have written, could they have had skill in Latin and so slaked their thirst for writing! Men who though they lacked acquaintance with the speech of Rome, were yet seized with such a passion for bequeathing some record of their history, that they encompassed huge boulders instead of scrolls, borrowing rocks for the usage of books.

Nor may the pains of the men of Thule be blotted in oblivion; for though they lack all that can foster luxury (so naturally barren is the soil), yet they make up for their neediness by their wit, by keeping continually every observance of soberness, and devoting every instant of their lives to perfecting our knowledge of the deeds of foreigners. Indeed, they account it a delight to learn and to consign to remembrance the history of all nations, deeming it as great a glory to set forth the excellences of others as to display their own. Their stores, which are stocked with attestations of historical events, I have examined somewhat closely, and have woven together no small portion of the present work by following their narrative, not despising the judgment of men whom I know to be so well versed in the knowledge of antiquity. And I have taken equal care to follow the statements of Absalon, and with obedient mind and pen to include both his own doings and other men's doings of which he learnt; treasuring the witness of his august narrative as though it were some teaching from the skies.

Wherefore, Waldemar,* healthful Prince and Father of us all, shining light of thy land, whose lineage, most glorious from times of old, I am to relate, I beseech thee let thy grace attend the faltering course of this work; for I am fettered under the weight of my purpose, and dread that I may rather expose my unskillfulness and the feebleness of my parts, than portray thy descent as I duly should. For, not to speak of thy rich inheritance from thy fathers, thou hast nobly increased thy realm by con-

---

*Waldemar] the Second (1203-42). Saxo does not reach his history.

quering thy neighbours, and in the toil of spreading thy sovereignty hast encompassed the ebbing and flowing waves of Elbe, thus adding to thy crowded roll of honours no mean portion of fame. And after outstripping the renown and repute of thy forerunners by the greatness of thy deeds, thou didst not forbear to make armed assault even upon part of the Roman empire. And though thou art deemed to be well endowed with courage and generosity, thou hast left it in doubt whether thou dost more terrify to thy foes in warfare or melt thy people by thy mildness. Also thy most illustrious grandsire, who was sanctioned with the honours of public worship, and earned the glory of immortality by an unmerited death, now dazzles by the refulgence of his holiness those whom living he annexed in his conquests. And from his most holy wounds more virtue than blood hath flowed.

Moreover I, bound by an old and inherited duty of obedience, have set my heart on fighting for thee, if it be only with all the forces of my mind; my father and grandfather being known to have served thy illustrious sire in camp with loyal endurance of the toils of war. Relying therefore on thy guidance and regard, I have resolved to begin with the position and configuration of our own country; for I shall relate all things as they come more vividly, if the course of this history first traverse the places to which the events belong, and take their situation as the starting-point for its narrative.

The extremes, then, of this country are partly bounded by a frontier of another land, and partly enclosed by the waters of the adjacent sea. The interior is washed and

encompassed by the ocean; and this, through the circuitous winds of the interstices, now straitens into the nar-
rows of a firth, now advances into ampler bays, forming
a number of islands. Hence Denmark is cut in pieces by
the intervening waves of ocean, and has but few portions
of firm and continuous territory; these being divided by
the mass of waters that break them up, in ways varying
with the different angle of the bend of the sea. Of all
these, Jutland, being the largest and first settled, holds
the chief place in the Danish kingdom. It both lies foremost and stretches furthest, reaching to the frontiers of
Teutonland, from contact with which it is severed by the
bed of the river Eyder. Northwards it swells somewhat
in breadth, and runs out to the shore of the Noric Channel (Skagerrak). In this part is to be found the fjord
called Liim, which is so full of fish that it seems to yield
the natives as much food as the whole soil.

Close by this fjord also lies Lesser (North) Friesland,
which curves in from the promontory of Jutland in a
cove of sinking plains and shelving lap, and by the favour
of the flooding ocean yields immense crops of grain.
But whether this violent inundation bring the inhabitants
more profit or peril, remains a vexed question. For when
the (dykes of the) estuaries, whereby the waves of the
sea are commonly checked among that people, are broken
through by the greatness of the storm, such a mass of
waters is wont to overrun the fields that it sometimes
overwhelms not only the tilled lands, but people and their
dwellings likewise.

Eastwards, after Jutland, comes the Isle of Funen,

cut off from the mainland by a very narrow sound of sea. This faces Jutland on the west, and on the east Zealand, which is famed for its remarkable richness in the necessaries of life. This latter island, being by far the most delightful of all the provinces of our country, is held to occupy the heart of Denmark, being divided by equal distances from the extreme frontier; on its eastern side the sea breaks through and cuts off the western side of Skaane; and this sea commonly yields each year an abundant haul to the nets of the fishers. Indeed, the whole sound is apt to be so thronged with fish that any craft which strikes on them is with difficulty got off by hard rowing, and the prize is captured no longer by tackle, but by simple use of the hands.

Moreover, Halland and Bleking, shooting forth from the mass of the Skaane like two branches from a parent trunk, are linked to Gothland and to Norway, though with wide deviations of course, and with various gaps consisting of fjords. Now in Bleking is to be seen a rock which travellers can visit, dotted with letters in a strange character. For there stretches from the southern sea into the desert of Vaarnsland a road of rock, contained between two lines a little way apart and very prolonged, between which is visible in the midst a level space, graven all over with characters made to be read. And though this lies so unevenly as sometimes to break through the tops of the hills, sometimes to pass along the valley bottoms, yet it can be discerned to preserve continuous traces of the characters. Now Waldemar, well-starred son of holy Canute, marvelled at these, and

desired to know their purport, and sent men to go along
the rock and gather with close search the series of the
characters that were to be seen there; they were then to
denote them with certain marks, using letters of similar
shape. These men could not gather any sort of interpretation of them, because owing to the hollow space of the
graving being partly smeared up with mud and partly
worn by the feet of travellers in the trampling of the
road, the long line that had been drawn became blurred.
Hence it is plain that crevices, even in the solid rock, if
long drenched with wet, become choked either by the
solid washings of dirt or the moistening drip of showers.

But since this country, by its closeness of language as
much as of position, includes Sweden and Norway, I
will record their divisions and their climates also as I
have those of Denmark. These territories, lying under
the northern pole, and facing Boötes and the Great Bear,
reach with their utmost outlying parts the latitude of
the freezing zone; and beyond these the extraordinary
sharpness of the cold suffers not human habitation. Of
these two, Norway has been allotted by the choice of
nature a forbidding rocky site. Craggy and barren, it is
beset all around by cliffs, and the huge desolate boulders
give it the aspect of a rugged and a gloomy land; in its
furthest part the day-star is not hidden even by night;
so that the sun, scorning the vicissitudes of day and
night, ministers in unbroken presence an equal share of
his radiance to either season.

On the west of Norway comes the island called Iceland, with the mighty ocean washing round it: a land

very squalid to dwell in, but noteworthy for marvels, both strange occurrences and objects that pass belief. A spring is there which, by the malignant reek of its water, destroys the original nature of anything whatsoever. Indeed, all that is sprinkled with the breath of its vapour is changed into the hardness of stone. It remains a doubt whether it be more marvellous or more perilous, that soft and flowing water should be invested with such a stiffness, as by a sudden change to transmute into the nature of stone whatsoever is put to it and drenched with its reeking fume, nought but the shape surviving. Here also are said to be other springs, which now are fed with floods of rising water, and, overflowing in full channels, cast a mass of spray upwards; and now again their bubbling flags, and they can scarce be seen below at the bottom, and are swallowed into deep hiding far under ground. Hence, when they are gushing over, they bespatter everything about them with the white spume, but when they are spent the sharpest eye cannot discern them. In this island there is likewise a mountain, whose floods of incessant fire make it look like a glowing rock, and which, by belching out flames, keeps its crest in an everlasting blaze. This thing awakens our wonder as much as those aforesaid; namely, when a land lying close to the extreme of cold can have such abundance of matter to keep up the heat, as to furnish eternal fires with unseen fuel, and supply an endless provocative to feed the burning. To this isle also, at fixed and appointed seasons, there drifts a boundless mass of ice, and when it approaches and begins to dash upon the rugged reefs, then,

just as if the cliffs rang reply, there is heard from the deep a roar of voices and a changing din of extraordinary clamour. Whence it is supposed that spirits, doomed to torture for the iniquity of their guilty life, do here pay, by that bitter cold, the penalty of their sins. And so any portion of this mass that is cut off when the aforesaid ice breaks away from the land, soon slips its bonds and bars, though it be made fast with ever so great joins and knots. The mind stands dazed in wonder, that a thing which is covered with bolts past picking, and shut in by manifold and intricate barriers, should so depart after that mass whereof it was a portion, as by its enforced and inevitable flight to baffle the wariest watching. There also, set among the ridges and crags of the mountains, is another kind of ice which is known periodically to change and in a way reverse its position, the upper parts sinking to the bottom, and the lower again returning to the top. For proof of this story it is told that certain men, while they chanced to be running over the level of ice, rolled into the abyss before them, and into the depths of the yawning crevasses, and were a little later picked up dead without the smallest chink of ice above them. Hence it is common for many to imagine that the urn of the sling of ice first swallows them, and then a little after turns upside down and restores them. Here also, is reported to bubble up the water of a pestilent flood, which if a man taste, he falls struck as though by poison. Also there are other springs, whose gushing waters are said to resemble the quality of the bowl of Ceres. There are also fires, which, though

they cannot consume linen, yet devour so fluent a thing
as water.  Also there is a rock, which flies over moun-
tain-steeps, not from any outward impulse, but of its
innate and proper motion.

And now to unfold somewhat more thoroughly our
delineation of Norway.  It should be known that on
the east it is conterminous with Sweden and Gothland,
and is bounded on both sides by the waters of the neighbouring ocean.  Also on the north it faces a region whose
position and name are unknown, and which lacks all
civilisation, but teems with peoples of monstrous strangeness; and a vast interspace of flowing sea severs it from
the portion of Norway opposite.  This sea is found hazardous for navigation, and suffers few that venture thereon to return in peace.

Moreover, the upper bend of the ocean, which cuts
through Denmark and flows past it, washes the southern
side of Gothland with a gulf of some width; while its
lower channel, passing the northern sides of Gothland
and Norway, turns eastwards, widening much in breadth,
and is bounded by a curve of firm land.  This limit of
the sea the elders of our race called Grandvik.  Thus
between Grandvik and the Southern Sea there lies a
short span of mainland, facing the seas that wash on
either shore; and but that nature had set this as a boundary where the billows almost meet, the tides of the two
seas would have flowed into one, and cut off Sweden
and Norway into an island.  The regions on the east
of these lands are inhabited by the Skric-Finns.  This
people is used to an extraordinary kind of carriage, and

in its passion for the chase strives to climb untrodden mountains, and attains the coveted ground at the cost of a slippery circuit. For no crag juts out so high, but they can reach its crest by fetching a cunning compass. For when they first leave the deep valleys, they glide twisting and circling among the bases of the rocks, thus making the route very roundabout by dint of continually swerving aside, until, passing along the winding curves of the tracks, they conquer the appointed summit. This same people is wont to use the skins of certain beasts for merchandise with its neighbours.

Now Sweden faces Denmark and Norway on the west, but on the south and on much of its eastern side it is skirted by the ocean. Past this eastward is to be found a vast accumulation of motley barbarism.

That the country of Denmark was once cultivated and worked by giants, is attested by the enormous stones attached to the barrows and caves of the ancients. Should any man question that this is accomplished by superhuman force, let him look up at the tops of certain mountains and say, if he knows how, what man hath carried such immense boulders up to their crests. For anyone considering this marvel will mark that it is inconceivable how a mass, hardly at all or but with difficulty movable upon a level, could have been raised to so mighty a peak of so lofty a mountain by mere human effort, or by the ordinary exertion of human strength. But as to whether, after the Deluge went forth, there existed giants who could do such deeds, or men endowed beyond others with bodily force, there is scant tradition to tell us.

89

But, as our countrymen aver, those who even to-day are said to dwell in that rugged and inaccessible desert aforesaid, are, by the mutable nature of their bodies, vouchsafed the power of being now near, now far, and of appearing and vanishing in turn. The approach to this desert is beset with perils of a fearful kind, and has seldom granted to those who attempted it an unscathed return. Now I will let my pen pass to my theme.

# BOOK ONE.

Now DAN and ANGUL, with whom the stock of the
Danes begins, were begotten of Humble, their father, and
were the governors and not only the founders of our
race. (Yet Dudo, the historian of Normandy, considers
that the Danes are sprung and named from the Danai.)
And these two men, though by the wish and favour of
their country they gained the lordship of the realm, and,
owing to the wondrous deserts of their bravery, got
the supreme power by the consenting voice of their
countrymen, yet lived without the name of king: the
usage whereof was not then commonly resorted to by
any authority among our people.

Of these two, Angul, the fountain, so runs the tradition, of the beginnings of the Anglian race, caused his
name to be applied to the district which he ruled. This
was an easy kind of memorial wherewith to immortalise
his fame: for his successors a little later, when they
gained possession of Britain, changed the original name
of the island for a fresh title, that of their own land.
This action was much thought of by the ancients: witness Bede, no mean figure among the writers of the
Church, who was a native of England, and made it his
care to embody the doings of his country in the most
hallowed treasury of his pages; deeming it equally a

religious duty to glorify in writing the deeds of his land, and to chronicle the history of the Church.

From Dan, however, so saith antiquity, the pedigrees of our kings have flowed in glorious series, like channels from some parent spring. Grytha, a matron most highly revered among the Teutons, bore him two sons, HUMBLE and LOTHER.

The ancients, when they were to choose a king, were wont to stand on stones planted in the ground, and to proclaim their votes, in order to foreshadow from the steadfastness of the stones that the deed would be lasting. By this ceremony Humble was elected king at his father's death, thus winning a novel favour from his country; but by the malice of ensuing fate he fell from a king into a common man. For he was taken by Lother in war, and bought his life by yielding up his crown; such, in truth, were the only terms of escape offered him in his defeat. Forced, therefore, by the injustice of a brother to lay down his sovereignty, he furnished the lesson to mankind, that there is less safety, though more pomp, in the palace than in the cottage. Also, he bore his wrong so meekly that he seemed to rejoice at his loss of title as though it were a blessing; and I think he had a shrewd sense of the quality of a king's estate. But Lother played the king as insupportably as he had played the soldier, inaugurating his reign straightway with arrogance and crime; for he counted it uprightness to strip all the most eminent of life or goods, and to clear his country of its loyal citizens, thinking all his equals in birth his rivals for the crown. He was soon

chastised for his wickedness; for he met his end in an
insurrection of his country; which had once bestowed on
him his kingdom, and now bereft him of his life.

SKIOLD, his son, inherited his natural bent, but not his
behaviour; avoiding his inborn perversity by great dis-
cretion in his tender years, and thus escaping all traces
of his father's taint. So he appropriated what was alike
the more excellent and the earlier share of the family
character; for he wisely departed from his father's sins,
and became a happy counterpart of his grandsire's virtues. This man was famous in his youth among the
huntsmen of his father for his conquest of a monstrous
beast: a marvellous incident, which augured his future
prowess. For he chanced to obtain leave from his guardians, who were rearing him very carefully, to go and
see the hunting. A bear of extraordinary size met him; he
had no spear, but with the girdle that he commonly wore
he contrived to bind it, and gave it to his escort to kill.
More than this, many champions of tried prowess were
at the same time of his life vanquished by him singly;
of these Attal and Skat were renowned and famous.
While but fifteen years of age he was of unusual bodily
size and displayed mortal strength in its perfection, and
so mighty were the proofs of his powers that the rest of
the kings of the Danes were called after him by a common title, the SKIOLDUNGS. Those who were wont to
live an abandoned and flaccid life, and to sap their self-
control by wantonness, this man vigilantly spurred to the
practice of virtue in an active career. Thus the ripeness
of Skiold's spirit outstripped the fulness of his strength,

and he fought battles at which one of his tender years could scarce look on. And as he thus waxed in years and valour he beheld the perfect beauty of Alfhild, daughter of the King of the Saxons, sued for her hand, and, for her sake, in the sight of the armies of the Teutons and the Danes, challenged and fought with Skat, governor of Allemannia, and a suitor for the same maiden; whom he slew, afterwards crushing the whole nation of the Allemannians, and forcing them to pay tribute, they being subjugated by the death of their captain. Skiold was eminent for patriotism as well as arms. For he annulled unrighteous laws, and most heedfully executed whatsoever made for the amendment of his country's condition. Further, he regained by his virtue the realm that his father's wickedness had lost. He was the first to proclaim the law abolishing manumissions. A slave, to whom he had chanced to grant his freedom, had attempted his life by stealthy treachery, and he exacted a bitter penalty; as though it were just that the guilt of one freedman should be visited upon all. He paid off all men's debts from his own treasury, and contended, so to say, with all other monarchs in courage, bounty, and generous dealing. The sick he used to foster, and charitably gave medicines to those sore stricken; bearing witness that he had taken on him the care of his country and not of himself. He used to enrich his nobles not only with home taxes, but also with plunder taken in war; being wont to aver that the prize-money should flow to the soldiers, and the glory to the general.

Thus delivered of his bitterest rival in wooing, he took

as the prize of combat the maiden, for the love of whom he had fought, and wedded her in marriage. Soon after, he had by her a son, GRAM, whose wondrous parts savoured so strongly of his father's virtues that he was deemed to tread in their very footsteps. The days of Gram's youth were enriched with surpassing gifts of mind and body, and he raised them to the crest of renown. Posterity did such homage to his greatness that in the most ancient poems of the Danes royal dignity is implied in his very name. He practiced with the most zealous training whatsoever serves to sharpen and strengthen the bodily powers. Taught by the fencers, he trained himself by sedulous practice to parrying and dealing blows. He took to wife the daughter of his upbringer, Roar, she being his foster-sister and of his own years, in order the better to show his gratefulness for his nursing. A little while after he gave her in marriage to a certain Bess, since he had ofttimes used his strenuous service. In this partner of his warlike deeds he put his trust; and he has left it a question whether he has won more renown by Bess's valour or his own.

Gram, chancing to hear that Groa, daughter of Sigtryg, King of the Swedes, was plighted to a certain giant, and holding accursed an union so unworthy of the blood royal, entered on a Swedish war; being destined to emulate the prowess of Hercules in resisting the attempts of monsters. He went into Gothland, and, in order to frighten people out of his path, strode on clad in goats' skins, swathed in the motley hides of beasts, and grasping in his right hand a dreadful weapon, thus feigning the

95

attire of a giant; when he met Groa herself riding with
a very small escort of women on foot, and making her
way, as it chanced, to the forest-pools to bathe, she
thought it was her betrothed who had hastened to meet
her, and was scared with feminine alarm at so strange a
garb: so, flinging up the reins, and shaking terribly all
over, she began in the song of her country, thus:

"I see that a giant, hated of the king, has come, and
darkens the highways with his stride. Or my eyes play
me false; for it has oft befallen bold warriors to skulk
behind the skin of a beast."

Then began Bess: "Maiden, seated on the shoulders of
the steed, tell me, pouring forth in thy turn words of
answer, what is thy name, and of what line art thou
born?"

Groa replied: "Groa is my name; my sire is a king,
glorious in blood, gleaming in armour. Disclose to us,
thou also, who thou art, or whence sprung!"

To whom Bess: "I am Bess, brave in battle, ruthless
to foes, a terror to nations, and oft drenching my right
hand in the blood of foes."

Then said Groa: "Who, prithee, commands your lines?
Under what captain raise ye the war-standards? What
prince controls the battle? Under whose guidance is the
war made ready?"

Bess in answer: "Gram, the blest in battle, rules the
array: force nor fear can swerve him; flaming pyre and
cruel sword and ocean billow have never made him
afraid. Led by him, maiden, we raise the golden stan-
dards of war."

Groa once more: "Turn your feet and go back hence, lest Sigtryg vanquish you all with his own array, and fasten you to a cruel stake, your throats haltered with the cord, and doom your carcases to the stiff noose, and, glaring evilly, thrust out your corpses to the hungry raven."

Bess again: "Gram, ere he shall shut his own eyes in death, shall first make him a ghost, and, smiting him on the crest, shall send him to Tartarus. We fear no camp of the Swedes. Why threaten us with ghastly dooms, maiden?"

Groa answered him: "Behold, I will ride thence to see again the roof of my father which I know, that I may not rashly set eyes on the array of my brother who is coming. And I pray that your death-doom may tarry for you who abide."

Bess replied: "Daughter, to thy father go back with good cheer; nor imprecate swift death upon us, nor let choler shake thy bosom. For often has a woman, harsh at first and hard to a wooer, yelded the second time."

Whereupon Gram could brook no longer to be silent, and pitching his tones gruffly, so as to mimic a gruesome and superhuman voice, accosted the maiden thus:

"Let not the maiden fear the brother of the fleet giant, nor turn pale because I am nigh her. For I am sent by Grip, and never seek the couch and embrace of damsels save when their wish matches mine."

Groa answered: "Who so mad as to wish to be the leman of giants? Or what woman could love the bed that genders monsters? Who could be the wife of de-

97

mons, and know the seed whose fruit is monstrous? Or
who would fain share her couch with a barbarous giant?
Who caresses thorns with her fingers? Who would
mingle honest kisses with mire? Who would unite shaggy
limbs to smooth ones which correspond not? Full ease
of love cannot be taken when nature cries out against it:
nor doth the love customary in the use of women sort
with monsters."

Gram rejoined: "Oft with conquering hand I have
tamed the necks of mighty kings, defeating with stronger
arm their insolent pride. Thence take red-glowing gold,
that the troth may be made firm by the gift, and that the
faith to be brought to our wedlock may stand fast."

Thus speaking, he cast off his disguises, and revealed
his natural comeliness; and by a single sight of him he
filled the damsel with well-nigh as much joy as he had
struck her with fear before at his counterfeit. She was
even incited to his embraces by the splendour of his
beauty; nor did he fail to offer her the gifts of love.

Having won Groa, Bess proceeded and learnt that the
road was beset by two robbers. These he slew simply by
charging them as they rushed covetously forth to despoil
him. This done, loth to seem to have done any service
to the soil of an enemy, he put timbers under the carcases of the slain, fastened them thereto, and stretched
them so as to counterfeit an upright standing position;
so that in their death they might menace in seeming those
whom their life had harmed in truth; and that, terrible
even after their decease, they might block the road in
effigy as much as they had once in deed. Whence it

appears that in slaying the robbers he took thought for himself and not for Sweden: for he betokened by so singular an act how great a hatred of Sweden filled him. Having heard from the diviners that Sigtryg could only be conquered by gold, he straightway fixed a knob of gold to a wooden mace, equipped himself therewith in the war wherein he attacked the king, and obtained his desire. This exploit was besung by Bess in a most zealous strain of eulogy:

"Gram, the fierce wielder of the prosperous mace, knowing not the steel, rained blows on the outstretched sword, and with a stock beat off the lances of the mighty.

"Following the decrees and will of the gods, he brought low the glory of the powerless Swedes, doing their king to death and crushing him with the stiff gold.

"For he pondered on the arts of war: he wielded in his clasp the ruddy-flashing wood, and victoriously with noble stroke made their fallen captain writhe.

"Shrewdly he conquered with the hardness of gold him whom fate forbade should be slain by steel; unsworded, waging war with the worthier metal.

"This treasure, for which its deviser claims glory and the height of honour, shall abide yet more illustrious hereafter, known far and wide in ampler fame."

Having now slain Sigtryg, the King of Sweden, Gram desired to confirm his possession of the empire which he had won in war; and therefore, suspecting Swarin the governor of Gothland of aspiring to the crown, he challenged him to combat, and slew him. This man's brethren, of whom he had seven lawfully born, and nine the

99

sons of a concubine, sought to avenge their brother's death, but Gram, in an unequal contest, cut them off.

Gram, for his marvellous prowess, was granted a share in the sovereignty by his father, who was now in extreme age, and thought it better and likewise more convenient to give his own blood a portion of the supremacy of the realm, than now in the setting of his life to administer it without a partner. Therefore Ring, a nobly-born Zealander, stirred the greater part of the Danes with desire for insurrection; fancying that one of these men was unripe for his rank, and that the other had run the course of his powers, alleging the weakness in years of both, and declaring that the wandering wit of an old man made the one, and that of a boy the other, unfit for royal power. But they fought and crushed him, making him an example to all men, that no season of life is to be deemed incompatible with valour.

Many other deeds also King Gram did. He declared war against Sumble, King of the Finns; but when he set eyes upon the King's daughter, Signe, he laid down his arms, the foeman turned into the suitor, and, promising to put away his own wife, he plighted troth with her. But, while much busied with a war against Norway, which he had taken up against King Swipdag for debauching his sister and his daughter, he heard from a messenger that Signe had, by Sumble's treachery, been promised in marriage to Henry, King of Saxony. Then, inclining to love the maiden more than his soldiers, he left his army, privily made his way to Finland, and came in upon the wedding, which was already begun. Putting

on a garb of the utmost meanness, he lay down at the table in a seat of no honour. When asked what he brought, he professed skill in leechcraft. At last, when all were drenched in drunkenness, he gazed at the maiden, and amid the revels of the riotous banquet, cursing deep the fickleness of women, and vaunting loud his own deeds of valour, he poured out the greatness of his wrath in a song like this:

"Singly against eight at once I drove the darts of death, and smote nine with a back-swung sword, when I slew Swarin, who wrongfully assumed his honours and tried to win fame unmerited; wherefore I have oft dyed in foreign blood my blade red with death and reeking with slaughter, and have never blenched at the clash of dagger or the sheen of helmet. Now Signe, the daughter of Sumble, vilely spurns me, and endures vows not mine, cursing her ancient troth; and, conceiving an ill-ordered love, commits a notable act of female lightness; for she entangles, lures, and bestains princes, rebuffing beyond all others the lordly of birth; yet remaining firm to none, but ever wavering, and bringing to birth impulses doubtful and divided."

And as he spoke he leapt up from where he lay, and there he cut Henry down while at the sacred board and the embraces of his friends, carried off his bride from amongst the bridesmaids, felled most of the guests, and bore her off with him in his ship. Thus the bridal was turned into a funeral; and the Finns might learn the lesson, that hands should not be laid upon the loves of other men.

After this, SWIPDAG, King of Norway, destroyed Gram, who was attempting to avenge the outrage on his sister and the attempt on his daughter's chastity. This battle was notable for the presence of the Saxon forces, who were incited to help Swipdag, not so much by love of him, as by desire to avenge Henry.

Guthorm and HADDING, the sons of Gram (Groa being the mother of the first and Signe of the second), were sent over to Sweden in a ship by their foster-father, Brage (Swipdag being now master of Denmark), and put in charge of the giants Wagnhofde and Hafle, for guard as well as rearing.

As I shall have briefly to relate doings of these folk, and would fain not seem to fabricate what conflicts with common belief or outsteps the faithful truth, it is worth the knowing that there were in old times three kinds of magicians who by diverse sleights practiced extraordinary marvels. The first of these were men of monstrous stock, termed by antiquity giants; these by their exceeding great bodily stature surpassed the size natural to mankind. Those who came after these were the first who gained skill in divination from entrails, and attained the Pythonic art. These surpassed the former in briskness of mental parts as much as they fell behind them in bodily condition. Constant wars for the supremacy were waged between these and the giants; till at last the sorcerers prevailed, subdued the tribe of giants by arms, and acquired not merely the privilege of ruling, but also the repute of being divine. Both of these kinds had extreme skill in deluding the eyesight, knowing how to obscure

their own faces and those of others with divers semblances, and to darken the true aspects of things with beguiling shapes. But the third kind of men, springing from the natural union of the first two, did not answer to the nature of their parents either in bodily size or in practice of magic arts; yet these gained credit for divinity with minds that were befooled by their jugglings.

Nor must we marvel if, tempted by the prodigious miracles of these folk, the barbaric world fell to worshipping a false religion, when others like unto these, who were mere mortals, but were reverenced with divine honours, beguiled even the shrewdness of the Latins. I have touched on these things lest, when I relate of sleights and marvels, I be checked by the disbelief of the reader. Now I will leave these matters and return to my theme.

Swipdag, now that he had slain Gram, was enriched with the realms of Denmark and Sweden; and because of the frequent importunities of his wife he brought back from banishment her brother Guthorm, upon his promising tribute, and made him ruler of the Danes. But Hadding preferred to avenge his father rather than take a boon from his foe.

This man's nature so waxed and throve that in the early season of his youth he was granted the prime of manhood. Leaving the pursuit of pleasure, he was constantly zealous in warlike exercises; remembering that he was the son of a fighting father, and was bound to spend his whole span of life in approved deeds of war-

fare. Hardgrep, daughter of Wagnhofde, tried to en-
feeble his firm spirit with her lures of love, contending
and constantly averring that he ought to offer the first
dues of the marriage bed in wedlock with her, who had
proffered to his childhood most zealous and careful fostering, and had furnished him with his first rattle.·

Nor was she content with admonishing in plain words,
but began a strain of song as follows:

"Why doth thy life thus waste and wander? Why
dost thou pass thy years unwed, following arms, thirsting for throats? Nor does my beauty draw thy vows.
Carried away by excess of frenzy, thou art little prone
to love. Steeped in blood and slaughter, thou judgest
wars better than the bed, nor refreshest thy soul with
incitements. Thy fierceness finds no leisure; dalliance is
far from thee, and savagery fostered. Nor is thy hand
free from blasphemy while thou loathest the rites of love.
Let this hateful strictness pass away, let that loving
warmth approach, and plight the troth of love to me,
who gave thee the first breasts of milk in childhood, and
helped thee, playing a mother's part, duteous to thy
needs."

When he answered that the size of her body was un-
wieldy for the embraces of a mortal, since doubtless her
nature was framed in conformity to her giant stock, she
said:

"Be not moved by my unwonted look of size. For my
substance is sometimes thinner, sometimes ampler; now
meagre, now abundant; and I alter and change at my
pleasure the condition of my body, which is at one time

shrivelled up and at another time expanded: now my tallness rises to the heavens, and now I settle down into a
human being, under a more bounded shape."

As he still faltered, and was slow to believe her words,
she added the following song:

"Youth, fear not the converse of my bed. I change
my bodily outline in twofold wise, and am wont to enjoin
a double law upon my sinews. For I conform to shapes
of different figure in turn, and am altered at my own
sweet will: now my neck is star-high, and soars nigh to
the lofty Thunderer; then it falls and declines to human
strength, and plants again on earth that head which was
near the firmament. Thus I lightly shift my body into
diverse phases, and am beheld in varying wise; for
changefully now cramped stiffness draws in my limbs,
now the virtue of my tall body unfolds them, and suffers
them to touch the cloud-tops. Now I am short and
straitened, now stretch out with loosened knee; and I
have mutably changed myself like wax into strange aspects. He who knows of Proteus should not marvel at
me. My shape never stays the same, and my aspect is
twofold: at one time it contrasts its outstretched limbs,
at another shoots them out when closed; now disentang-
ling the members and now rolling them back into a
coil. I dart out my ingathered limbs, and presently,
while they are strained, I wrinkle them up, dividing my
countenance between shapes twain, and adopting two
forms: with the greater of these I daunt the fierce, while
with the shorter I seek the embraces of men."

By thus averring she obtained the embraces of Had-

ding; and her love for the youth burned so high that
when she found him desirous of revisiting his own land,
she did not hesitate to follow him in man's attire, and
counted it as joy to share his hardships and perils. While
upon the journey she had undertaken, she chanced to
enter in his company, in order to pass the night, a dwelling, the funeral of whose dead master was being conducted with melancholy rites. Here, desiring to pry
into the purposes of heaven by the help of a magical
espial, she graved on wood some very dreadful spells,
and caused Hadding to put them under the dead man's
tongue; thus forcing him to utter, with the voice so
given, a strain terrible to hear:

"Perish accursed he who hath dragged me back from
those below, let him be punished for calling a spirit out
of bale!

"Whoso hath called me, who am lifeless and dead,
back from the abode below, and hath brought me again
into upper air, let him pay full penalty with his own death
in the dreary shades beneath livid Styx. Behold, counter
to my will and purpose, I must declare some bitter tidings. For as ye go away from this house ye will come
to the narrow path of a grove, and will be a prey to
demons all about. Then she who hath brought our death
back from out of void, and has given us a sight of this
light once more, by her prayers wondrously drawing
forth the ghost and casting it into the bonds of the body,
shall bitterly bewail her rash enterprise.

"Perish accursed he who hath dragged me back from
those below, let him be punished for calling a spirit out
of bale!

"For when the black pestilence of the blast that engenders monsters has crushed out the inmost entrails with stern effort, and when their hand has swept away the living with cruel nail, tearing off limbs and rending ravished bodies; then Hadding, thy life shall survive, nor shall the nether realms bear off thy ghost, nor thy spirit pass heavily to the waters of Styx; but the woman who hath made the wretched ghost come back hither, crushed by her own guilt, shall appease our dust; she shall be dust herself.

"Perish accursed he who hath dragged me back from those below, let him be punished for calling a spirit out of bale!"

So, while they were passing the night in the forest foretold them, in a shelter framed of twigs, a hand of extraordinary size was seen to wander over the inside of the dwelling. Terrified at this portent, Hadding entreated the aid of his nurse. Then Hardgrep, expanding her limbs and swelling to a mighty bigness, gripped the hand fast and held it to her foster-child to hew off. What flowed from the noisesome wounds he dealt was not so much blood as corrupt matter. But she paid the penalty of this act, presently being torn in pieces by her kindred of the same stock; nor did her constitution or her bodily size help her against feeling the attacks of her foes' claws.

Hadding, thus bereft of his foster-mother, chanced to be made an ally in a solemn covenant to a rover, Lysir, by a certain man of great age that had lost an eye, who took pity on his loneliness. Now the ancients, when about to make a league, were wont to besprinkle their footsteps

with blood of one another, so to ratify their pledge of
friendship by reciprocal barter of blood. Lysir and Hadding, being bound thus in the strictest league, declared
war against Loker, the tyrant of the Kurlanders. They
were defeated; and the old man aforementioned took
Hadding, as he fled on horseback, to his own house, and
there refreshed him with a certain pleasant draught,
telling him that he would find himself quite brisk and
sound in body. . This prophetic advice he confirmed by a
song as follows:

"As thou farest hence, a foe, thinking thee a deserter,
will assail thee, that he may keep thee bound and cast
thee to be devoured by the mangling jaws of beasts. But
fill thou the ears of the warders with divers tales, and
when they have done the feast and deep sleep holds them,
snap off the fetters upon thee and the loathly chains. Turn
thy feet thence, and when a little space has fled, with all
thy might rise up against a swift lion who is wont to toss
the carcases of the prisoners, and strive with thy stout
arms against his savage shoulders, and with naked sword
search his heart-strings. Straightway put thy throat to
him and drink the steaming blood, and devour with ravenous jaws the banquet of his body. Then renewed
strength will come to thy limbs, then shall undreamed-of
might enter thy sinews, and an accumulation of stout
force shall bespread and nerve thy frame throughout.
I myself will pave the path to thy prayers, and will subdue the henchmen in sleep, and keep them snoring
throughout the lingering night."

And as he spoke, he took back the young man on his

horse, and set him where he had found him. Hadding
cowered trembling under his mantle; but so extreme was
his wonder at the event, that with keen vision he peered
through its holes. And he saw that before the steps of
the horse lay the sea; but was told not to steal a glimpse
of the forbidden thing, and therefore turned aside his
amazed eyes from the dread spectacle of the roads that
he journeyed. Then he was taken by Loker, and found
by very sure experience that every point of the prophecy
was fulfilled upon him. So he assailed Handwan, king
of the Hellespont, who was entrenched behind an im-
pregnable defence of wall in his city Duna, and withstood him not in the field, but with battlements. Its
summit defying all approach by a besieger, he ordered
that the divers kinds of birds who were wont to nest in
that spot should be caught by skilled fowlers, and he
caused wicks which had been set on fire to be fastened
beneath their wings. The birds sought the shelter of
their own nests, and filled the city with a blaze; all the
townsmen flocked to quench it, and left the gates defenceless. He attacked and captured Handwan, but suffered him to redeem his life with gold for ransom. Thus,
when he might have cut off his foe, he preferred to
grant him the breath of life; so far did his mercy qualify
his rage.

After this he prevailed over a great force of men of
the East, and came back to Sweden. Swipdag met him
with a great fleet off Gottland; but Hadding attacked and
destroyed him. And thus he advanced to a lofty pitch
of renown, not only by the fruits of foreign spoil, but by

the trophies of his vengeance for his brother and his father. And he exchanged exile for royalty, for he became king of his own land as soon as he regained it.

At this time there was one Odin, who was credited over all Europe with the honour, which was false, of godhead, but used more continually to sojourn at Upsala; and in this spot, either from the sloth of the inhabitants or from its own pleasantness, he vouchsafed to dwell with somewhat especial constancy. The kings of the North, desiring more zealously to worship his deity, embounded his likeness in a golden image; and this statue, which betokened their homage, they transmitted with much show of worship to Byzantium, fettering even the effigied arms with a serried mass of bracelets. Odin was overjoyed at such notoriety, and greeted warmly the devotion of the senders. But his queen Frigga, desiring to go forth more beautified, called smiths, and had the gold stripped from the statue. Odin hanged them, and mounted the statue upon a pedestal, which by the marvellous skill of his art he made to speak when a mortal touched it. But still Frigga preferred the splendour of her own apparel to the divine honours of her husband, and submitted herself to the embraces of one of her servants; and it was by this man's device she broke down the image, and turned to the service of her private wantonness that gold which had been devoted to public idolatry. Little thought she of practicing unchastity, that she might the easier satisfy her greed, this woman so unworthy to be the consort of a god; but what should I here add, save that such a godhead was worthy of such a wife? So

great was the error that of old befooled the minds of men. Thus Odin, wounded by the double trespass of his wife, resented the outrage to his image as keenly as that to his bed; and, ruffled by these two stinging dishonours, took to an exile overflowing with noble shame, imagining so to wipe off the slur of his ignominy. When he had retired, one Mit-othin, who was famous for his juggling tricks, was likewise quickened, as though by inspiration from on high, to seize the opportunity of feigning to be a god; and, wrapping the minds of the barbarians in fresh darkness, he led them by the renown of his jugglings to pay holy observance to his name. He said that the wrath of the gods could never be appeased nor the outrage to their deity expiated by mixed and indiscriminate sacrifices, and therefore forbade that prayers for this end should be put up without distinction, appointing to each of those above his especial drink-offering. But when Odin was returning, he cast away all help of jugglings, went to Finland to hide himself, and was there attacked and slain by the inhabitants. Even in his death his abominations were made manifest, for those who came nigh his barrow were cut off by a kind of sudden death; and after his end, he spread such pestilence that he seemed almost to leave a filthier record in his death than in his life: it was as though he would extort from the guilty a punishment for his slaughter. The inhabitants, being in this trouble, took the body out of the mound, beheaded it, and impaled it through the breast with a sharp stake; and herein that people found relief.

The death of Odin's wife revived the ancient splendour of his name, and seemed to wipe out the disgrace upon his deity; so, returning from exile, he forced all those, who had used his absence to assume the honours of divine rank, to resign them as usurped; and the gangs of sorcerers that had arisen he scattered like a darkness before the advancing glory of his godhead. And he forced them by his power not only to lay down their divinity, but further to quit the country, deeming that they, who tried to foist themselves so iniquitously into the skies, ought to be outcasts from the earth.

Meanwhile Asmund, the son of Swipdag, fought with Hadding to avenge his father. And when he heard that Henry his son, his love for whom he set even before his own life, had fallen fighting valiantly, his soul longed for death, and loathed the light of day, and made a song in a strain like this:

"What brave hath dared put on my armour? The sheen of the helmet serves not him who tottereth, nor doth the breastplate fitly shelter him that is sore spent. Our son is slain, let us riot in battle; my eager love for him driveth me to my death, that I may not be left outliving my dear child. In each hand I am fain to grasp the sword; now without shield let us ply our warfare bare-breasted, with flashing blades. Let the rumour of our rage beacon forth: boldly let us grind to powder the column of the foe; nor let the battle be long and chafe us; nor let our onset be shattered in rout and be still."

When he had said this, he gripped his hilt with both hands, and, fearless of peril, swung his shield upon his

back and slew many. Hadding therefore called on the powers with which he was allied to protect him, and on a sudden Wagnhofde rode up to fight on his side. And when Asmund saw his crooked sword, he cried out, and broke into the following strain:

"Why fightest thou with curved sword? The short sword shall prove thy doom, the javelin shall be flung and bring forth death. Thou shouldst conquer thy foe by thy hand, but thou trustest that he can be rent by spells; thou trustest more in words than vigour, and puttest thy strength in thy great resource. Why dost thus beat me back with thy shield, threatening with thy bold lance, when thou art so covered with wretched crimes and spotted all over? Thus hath the brand of shame bestained thee, rotting in sin, lubber-lipped."

While he thus clamoured, Hadding, flinging his spear by the thong, pierced him through. But Asmund lacked not comfort even for his death; for while his life flickered in the socket he wounded the foot of his slayer, and by this short instant of revenge he memorized his fall, punishing the other with an incurable limp. Thus crippling of a limb befell one of them and loss of life the other. Asmund's body was buried in solemn state at Upsala and attended with royal obsequies. His wife Gunnhild, loth to outlive him, cut off her own life with the sword, choosing rather to follow her lord in death than to forsake him by living. Her friends, in consigning her body to burial, laid her with her husband's dust, thinking her worthy to share the mound of the man, her love for whom she had set above life. So there lies

Gunnhild, clasping her lord somewhat more beautifully in the tomb than she had ever done in the bed.

After this Hadding, now triumphant, wasted Sweden. But Asmund's son, named Uffe, shrinking from a conflict, transported his army into Denmark, thinking it better to assail the house of his enemy than to guard his own, and deeming it a timely method of repelling his wrongs to retaliate upon his foe what he was suffering at his hands. Thus the Danes had to return and defend their own, preferring the safety of their land to lordship of a foreign realm; and Uffe went back to his own country, now rid of an enemy's arms.

Hadding, on returning from the Swedish war, perceived that his treasury, wherein he was wont to store the wealth he had gotten by the spoils of war, had been forced and robbed, and straightway hanged its keeper Glumer, proclaiming by a crafty device, that, if any of the culprits brought about the recovery of the stolen goods, he should have the same post of honour as Glumer had filled. Upon this promise, one of the guilty men became more zealous to reap the bounty than to hide his crime, and had the money brought back to the king. His confederates fancied he had been received into the king's closest friendship, and believed that the honours paid him were as real as they were lavish; and therefore they also, hoping to be as well rewarded, brought back their moneys and avowed their guilt. Their confession was received at first with promotion and favours, and soon visited with punishment, thus bequeathing a signal lesson against being too confiding. I should judge that men,

whose foolish blabbing brought them to destruction,
when wholesome silence could have ensured their safety,
well deserved to atone upon the gallows for their breach
of reticence.

After this Hadding passed the whole winter season in
the utmost preparation for the renewal of the war.
When the frosts had been melted by the springtide sun,
he went back to Sweden and there spent five years in
warfare. By dint of this prolonged expedition, his
soldiers, having consumed all their provision, were
reduced almost to the extremity of emaciation, and began
to assuage their hunger with mushrooms from the wood.
At last, under stress of extreme necessity, they devoured
their horses, and finally satisfied themselves with the
carcases of dogs. Worse still, they did not scruple to
feed upon human limbs. So, when the Danes were
brought unto the most desperate straits, there sounded in
the camp, in the first sleep of the night, and no man
uttering it, the following song:

"With foul augury have ye left the abode of your
country, thinking to harry these fields in War. What
idle notion mocks your minds? What blind self-confidence has seized your senses, that ye think this soil can
thus be won. The might of Sweden cannot yield or
quail before the War of the stranger; but the whole of
your column shall melt away when it begins to assault
our people in War. For when flight has broken up the
furious onset, and the straggling part of the fighters
wavers, then to those who prevail in the War is given
free scope to slay those who turn their backs, and they

have earned power to smite the harder when fate drives the renewer of the war headlong. Nor let him whom cowardice deters aim the spears."

This prophecy was accomplished on the morrow's dawn by a great slaughter of the Danes. On the next night the warriors of Sweden heard an utterance like this, none knowing who spake it:

"Why doth Uffe thus defy me with grievous rebellion? He shall pay the utmost penalty. For he shall be buried and transpierced under showers of lances, and shall fall lifeless in atonement for his insolent attempt. Nor shall the guilt of his wanton rancour be unpunished; and, as I forebode, as soon as he joins battle and fights, the points shall fasten in his limbs and strike his body everywhere, and his raw gaping wounds no bandage shall bind up; nor shall any remedy heal over thy wide gashes."

On that same night the armies fought; when two hairless old men, of appearance fouler than human, and displaying their horrid baldness in the twinkling starlight, divided their monstrous efforts with opposing ardour, one of them being zealous on the Danish side, and the other as fervent for the Swedes. Hadding was conquered and fled to Helsingland, where, while washing in the cold sea-water his body which was scorched with heat, he attacked and cut down with many blows a beast of unknown kind, and having killed it had it carried into camp. As he was exulting in this deed a woman met him and addressed him in these words:

"Whether thou tread the fields afoot, or spread canvas overseas, thou shalt suffer the hate of the gods, and

through all the world shalt behold the elements oppose thy purposes. Afield thou shalt fall, on sea thou shalt be tossed, an eternal tempest shall attend the steps of thy wandering, nor shall frost-bind ever quit thy sails; nor shall thy roof-tree roof thee, but if thou seekest it, it shall fall smitten by the hurricane; thy herd shall perish of bitter chill. All things shall be tainted, and shall lament that thy lot is there. Thou shalt be shunned like a pestilent tetter, nor shall any plague be fouler than thou. Such chastisement doth the power of heaven mete out to thee, for truly thy sacrilegious hands have slain one of the dwellers above, disguised in a shape that was not his: thus here art thou, the slayer of a benignant god! But when the sea receives thee, the wrath of the prison of Eolus shall be loosed upon thy head. The West and the furious North, the South wind shall beat thee down, shall league and send forth their blasts in rivalry; until with better prayers thou hast melted the sternness of heaven, and hast lifted with appeasement the punishment thou hast earned."

So, when Hadding went back, he suffered all things after this one fashion, and his coming brought disquiet upon all peaceful places. For when he was at sea a mighty storm arose and destroyed his fleet in a great tempest: and when, a shipwrecked man, he sought entertainment, he found a sudden downfall of that house. Nor was there any cure for his trouble, ere he atoned by sacrifice for his crime, and was able to return into favour with heaven. For, in order to appease the deities, he sacrificed dusky victims to the god Frey. This manner

of propitiation by sacrifice he repeated as an annual feast,
and left posterity to follow. This rite the Swedes call
Fröblod (the sacrifice or feast of Frey).

Hadding chanced to hear that a certain giant had taken
in troth Ragnhild, daughter of Hakon, King of the
Nitherians; and, loathing so ignominious a state of
affairs, and utterly abominating the destined union, he
forestalled the marriage by noble daring. For he went
to Norway and overcame by arms him that was so foul
a lover for a princess. For he thought so much more of
valour than of ease, that, though he was free to enjoy
all the pleasures of a king, he accounted it sweeter than
any delight to repel the wrongs done, not only to himself,
but to others. The maiden, not knowing him, ministered
with healing tendance to the man that had done her
kindness and was bruised with many wounds. And in
order that lapse of time might not make her forget him,
she shut up a ring in his wound, and thus left a mark on
his leg. Afterwards her father granted her freedom to
choose her own husband; so when the young men were
assembled at banquet, she went along them and felt their
bodies carefully, searching for the tokens she had stored
up long ago. All the rest she rejected, but Hadding she
discovered by the sign of the secret ring; then she
embraced him, and gave herself to be the wife of him who
had not suffered a giant to win her in marriage.

While Hadding was sojourning with her a marvellous
portent befell him. While he was at supper, a woman
bearing hemlocks was seen to raise her head beside the
brazier, and, stretching out the lap of her robe, seemed to

ask, "in what part of the world such fresh herbs had grown in winter?" The king desired to know; and, wrapping him in her mantle, she drew him with her underground, and vanished. I take it that the nether gods purposed that he should pay a visit in the flesh to the regions whither he must go when he died. So they first pierced through a certain dark misty cloud, and then advancing along a path that was worn away with long thoroughfaring, they beheld certain men wearing rich robes, and nobles clad in purple; these passed, they at last approached sunny regions which produced the herbs the woman had brought away. Going further, they came on a swift and tumbling river of leaden waters, whirling down on its rapid current divers sorts of missiles, and likewise made passable by a bridge. When they had crossed this, they beheld two armies encountering one another with might and main. And when Hadding inquired of the woman about their estate: "These," she said, "are they who, having been slain by the sword, declare the manner of their death by a continual rehearsal, and enact the deeds of their past life in a living spectacle." Then a wall hard to approach and to climb blocked their further advance. The woman tried to leap it, but in vain, being unable to do so even with her slender wrinkled body; then she wrung off the head of a cock which she chanced to be taking down with her, and flung it beyond the barrier of the walls; and forthwith the bird came to life again, and testified by a loud crow to recovery of its breathing.

Then Hadding turned back and began to make home-

wards with his wife; some rovers bore down on him, but by swift sailing he baffled their snares; for though it was almost the same wind that helped both, they were behind him as he clove the billows, and, as they had only just as much sail, could not overtake him.

Meantime Uffe, who had a marvellously fair daughter, decreed that the man who slew Hadding should have her. This sorely tempted one Thuning, who got together a band of men of Perm (Byarmenses), being fain so to win the desired advancement. Hadding was going to fall upon him, but while he was passing Norway in his fleet he saw upon the beach an old man signing to him, with many wavings of his mantle, to put into shore. His companions opposed it, and declared that it would be a ruinous diversion from their journey; but he took the man on board, and was instructed by him how to order his army. For this man, in arranging the system of the columns, used to take special care that the front row consisted of two, the second of four, while the third increased and was made up to eight, and likewise each row was double that in front of it. Also the old man bade the wings of the slingers go back to the extremity of the line, and put with them the ranks of the archers. So when the squadrons were arranged in the wedge, he stood himself behind the warriors, and from the wallet which was slung round his neck drew an arbalist. This seemed small at first, but soon projected with more prolonged tip, and accommodated ten arrows to its string at once, which were shot all at once at the enemy in a brisk volley, and inflicted as many wounds. Then the

men of Perm, quitting arms for cunning, by their spells loosed the sky in clouds of rain, and melted the joyous visage of the air in dismal drenching showers. But the old man, on the other hand, drove back with a cloud the heavy mass of storm which had arisen, and checked the dripping rain by this barrier of mist. Thus Hadding prevailed. But the old man, when he parted from him, foretold that the death whereby he would perish would be inflicted, not by the might of an enemy, but by his own hand. Also he forbade him to prefer obscure wars to such as were glorious, and border wars to those remote.

Hadding, after leaving him, was bidden by Uffe to Upsala on pretence of a interview; but lost all his escort by treachery, and made his escape sheltered by the night. For when the Danes sought to leave the house into which they had been gathered on pretext of a banquet, they found one awaiting them, who mowed off the head of each of them with his sword as it was thrust out of the door. For this wrongful act Hadding retaliated and slew Uffe; but put away his hatred and consigned his body to a sepulchre of notable handiwork, thus avowing the greatness of his foe by his pains to beautify his tomb, and decking in death with costly distinctions the man whom he used to pursue in his life with hot enmity. Then, to win the hearts of the people he had subdued, he appointed Hunding, the brother of Uffe, over the realm, that the sovereignty might seem to be maintained in the house of Asmund, and not to have passed into the hand of a stranger.

Thus his enemy was now removed, and he passed

several years without any stirring events and in utter disuse of arms; but at last he pleaded the long while he had been tilling the earth, and the immoderate time he had forborne from exploits on the seas; and seeming to think war a merrier thing than peace, he began to upbraid himself with slothfulness in a strain like this:

"Why loiter I thus in darksome hiding, in the folds of rugged hills, nor follow seafaring as of old? The continual howling of the band of wolves, and the plaintive cry of harmful beasts that rises to heaven, and the fierce impatient lions, all rob my eyes of sleep. Dreary are the ridges and the desolation to hearts that trusted to do wilder work. The stark rocks and the rugged lie of the ground bar the way to spirits who are wont to love the sea. It were better service to sound the firths with the oars, to revel in plundered wares, to pursue the gold of others for my coffer, to gloat over sea-gotten gains, than to dwell in rough lands and winding woodlands and barren glades."

Then his wife, loving a life in the country, and weary of the matin harmony of the sea-birds, declared how great joy she found in frequenting the woodlands, in the following strain:

"The shrill bird vexes me as I tarry by the shore, and with its chattering rouses me when I cannot sleep. Wherefore the noisy sweep of its boisterous rush takes gentle rest from my sleeping eye, nor doth the loud-chattering sea-mew suffer me to rest in the night, forcing its wearisome tale into my dainty ears; nor when I would lie down doth it suffer me to be refreshed, clamouring

with doleful modulation of its ill-boding voice. Safer
and sweeter do I deem the enjoyment of the woods.
How are the fruits of rest plucked less by day or night
than by tarrying tossed on the shifting sea?"

At this time one Toste emerged, from the obscure spot
of Jutland where he was born, into bloody notoriety.
For by all manner of wanton attacks upon the common
people he spread wide the fame of his cruelty, and gained
so universal a repute for rancour, that he was branded
with the name of the Wicked. Nor did he even refrain
from wrongdoing to foreigners, but, after foully harrying
his own land, went on to assault Saxony. The Saxon
general Syfrid, when his men were hard put to it in the
battle, entreated peace. Toste declared that he should
have what he asked, but only if he would promise to
become his ally in a war against Hadding. Syfrid
demurred, dreading to fulfill the condition, but by sharp
menaces Toste induced him to promise what he asked.
For threats can sometimes gain a request which soft-
dealing cannot compass. Hadding was conquered by
this man in an affair by land; but in the midst of his
flight he came on his enemy's fleet, and made it
unseaworthy by boring the sides; then he got a skiff and
steered it out to sea. Toste thought he was slain, but
though he sought long among the indiscriminate heaps
'of dead, could not find him, and came back to his fleet;
when he saw from afar off a light boat tossing on the
ocean billows. Putting out some vessels, he resolved to
give it chase, but was brought back by peril of shipwreck,
and only just reached the shore. Then he quickly took

some sound craft, and accomplished the journey which he had before begun. Hadding, seeing he was caught, proceeded to ask his companion whether he was a skilled and practised swimmer; and when the other said he was not, Hadding despairing of flight, deliberately turned the vessel over and held on inside to its hollow, thus making his pursuers think him dead. Then he attacked Toste, who, careless and unaware, was greedily watching over the remnants of his spoil; cut down his army, forced him to quit his plunder, and avenged his own rout by that of Toste.

But Toste lacked not heart to avenge himself. For, not having store enough in his own land to recruit his forces—so heavy was the blow he had received—he went to Britain, calling himself an ambassador. Upon his outward voyage, for sheer wantonness, he got his crew together to play dice, and when a wrangle arose from the throwing of the cubes, he taught them to wind it up with a fatal affray. And so, by means of this peaceful sport, he spread the spirit of strife through the whole ship, and the jest gave place to quarrelling, which engendered bloody combat. Also, fain to get some gain out of the misfortunes of others, he seized the moneys of the slain, and attached to him a certain rover then famous, named Koll; and a little after returned in his company to his own land, where he was challenged and slain by Hadding, who preferred to hazard his own fortune rather than that of his soldiers. For generals of antique valour were loth to accomplish by general massacre what could be decided by the lot of a few.

After these deeds the figure of Hadding's dead wife appeared before him in his sleep, and sang thus:

"A monster is born to thee that shall tame the rage of wild beasts, and crush with fierce mouth the fleet wolves." Then she added a little: "Take thou heed; from thee hath issued a bird of harm, in choler a wild screech-owl, in tongue a tuneful swan."

On the morrow the king, when he had shaken off slumber, told the vision to a man skilled in interpretations, who explained the wolf to denote a son that would be truculent and the word swan as signifying a daughter; and foretold that the son would be deadly to enemies and the daughter treacherous to her father. The result answered to the prophecy. Hadding's daughter, Ulfhild, who was wife to a certain private person called Guthorm, was moved either by anger at her match, or with aspirations to glory, and throwing aside all heed of daughterly love, tempted her husband to slay her father; declaring that she preferred the name of queen to that of princess. I have resolved to set forth the manner of her exhortation almost in the words in which she uttered it; they were nearly these:

"Miserable am I, whose nobleness is shadowed by an unequal yoke! Hapless am I, to whose pedigree is bound the lowliness of a peasant! Luckless issue of a king, to whom a common man is equal by law of marriage! Pitiable daughter of a prince, whose comeliness her spiritless father hath made over to base and contemptible embraces! Unhappy child of thy mother, with thy happiness marred by consorting with this bed! thy purity

is handled by the impurity of a peasant, thy nobility is bowed down by ignoble commonness, thy high birth is impaired by the estate of thy husband! But thou, if any pith be in thee, if valour reign in thy soul at all, if thou deem thyself fit husband for a king's daughter, wrest the sceptre from her father, retrieve thy lineage by thy valour, balance with courage thy lack of ancestry, requite by bravery thy detriment of blood. Power won by daring is more prosperous than that won by inheritance. Boldness climbs to the top better than inheritance, and worth wins power better than birth. Moreover, it is no shame to overthrow old age, which of its own weight sinks and totters to its fall. It shall be enough for my father to have borne the sceptre for so long; let the dotard's power fall to thee; if it elude thee, it will pass to another. Whatsoever rests on old age is near its fall. Think that his reign has been long enough, and be it thine, though late in the day, to be first. Further, I would rather have my husband than my father king—would rather be ranked a king's wife than daughter. It is better to embrace a monarch in one's home, than to give him homage from afar; it is nobler to be a king's bride than his courtier. Thou, too, must surely prefer thyself to thy wife's father for bearing the sceptre; for nature has made each one nearest to himself. If there be a will for the deed, a way will open; there is nothing but yields to the wit of man. The feast must be kept, the banquet decked, the preparations looked to, and my father bidden. The path to treachery shall be smoothed by a pretence of friendship, for nothing cloaks a snare

better than the name of kindred. · Also his soddenness
shall open a short way to his slaughter; for when the king
shall be intent upon the dressing of his hair, and his hand
is upon his beard and his mind upon stories; when he has
parted his knotted locks, either with hairpin or disentang-
ling comb, then let him feel the touch of the steel in his
flesh. Busy men commonly devise little precaution. Let
thy hand draw near to punish all his sins. It is a
righteous deed to put forth thy hand to avenge the
wretched!"

Thus Ulfhild importuned, and her husband was overcome by her promptings, and promised his help to the
treachery. But meantime Hadding was warned in a
dream to beware of his son-in-law's guile. He went to
the feast, which his daughter had made ready for him
with a show of love, and posted an armed guard hard by
to use against the treachery when need was. As he ate,
the henchman who was employed to do the deed of guile
silently awaited a fitting moment for his crime, his dagger
hid under his robe. The king, remarking him, blew on
the trumpet a signal to the soldiers who were stationed
near; they straightway brought aid, and he made the guile
recoil on its deviser.

Meanwhile Hunding, King of the Swedes, heard false
tidings that Hadding was dead, and resolved to greet
them with obsequies. So he gathered his nobles together,
and filled a jar of extraordinary size with ale, and had
this set in the midst of the feasters for their delight, and,
to omit no mark of solemnity, himself assumed a servant's
part, not hesitating to play the cupbearer. And while he

was passing through the palace in fulfillment of his office, he stumbled and fell into the jar, and, being choked by the liquor, gave up the ghost; thus atoning either to Orcus, whom he was appeasing by a baseless performance of the rites, or to Hadding, about whose death he had spoken falsely. Hadding, when he heard this, wished to pay like thanks to his worshipper, and, not enduring to survive his death, hanged himself in sight of the whole people.

# BOOK TWO.

HADDING was succeeded by FRODE, his son, whose fortunes were many and changeful. When he had passed the years of a stripling he displayed the fulness of a warrior's prowess; and being loth that this should be spoilt by slothfulness, he sequestered his mind from delights and perseveringly constrained it to arms. Warfare having drained his father's treasury, he lacked a stock of pay to maintain his troops, and cast about diligently for the supplies that he required; and while thus employed, a man of the country met him and roused his hopes by the following strain:

"Not far off is an island rising in delicate slopes, hiding treasure in its hills and ware of its rich booty. Here a noble pile is kept by the occupant of the mount, who is a snake wreathed in coils, doubled in many a fold, and with tail drawn out in winding whorls, shaking his manifold spirals and shedding venom. If thou wouldst conquer him, thou must use thy shield and stretch thereon bulls' hides, and cover thy body with the skins of kine, nor let thy limbs lie bare to the sharp poison; his slaver burns up what it bespatters. Though the three-forked tongue flicker and leap out of the gaping mouth, and with awful yawn menace ghastly wounds remember to keep the dauntless temper of thy mind; nor

let the point of the jagged tooth trouble thee, nor the starkness of the beast, nor the venom spat from the swift throat. Though the force of his scales spurn thy spears, yet know there is a place under his lowest belly whither thou mayst plunge the blade; aim at this with thy sword, and thou shalt probe the snake to his centre. Thence go fearless up to the hill, drive the mattock, dig and ransack the holes; soon fill thy pouch with treasure, and bring back to the shore thy craft laden."

Frode believed, and crossed alone to the island, loth to attack the beast with any stronger escort than that wherewith it was the custom for champions to attack. When it had drunk water and was repairing to its cave, its rough and sharp hide spurned the blow of Frode's steel. Also the darts that he flung against it rebounded idly, foiling the effort of the thrower. But when the hard back yielded not a whit, he noted the belly heedfully, and its softness gave entrance to the steel. The beast tried to retaliate by biting, but only struck the sharp point of its mouth upon the shield. Then it shot out its flickering tongue again and again, and gasped away life and venom together.

The money which the King found made him rich; and with this supply he approached in his fleet the region of the Kurlanders, whose king Dorn, dreading a perilous war, is said to have made a speech of the following kind to his soldiers:

"Nobles! Our enemy is a foreigner, begirt with the arms and the wealth of almost all the West; let us, by endeavouring to defer the battle for our profit, make him

a prey to famine, which is an inward malady; and he will find it very hard to conquer a peril among his own people. It is easy to oppose the starving. Hunger will be a better weapon against our foe than arms; famine will be the sharpest lance we shall hurl at him. For lack of food nourishes the pestilence that eats away men's strength, and lack of victual undermines store of weapons. Let this whirl the spears while we sit still; let this take up the prerogative and the duty of fighting. Unimperilled, we shall be able to imperil others; we can drain their blood and lose no drop of ours. One may defeat an enemy by inaction. Who would not rather fight safely than at a loss? Who would strive to suffer chastisement when he may contend unhurt? Our success in arms will be more prosperous if hunger joins battle first. Let hunger captain us, and so let us take the first chance of conflict. Let it decide the day in our stead, and let our camp remain free from the stir of war; if hunger retreat beaten, we must break off idleness. He who is fresh easily overpowers him who is shaken with languor. The hand that is flaccid and withered will come fainter to the battle. He whom any hardship has first wearied, will bring slacker hands to the steel. When he that is wasted with sickness engages with the sturdy, the victory hastens. Thus, undamaged ourselves, we shall be able to deal damage to others."

Having said this, he wasted all the places which he saw would be hard to protect, distrusting his power to guard them, and he so far forestalled the ruthlessness of the foe in ravaging his own land, that he left nothing untouched

which could be seized by those who came after. Then he shut up the greater part of his forces in a town of undoubted strength, and suffered the enemy to blockade him. Frode, distrusting his power of attacking this town, commanded several trenches of unwonted depth to be made within the camp, and the earth to be secretly carried out in baskets and cast quietly into the river bordering the walls. Then he had a mass of turf put over the trenches to hide the trap: wishing to cut off the unwary enemy by tumbling them down headlong, and thinking that they would be overwhelmed unawares by the slip of the subsiding earth. Then he feigned a panic, and proceeded to forsake the camp for a short while. The townsmen fell upon it, missed their footing everywhere, rolled forward into the pits, and were massacred by him under a shower of spears.

Thence he travelled and fell in with Trannon, the monarch of the Ruthenians. Desiring to spy out the strength of his navy, he made a number of pegs out of sticks, and loaded a skiff with them; and in this he approached the enemy's fleet by night, and bored the hulls of the vessels with an auger. And to save them from a sudden influx of the waves, he plugged up the open holes with the pegs he had before provided, and by these pieces of wood he made good the damage done by the auger. But when he thought there were enough holes to drown the fleet, he took out the plugs, thus giving instant access to the waters, and then made haste to surround the enemy's fleet with his own. The Ruthenians were beset with a double peril, and wavered whether they should first

withstand waves or weapons. Fighting to save their ships from the foe, they were shipwrecked. Within, the peril was more terrible than without: within, they fell back before the waves, while drawing the sword on those without. For the unhappy men were assaulted by two dangers at once; it was doubtful whether the swiftest way of safety was to swim or to battle to the end; and the fray was broken off at its hottest by a fresh cause of doom. Two forms of death advanced in a single onset; two paths of destruction offered united peril: it was hard to say whether the sword or the sea hurt them more. While one man was beating off the swords, the waters stole up silently and took him. Contrariwise, another was struggling with the waves, when the steel came up and encompassed him. The flooding waters were befouled with the gory spray. Thus the Ruthenians were conquered, and Frode made his way back home.

Finding that some envoys, whom he had sent into Russia to levy tribute, had been horribly murdered through the treachery of the inhabitants, Frode was stung by the double wrong and besieged closely their town Rotel. Loth that the intervening river should delay his capture of the town, he divided the entire mass of the waters by making new and different streams, thus changing what had been a channel of unknown depth into passable fords; not ceasing till the speed of the eddy, slackened by the division of its outlet, rolled its waves onward in fainter current, and winding along its slender reaches, slowly thinned and dwindled into a shallow. Thus he prevailed over the river; and the town, which

133

lacked natural defences, he overthrew, his soldiers breaking in without resistance. This done, he took his army to the city of Paltisca. Thinking no force could overcome it, he exchanged war for guile. He went into a dark and unknown hiding-place, only a very few being in the secret, and ordered a report of his death to be spread abroad, so as to inspire the enemy with less fear; his obsequies being also held, and a barrow raised, to give the tale credit. Even the soldiers bewailed his supposed death with a mourning which was in the secret of the trick. This rumour led Vespasius, the king of the city, to show so faint and feeble a defence, as though the victory was already his, that the enemy got a chance of breaking in, and slew him as he sported at his ease.

Frode, when he had taken this town, aspired to the empire of the East, and attacked the city of Handwan. This king, warned by Hadding's having once fired his town, accordingly cleared the tame birds out of all his houses, to save himself from the peril of like punishment. But Frode was not at a loss for new trickery. He exchanged garments with a serving-maid, and feigned himself to be a maiden skilled in fighting; and having thus laid aside the garb of man and imitated that of woman, he went to the town, calling himself a deserter. Here he reconnoitred everything narrowly, and on the next day sent out an attendant with orders that the army should be up at the walls, promising that he would see to it that the gates were opened. Thus the sentries were eluded and the city despoiled while it was buried in sleep; so that it paid for its heedlessness with destruction, and

134

was more pitiable for its own sloth than by reason of the valour of the foe. For in warfare nought is found to be more ruinous than that a man, made foolhardy by ease, should neglect and slacken his affairs and doze in arrogant self-confidence.

Handwan, seeing that the fortunes of his country were lost and overthrown, put all his royal wealth on shipboard and drowned it in the sea, so as to enrich the waves rather than his enemy. Yet it had been better to forestall the goodwill of his adversaries with gifts of money than to begrudge the profit of it to the service of mankind. After this, when Frode sent ambassadors to ask for the hand of his daughter, he answered, that he must take heed not to be spoiled by his thriving fortunes, or to turn his triumph into haughtiness; but let him rather bethink him to spare the conquered, and in this their abject estate to respect their former bright condition; let him learn to honour their past fortune in their present pitiable lot. Therefore, said Handwan, he must mind that he did not rob of his empire the man with whom he sought alliance, nor bespatter her with the filth of ignobleness whom he desired to honour with marriage: else he would tarnish the honour of the union with covetousness. The courtliness of this saying not only won him his conqueror for son-in-law, but saved the freedom of his realm.

Meantime Thorhild, wife of Hunding, King of the Swedes, possessed with a boundless hatred for her stepsons Ragnar and Thorwald, and fain to entangle them in divers perils, at last made them the king's shepherds. But Swanhwid, daughter of Hadding, wished

11    135

to arrest by woman's wit the ruin of natures so noble; and taking her sisters to serve as retinue, journeyed to Sweden. Seeing the said youths beset with sundry prodigies while busy watching at night over their flocks, she forbade her sisters, who desired to dismount, in a poem of the following strain:

"Monsters I behold taking swift leaps and flinging themselves over the night places. The demon is at war, and the unholy throng, devoted to the mischievous fray, battles in the mid-thoroughfare. Prodigies of aspect grim to behold pass by, and suffer no mortal to enter this country. The ranks galloping in headlong career through the void bid us stay our advance in this spot; they warn us to turn our rein and hold off from the accursed fields, they forbid us to approach the country beyond. A scowling horde of ghosts draws near, and scurries furiously through the wind, bellowing drearily to the stars. Fauns join Satyrs, and the throng of Pans mingles with the Spectres and battles with fierce visage. The Swart Ones meet the Woodland Spirits, and the pestilent Phantoms strive to share the path with the Witches. Furies poise themselves on the leap, and on them huddle the Phantoms, whom Foreboder (Fantua) joined to the Flatnoses (Satyrs), jostles. The path that the footfarer must tread brims with horror. It were safer to burden the back of the tall horse."

Thereon Ragnar declared that he was a slave of the king, and gave as reason of his departure so far from home that, when he had been banished to the country on his shepherd's business, he had lost the flock of which he

had charge, and despairing to recover it, had chosen rather to forbear from returning than to incur punishment. Also, loth to say nothing about the estate of his brother, he further spoke the following poem:

"Think us men, not monsters; we are slaves who drove our lingering flocks for pasture through the country. But while we took our pastime in gentle sports, our flock chanced to stray and went into far-off fields. And when our hope of finding them, our long quest failed, trouble came upon the mind of the wretched culprits. And when sure tracks of our kine were nowhere to be seen, dismal panic filled our guilty hearts. That is why, dreading the penal stripe of the rod, we thought it doleful to return to our own roof. We supposed it safer to hold aloof from the familiar hearth than to bear the hand of punishment. Thus we are fain to put off the punishment; we loathe going back and our wish is to lie hid here and escape our master's eye. This will aid us to elude the avenger of his neglected flock; and this is the one way of escape that remains safe for us."

Then Swanhwid gazed intently, and surveying his features, which were very comely, admired them ardently, and said:

"The radiant flashing of thine eyes is eloquent that thou art of kingly and not of servile stock. Beauty announces blood, and loveliness of soul glitters in the flash of the eyes. A keen glance betokens lordly birth, and it is plain that he whom fairness, that sure sign of nobleness, commends, is of no mean station. The outward alertness of thine eyes signifies a spirit of

137

radiance within. Face vouches for race; and the lustre of forefathers is beheld in the brightness of the countenance. For an aspect so benign and noble could never have issued from base parentage. The grace of thy blood makes thy brow mantle with a kindred grace, and the estate of thy birth is reflected in the mirror of thy countenance. It is no obscure craftsman, therefore, that has finished the portrait of so choice a chasing. Now therefore turn aside with all speed, seek constantly to depart out of the road, shun encounters with monsters, lest ye yield your most gracious bodies to be the prey and pasture of the vilest hordes."

But Ragnar was seized with great shame for his unsightly attire, which he thought was the only possible device to disguise his birth. So he rejoined, "That slaves were not always found to lack manhood; that a strong hand was often hidden under squalid raiment, and sometimes a stout arm was muffled under a dusky cloak; thus the fault of nature was retrieved by valour, and deficiency in race requited by nobleness of spirit. He therefore feared the might of no supernatural prowess, save of the god Thor only, to the greatness of whose force nothing human or divine could fitly be compared. The hearts of men ought not to be terrified at phantoms, which were only awful from their ghastly foulness, and whose semblances, marked by counterfeit ghostliness, were wont for a moment to borrow materiality from the fluent air. Swanhwid therefore erred in trying, womanlike, to sap the firm strength of men, and to melt in unmanly panic that might which knew not defeat."

Swanhwid marvelled at the young man's steadfastness, and cast off the cloud of mist which overshadowed her, dispelling the darkness which shrouded her face, till it was clear and cloudless. Then, promising that she would give him a sword fitted for divers kinds of battle, she revealed the marvellous maiden beauty of her lustrous limbs. Thus was the youth kindled, and she plighted her troth with him, and proffering the sword, she thus began:

"King, in this sword, which shall expose the monsters to thy blows, take the first gift of thy betrothed. Show thyself duly deserving hereof; let hand rival sword, and aspire to add lustre to its weapon. Let the might of steel strengthen the defenceless point of thy wit, and let spirit know how to work with hand. Let the bearer match the burden: and that thy deed may sort with thy blade, let equal weight in each be thine. What avails the javelin when the breast is weak and faint, and the quivering hands have dropped the lance? Let steel join soul, and be both the body's armour! Let the right hand be linked with its hilt in alliance. These fight famous battles, because they always keep more force when together; but less when parted. Therefore if it be joy to thee to win fame by the palm of war, pursue with daring whatsoever is hard pressed by thy hand."

After thus discoursing long in harmoniously-adjusted strains, she sent away her retinue, and passed all the night in combat against the foulest throngs of monsters; and at return of daybreak she perceived fallen all over the fields diverse shapes of phantoms, and figures extra-

ordinary to look on; and among them was seen the semblance of Thorhild herself covered with wounds. All these she piled in a heap and burnt, kindling a huge pyre, lest the foul stench of the filthy carcases might spread in pestilent vapour and hurt those who came nigh with its taint of corruption. This done, she won the throne of Sweden for Ragnar, and Ragnar for her husband. And though he deemed it uncomely to inaugurate his first campaign with a wedding, yet, moved by gratitude for the preservation of his safety, he kept his promise.

Meantime one Ubbe, who had long since wedded Ulfhild the sister of Frode, trusting in the high birth of his wife, seized the kingdom of Denmark, which he was managing carelessly as deputy. Frode was thus forced to quit the wars of the East, and fought a great battle in Sweden with his sister Swanhwid, in which he was beaten. So he got on board a skiff, and sailed stealthily in a circuit, seeking some way of boring through the enemy's fleet. When surprised by his sister and asked why he was rowing silently and following divers meandering courses, he cut short her inquiry by a similar question; for Swanhwid had also, at the same time of the night, taken to sailing about alone, and was stealthily searching out all the ways of approach and retreat through devious and dangerous windings. So she reminded her brother of the freedom he had given her long since, and went on to ask him that he should allow her full enjoyment of the husband she had taken; since, before he started on the Russian war, he had given her the boon

of marrying as she would; and that he should hold valid after the event what he had himself allowed to happen. These reasonable entreaties touched Frode, and he made a peace with Ragnar, and forgave, at his sister's request, the wrongdoing which Ragnar seemed to have begun because of her wantonness. They presented him with a force equal to that which they had caused him to lose: a handsome gift in which he rejoiced as compensation for so ugly a reverse.

Ragnar, entering Denmark, captured Ubbe, had him brought before him, and pardoned him, preferring to visit his ill deserts with grace rather than chastisement; because the man seemed to have aimed at the crown rather at his wife's instance than of his own ambition, and to have been the imitator and not the cause of the wrong. But he took Ulfhild away from him and forced her to wed his friend Scot, the same man that founded the Scottish name; esteeming change of wedlock a punishment for her. As she went away he even escorted her in the royal chariot, requiting evil with good; for he regarded the kinship of his sister rather than her disposition, and took more thought for his own good name than of her iniquity. But the fair deeds of her brother did not make her obstinate and wonted hatred slacken a whit; she wore the spirit of her new husband with her design of slaying Frode and mastering the sovereignty of the Danes. For whatsoever design the mind has resolutely conceived, it is slow to quit; nor is a sin that is long schemed swept away by the stream of years. For the temper of later life follows the mind of childhood; nor do the traces easily fade

of vices which have been stamped upon the character in the impressible age. Finding the ears of her husband deaf, she diverted her treachery from her brother against her lord, hiring bravoes to cut his thoat while he slept. Scot was told about this by a waiting-woman, and retired to bed in his cuirass on the night on which he had heard the deed of murder was to be wrought upon him. Ulfhild asked him why he had exchanged his wonted ways to wear the garb of steel; he rejoined that such was just then his fancy. The agents of the treachery, when they imagined him in a deep sleep, burst in; but he slipped from his bed and cut them down. The result was, that he prevented Ulfhild from weaving plots against her brother, and also left a warning to others to beware of treachery from their wives.

Meantime the design occurred to Frode of a campaign against Friesland; he was desirous to dazzle the eyes of the West with the glory he had won in conquering the East. He put out to ocean, and his first contest was with Witthe, a rover of the Frisians; and in this battle he bade his crews patiently bear the first brunt of the enemy's charge by merely opposing their shields, ordering that they should not use their missiles before they perceived that the shower of the enemy's spears was utterly spent. This the Frisians hurled as vehemently as the Danes received it impassively; for Witthe supposed that the long-suffering of Frode was due to a wish for peace. High rose the blast of the trumpet, and loud whizzed the javelins everywhere, till at last the heedless Frisians had not a single lance remaining, and they were con-

quered, overwhelmed by the missiles of the Danes. They
fled hugging the shore, and were cut to pieces amid the
circuitous windings of the canals. Then Frode explored
the Rhine in his fleet, and laid hands on the farthest parts
of Germany. Then he went back to the ocean, and
attacked the Frisian fleet, which had struck on shoals;
and thus he crowned shipwreck with slaughter. Nor
was he content with the destruction of so great an army
of his foes, but assailed Britain, defeated its king, and
attacked Melbrik, the Governor of the Scottish district.
Just as he was preparing to fight him, he heard from a
scout that the King of the Britons was at hand, and could
not look to his front and his rear both at once. So he
assembled the soldiers, and ordered that they should
abandon their chariots, fling away all their goods, and
scatter everywhere over the fields the gold which they
had about them; for he declared that their one chance was
to squander their treasure; and that, now they were
hemmed in, their only remaining help was to tempt the
enemy from combat to covetousness. They ought cheer-
fully to spend on so extreme a need the spoil they had
gotten among foreigners; for the enemy would drop it
as eagerly, when it was once gathered, as they would
snatch it when they first found it; for it would be to them
more burden than profit.

Then Thorkill, who was a more notable miser and a
better orator than them all, dishelming and leaning on his
shield, said:

"O King! most of us who rate high what we have
bought with our life-blood find thy bidding hard. We

take it ill that we should fling away what we have won
with utmost hazard; and men are loth to forsake what
they have purchased at peril of their lives.  For it is utter
madness to spurn away like women what our manly hearts
and hands have earned, and enrich the enemy beyond their
hopes.  What is more odious than to anticipate the
fortune of war by despising the booty which is ours, and,
in terror of an evil that may never come, to quit a good
which is present and assured?  Shall we scatter our gold
upon the earth, ere we have set eyes upon the Scots?
Those who faint at the thought of warring when they are
out for war, what manner of men are they to be thought
in the battle?  Shall we be a derision to our foes, we who
were their terror?  Shall we take scorn instead of glory?
The Briton will marvel that he was conquered by men
whom he sees fear is enough to conquer.  We struck
them before with panic; shall we be panic-stricken by
them?  We scorned them when before us; shall we dread
them when they are not here?  When will our bravery
win the treasure which our cowardice rejects?  Shall
we shirk the fight, in scorn of the money which we fought
to win, and enrich those whom we should rightly have
impoverished?  What deed more despicable can we do
than to squander gold on those whom we should smite
with steel?  Panic must never rob us of the spoils of
valour; and only war must make us quit what in warfare
we have won.  Let us sell our plunder at the price at
which we bought it; let the purchase-money be weighed
out in steel.  It is better to die a noble death, than to
moulder away too much in love with the light life.  In

a fleeting instant of time life forsakes us, but shame pursues us past the grave. Further, if we cast away this gold, the greater the enemy thinks our fear, the hotter will be his chase. Besides, whichever the issue of the day, the gold is not hateful to us. Conquerors, we shall triumph in the treasure which now we bear; conquered, we shall leave it to pay our burying."

So spoke the old man; but the soldiers regarded the advice of their king rather than of their comrade, and thought more of the former than of the latter counsel. So each of them eagerly drew his wealth, whatever he had, from his pouch; they unloaded their ponies of the various goods they were carrying; and having thus cleared their money-bags, girded on their arms more deftly. They went on, and the Britons came up, but broke away after the plunder which lay spread out before them. Their king, when he beheld them too greedily busied with scrambling for the treasure, bade them "take heed not to weary with a load of riches those hands which were meant for battle, since they ought to know that a victory must be culled ere it is counted. Therefore let them scorn the gold and give chase to the possessors of the gold; let them admire the lustre, not of lucre, but of conquest; remembering, that a trophy gave more reward than gain. Courage was worth more than dross, if they measured aright the quality of both; for the one furnished outward adorning, but the other enhanced both outward and inward grace. Therefore they must keep their eyes far from the sight of money, and their soul from covetousness, and devote it to the pursuits of war. Further,

they should know that the plunder had been abandoned by the enemy of set purpose, and that the gold had been scattered rather to betray them than to profit them. Moreover, the honest lustre of the silver was only a bait on the barb of secret guile. It was not thought to be that they, who had first forced the Britons to fly, would lightly fly themselves. Besides, nothing was more shameful than riches which betrayed into captivity the plunderer whom they were supposed to enrich. For the Danes thought that the men to whom they pretended to have offered riches ought to be punished with sword and slaughter. Let them therefore feel that they were only giving the enemy a weapon if they seized what he had scattered. For if they were caught by the look of the treasure that had been exposed, they must lose, not only that, but any of their own money that might remain. What could it profit them to gather what they must straightway disgorge? But if they refuse to abase themselves before money, they would doubtless abase the foe. Thus it was better for them to stand erect in valour than be grovelling in greed; with their souls not sinking into covetousness, but up and doing for renown. In the battle they would have to use not gold but swords."

As the king ended, a British knight, shewing them all his lapful of gold, said:

"O King! From thy speech can be gathered two feelings; and one of them witnesses to thy cowardice and the other to thy illwill: inasmuch as thou forbiddest us the use of the wealth because of the enemy, and also thinkest it better that we should serve thee needy

than rich. What is more odious than such a wish? What more senseless than such a counsel? We recognise these as the treasures of our own homes, and having done so, shall we falter to pick them up? We were on our way to regain them by fighting, we were zealous to win them back by our blood: shall we shun them when they are restored unasked? Shall we hesitate to claim our own? Which is the greater coward, he who squanders his winnings, or he who is fearful to pick up what is squandered? Look how chance has restored what compulsion took! These are, not spoils from the enemy, but from ourselves; the Dane took gold from Britain, he brought none. Beaten and loth we lost it; it comes back for nothing, and shall we run away from it? Such a gift of fortune it were a shame to take in an unworthy spirit. For what were madder than to spurn wealth that is set openly before us, and to desire it when it is shut up and kept from us? Shall we squeamishly yield what is set under our eyes, and clutch at it when it vanishes? Shall we seek distant and foreign treasure, refraining from what is made public property? If we disown what is ours, when shall we despoil the goods of others? No anger of heaven can I experience which can force me to unload of its lawful burden the lap which is filled with my father's and my grandsire's gold. I know the wantonness of the Danes: never would they have left jars full of wine had not fear forced them to flee. They would rather have sacrificed their life than their liquor. This passion we share with them, and herein we are like them. Grant that their flight is feigned; yet they will light

upon the Scots ere they can come back. This gold shall never rust in the country, to be trodden underfoot of swine or brutes: it will better serve the use of men. Besides, if we plunder the spoil of the army that prevailed over us, we transfer the luck of the conqueror to ourselves. For what surer omen of triumph could be got, than to bear off the booty before the battle, and to capture ere the fray the camp which the enemy have forsaken? Better conquer by fear than by steel."

The knight had scarce ended, when behold; the hands of all were loosed upon the booty and everywhere plucked up the shining treasure. There you might have marvelled at their disposition of filthy greed, and watched a portentous spectacle of avarice. You could have seen gold and grass clutched up together; the birth of domestic discord; fellow-countrymen in deadly combat, heedless of the foe; neglect of the bonds of comradeship and of reverence for ties; greed the object of all minds, and friendship of none.

Meantime Frode traversed in a great march the forest which separates Scotland and Britain, and bade his soldiers arm. When the Scots beheld his line, and saw that they had only a supply of light javelins, while the Danes were furnished with a more excellent style of armour, they forestalled the battle by flight. Frode pursued them but a little way, fearing a sally of the British, and on returning met Scot, the husband of Ulfhild, with a great army; he had been brought from the utmost ends of Scotland by the desire of aiding the Danes. Scot entreated him to abandon the pursuit of the

Scottish and turn back into Britain. So he eagerly regained the plunder which he had cunningly sacrificed; and got back his wealth with the greater ease, that he had so tranquilly let it go. Then did the British repent of their burden and pay for their covetousness with their blood. They were sorry to have clutched at greed with insatiate arms. and ashamed to have hearkened to their own avarice rather than to the counsel of their king.

Then Frode attacked London, the most populous city of Britain; but the strength of its walls gave him no chance of capturing it. Therefore he feigned to be dead, and his guile strengthened him. For Daleman, the governor of London, on hearing the false news of his death, accepted the surrender of the Danes, offered them a native general, and suffered them to enter the town, that they might choose him out of a great throng. They feigned to be making a careful choice, but beset Daleman in a night surprise and slew him.

When he had done these things, and gone back to his own land, one Skat entertained him at a banquet, desirous to mingle his toilsome warfare with joyous licence. Frode was lying in his house, in royal fashion, upon cushions of cloth of gold, and a certain Hunding challenged him to fight. Then, though he had bent his mind to the joys of wassail, he had more delight in the prospect of a fray than in the presence of a feast, and wound up the supper with a duel and the duel with a triumph. In the combat he received a dangerous wound; but a taunt of Hakon the champion again roused him, and, slaying his challenger, he took vengeance for the disturb-

ance of his rest. Two of his chamber-servants were openly convicted of treachery, and he had them tied to vast stones and drowned in the sea; thus chastising the weighty guilt of their souls by fastening boulders to their bodies. Some relate that Ulfhild gave him a coat which no steel could pierce, so that when he wore it no missile's point could hurt him. Nor must I omit how Frode was wont to sprinkle his food with brayed and pounded atoms of gold, as a resource against the usual snares of poisoners. While he was attacking Ragnar, the King of Sweden, who had been falsely accused of treachery, he perished, not by the spears, but stifled in the weight of his arms and by the heat of his own body.

Frode left three sons, HALFDAN, Ro, and Skat, who were equal in valour, and were seized with an equal desire for the throne. All thought of sway, none was constrained by brotherly regard: for love of others forsaketh him who is eaten up with love of self, nor can any man take thought at once for his own advancement and for his friendship with others. Halfdan, the eldest son, disgraced his birth with the sin of slaying his brethren, winning his kingdom by the murder of his kin; and, to complete his display of cruelty, arrested their adherents, first confining them in bonds, and presently hanging them. The most notable thing in the fortunes of Halfdan was this, that though he devoted every instant of his life to the practice of cruel deeds, yet he died of old age, and not by the steel.

Halfdan's sons were Ro and HELGE. Ro is said to have been the founder of Roskild, which was later increased

in population and enhanced in power by Sweyn, who was famous for the surname Forkbeard. Ro was short and spare, while Helge was rather tall of stature. Dividing the realm with his brother, Helge was allotted the domain of the sea; and attacking Skalk, the King of Sklavia, with his naval force, he slew him. Having reduced Sklavia into a province, he scoured the various arms of the sea in a wandering voyage. Savage of temper as Helge was, his cruelty was not greater than his lust. For he was so immoderately prone to love, that it was doubtful whether the heat of his tyranny or of his concupiscence was the greater. In Thorey he ravished the maiden Thora, who bore a daughter, to whom she afterwards gave the name of Urse. Then he conquered in battle, before the town of Stad, the son of Syrik, King of Saxony, Hunding, whom he challenged, attacked, and slew in duel. For this he was called Hunding's-Bane, and by that name gained glory of his victory. He took Jutland out of the power of the Saxons, and entrusted its management to his generals, Heske, Eyr, and Ler. In Saxony he enacted that the slaughter of a freedman and of a noble should be visited with the same punishment; as though he wished it to be clearly known that all the households of the Teutons were held in equal slavery, and that the freedom of all was tainted and savoured equally of dishonour.

Then Helge went freebooting to Thorey. But Thora had not ceased to bewail her lost virginity, and planned a shameful device in abominable vengeance for her rape. For she deliberately sent down to the beach her daughter,

who was of marriageable age, and prompted her father to deflower her. And though she yielded her body to the treacherous lures of delight, yet she must not be thought to have abjured her integrity of soul, inasmuch as her fault had a ready excuse by virtue of her ignorance. Insensate mother, who allowed the forfeiture of her child's chastity in order to avenge her own; caring nought for the purity of her own blood, so she might stain with incest the man who had cost her her own maidenhood at first! Infamous-hearted woman, who, to punish her defiler, measured out as it were a second defilement to herself, whereas she clearly by the selfsame act rather swelled than lessened the transgression! Surely, by the very act wherewith she thought to reach her revenge, she accumulated guilt; she added a sin in trying to remove a crime: she played the stepdame to her own offspring, not sparing her daughter abomination in order to atone for her own disgrace. Doubtless her soul was brimming over with shamelessness, since she swerved so far from shamefastness, as without a blush to seek solace for her wrong in her daughter's infamy. A great crime, with but one atonement; namely, that the guilt of this intercourse was wiped away by a fortunate progeny, its fruits being as delightful as its repute was evil.

ROLF, the son of Urse, retrieved the shame of his birth by signal deeds of valour; and their exceeding lustre is honoured with bright laudation by the memory of all succeeding time. For lamentation sometimes ends in laughter, and foul beginnings pass to fair issues. So that the father's fault, though criminal, was fortunate, being

afterwards atoned for by a son of such marvellous splendour.

Meantime Ragnar died in Sweden; and Swanhwid his wife passed away soon after of a malady which she had taken from her sorrow, following in death the husband from whom she had not endured severance in life. For it often happens that some people desire to follow out of life those whom they loved exceedingly when alive. Their son Hothbrodd succeeded them. Fain to extend his empire, he warred upon the East, and after a huge massacre of many peoples begat two sons, Athisl and Hother, and appointed as their tutor a certain Gewar, who was bound to him by great services. Not content with conquering the East, he assailed Denmark, challenged its king, Ro, in three battles, and slew him. Helge, when he heard this, shut up his son Rolf in Leire, wishing, however he might have managed his own fortunes, to see to the safety of his heir. When Hothbrodd sent in governors, wanting to free his country from alien rule, he posted his people about the city and prevailed and slew them. Also he annihilated Hothbrodd himself and all his forces in a naval battle; so avenging fully the wrongs of his country as well as of his brother. Hence he who had before won a nickname for slaying Hunding, now bore a surname for the slaughter of Hothbrodd. Besides, as if the Swedes had not been enough stricken in the battles, he punished them by stipulating for most humiliating terms; providing by law that no wrong done to any of them should receive amends according to the form of legal covenants. After these deeds, ashamed of his former

infamy, he hated his country and his home, went back to
the East, and there died. Some think that he was affected
by the disgrace which was cast in his teeth, and did himself to death by falling upon his drawn sword.

He was succeeded by his son ROLF, who was comely
with every gift of mind and body, and graced his mighty
stature with as high a courage. In his time Sweden was
subject to the sway of the Danes; wherefore Athisl, the
son of Hothbrodd, in pursuit of a crafty design to set
his country free, contrived to marry Rolf's mother, Urse,
thinking that his kinship by marriage would plead for
him, and enable him to prompt his stepson more effectually to relax the tribute; and fortune prospered his
wishes. But Athisl had from his boyhood been imbued
with a hatred of liberality, and was so grasping of
money, that he accounted it a disgrace to be called open-
handed. Urse, seeing him so steeped in filthy covetousness, desired to be rid of him; but, thinking that she
must act by cunning, veiled the shape of her guile with
a marvellous skill. Feigning to be unmotherly, she spurred on her husband to grasp his freedom, and urged and
tempted him to insurrection; causing her son to be summoned to Sweden with a promise of vast gifts. For she
thought that she would best gain her desire if, as soon
as her son had got his stepfather's gold, she could
snatch up the royal treasures and flee, robbing her husband of bed and money to boot. For she fancied that
the best way to chastise his covetousness would be to
steal away his wealth. This deep guilefulness was hard
to detect, from such recesses of cunning did it spring;

because she dissembled her longing for a change of wedlock under a show of aspiration for freedom. Blind-
witted husband, fancying the mother kindled against the
life of the son, never seeing that it was rather his own
ruin being compassed! Doltish lord, blind to the obstinate scheming of his wife, who, out of pretended
hatred of her son, devised opportunity for change of wedlock! Though the heart of woman should never be
trusted, he believed in a woman all the more insen-
sately, because he supposed her faithful to himself and
treacherous to her son.

Accordingly, Rolf, tempted by the greatness of the
gifts, chanced to enter the house of Athisl. He was not
recognised by his mother owing to his long absence and
the cessation of their common life; so in jest he first
asked for some victual to appease his hunger. She advised him to ask the king for a luncheon. Then he
thrust out a torn piece of his coat, and begged of her
the service of sewing it up. Finding his mother's ears
shut to him, he observed, "That it was hard to discover
a friendship that was firm and true, when a mother refused her son a meal, and a sister refused a brother the
help of her needle." Thus he punished his mother's
error, and made her blush deep for her refusal of kindness. Athisl, when he saw him reclining close to his
mother at the banquet, taunted them both with wantonness, declaring that it was an impure intercourse of
brother and sister. Rolf repelled the charge against his
honour by an appeal to the closest of natural bonds, and
answered, that it was honourable for a son to embrace

a beloved mother. Also, when the feasters asked him
what kind of courage he set above all others, he named
Endurance. When they also asked Athisl, what was the
virtue which above all he desired most devotedly, he
declared, Generosity. Proofs were therefore demanded
of bravery on the one hand and munificence on the other,
and Rolf was asked to give an evidence of courage first.
He was placed to the fire, and defending with his target
the side that was most hotly assailed, had only the firm-
ness of his endurance to fortify the other, which had no
defence. How dexterous, to borrow from his shield
protection to assuage the heat, and to guard his body,
which was exposed to the flames, with that which sometime sheltered it amid the hurtling spears! But the
glow was hotter than the fire of spears; as though it
could not storm the side that was entrenched by the
shield, yet it assaulted the flank that lacked its protection. But a waiting-maid who happened to be standing
near the hearth, saw that he was being roasted by the
unbearable heat upon his ribs; so taking the stopper out
of a cask, she spilt the liquid and quenched the flame, and
by the timely kindness of the shower checked in its career
the torturing blaze. Rolf was lauded for supreme endurance, and then came the request for Athisl's gifts.
And they say that he showered treasures on his stepson,
and at last, in order to crown the gift, bestowed on him
an enormously heavy necklace.

Now Urse, who had watched her chance for the deed
of guile, on the third day of the banquet, without her
husband ever dreaming of such a thing, put all the king's

wealth into carriages, and going out stealthily, stole away from her own dwelling and fled in the glimmering twilight, departing with her son. Thrilled with fear of her husband's pursuit, and utterly despairing of escape beyond, she begged and bade her companions to cast away the money, declaring that they must lose either life or riches; the short and only path to safety lay in flinging away the treasure, nor could any aid to escape be found save in the loss of tHeir possessions. Therefore, said she, they must follow the example of the manner in which Frode was said to have saved himself among the Britons. She added, that it was not paying a great price to lay down the Swedes' own goods for them to regain; if only they could themselves gain a start in flight, by the very device which would check the others in their pursuit, and if they seemed not so much to abandon their own possessions as to restore those of other men. Not a moment was lost; in order to make the flight swifter, they did the bidding of the queen. The gold is cleared from their purses; the riches are left for the enemy to seize. Some declare that Urse kept back the money, and strewed the tracks of Her flight with copper that was gilt over. For it was thought credible that a woman who could scheme such great deeds could also have painted with lying lustre the metal that was meant to be lost, mimicking riches of true worth with the sheen of spurious gold. So Athisl, when he saw the necklace that he had given to Rolf left among the other golden ornaments, gazed fixedly upon the dearest treasure of his avarice, and, in order to pick up the plunder,

glued his knees to the earth and deigned to stoop his royalty unto greed. Rolf, seeing him lie abjectly on his face in order to gather up the money, smiled at the sight of a man prostrated by his own gifts, just as if he were seeking covetously to regain what he had craftily yielded up. The Swedes were content with their booty, and Rolf quickly retired to his ships, and managed to escape by rowing violently.

Now they relate that Rolf used with ready generosity to grant at the first entreaty whatsoever he was begged to bestow, and never put off the request till the second time of asking. For he preferred to forestall repeated supplication by speedy liberality, rather than mar his kindness by delay. This habit brought him a great concourse of champions; valour having commonly either rewards for its food or glory for its spur.

At this time, a certain Agnar, son of Ingild, being about to wed Rute, the sister of Rolf, celebrated his bridal with a great banquet. The champions were rioting at this banquet with every sort of wantonness, and flinging from all over the room knobbed bones at a certain Hjalte; but it chanced that his messmate, named Bjarke, received a violent blow on the head through the ill aim of the thrower; at whom, stung both by the pain and the jeering, he sent the bone back, so that he twisted the front of his head to the back, and wrung the back of it to where the front had been; punishing the wryness of the man's temper by turning his face sidelong. This deed moderated their wanton and injurious jests, and drove the champions to quit the place. The bridegroom,

nettled at this affront to the banquet, resolved to fight
Bjarke, in order to seek vengeance by means of a duel
for the interruption of their mirth. At the outset of the
duel there was a long dispute, which of them ought to
have the chance of striking first. For of old, in the
ordering of combats, men did not try to exchange their
blows thick and fast; but there was a pause, and at the
same time a definite succession in striking: the contest
being carried on with few strokes, but those terrible,
so that honour was paid more to the mightiness than
to the number of the blows. Agnar, being of higher
rank, was put first; and the blow which he dealt is said
to have been so furious, that he cut through the front
of the helmet, wounded the skin on the scalp, and had to
let go his sword, which became locked in the vizor-
holes. Then Bjarke, who was to deal the return-stroke,
leaned his foot against a stock, in order to give the
freer poise to his steel, and passed his fine-edged blade
through the midst of Agnar's body. Some declare that
Agnar, in supreme suppression of his pain, gave up the
ghost with his lips relaxed into a smile. The champions
passionately sought to avenge him, but were visited by
Bjarke with like destruction; for he used a sword of
wonderful sharpness and unusual length which he called
Lövi. While he was triumphing in these deeds of prowess, a beast of the forest furnished him fresh laurels.
For he met a huge bear in a thicket, and slew it with a
javelin; and then bade his companion Hjalte put his
lips to the beast and drink the blood that came out, that
he might be the stronger afterwards. For it was be-

lieved that a draught of this sort caused an increase of bodily strength. By these valorous achievements he became intimate with the most illustrious nobles, and even, became a favourite of the king; took to wife his sister Rute, and had the bride of the conquered as the prize of the conquest. When Rolf was harried. by Athisl he avenged himself on him in battle and overthrew Athisl in war. Then Rolf gave his sister Skulde in marriage to a youth of keen wit, called Hiartuar, and made him governor of Sweden, ordaining a yearly tax; wishing to soften the loss of freedom to him by the favour of an alliance with himself.

Here let me put into my work a thing that it is mirthful to record. A youth named Wigg, scanning with attentive eye the bodily size of Rolf, and smitten with great wonder thereat, proceeded to inquire in jest who was that "Krage" whom Nature in her bounty had endowed with such towering stature? meaning humorously to banter his uncommon tallness. For "Krage" in the Danish tongue means a tree-trunk, whose branches are pollarded, and whose summit is climbed in such wise that the foot uses the lopped timbers as supports, as if leaning on a ladder, and, gradually advancing to the higher parts, finds the shortest way to the top. Rolf accepted this random word as though it were a name of honour for him, and rewarded the wit of the saying with a heavy bracelet. Then Wigg, thrusting out his right arm decked with the bracelet, put his left behind his back in affected shame, and walked with a ludicrous gait, declaring that he, whose lot had so long been poverty-

stricken, was glad of a scanty gift. When he was asked
why he was behaving so, he said that the arm which
lacked ornament and had no splendour to boast of was
mantling with the modest blush of poverty to behold the
other. The ingenuity of this saying won him a present
to match the first. For Rolf made him bring out to view,
like the other, the hand which he was hiding. Nor was
Wigg heedless to repay the kindness; for he promised,
uttering a strict vow, that, if it befell Rolf to perish by
the sword, he would himself take vengeance on his
slayers. Nor should it be omitted that in old time nobles
who were entering the court used to devote to their
rulers the first-fruits of their service by vowing some
mighty exploit; thus bravely inaugurating their first
campaign.

Meantime, Skulde was stung with humiliation at the
payment of the tribute, and bent her mind to devise deeds
of horror. Taunting her husband with his ignominious
estate, she urged and egged him to break off his servitude,
induced him to weave plots against Rolf, and filled his
mind with the most abominable plans of disloyalty, declaring that everyone owed more to their freedom than
to kinship. Accordingly, she ordered huge piles of arms
to be muffled up under divers coverings, to be carried by
Hiartuar into Denmark, as if they were tribute: these
would furnish a store wherewith to slay the king by night.
So the vessels were loaded with the mass of pretended
tribute, and they proceeded to Leire, a town which Rolf
had built and adorned with the richest treasure of his
realm, and which, being a royal foundation and a royal

seat, surpassed in importance all the cities of the neighbouring districts. The king welcomed the coming of
Hiartuar with a splendid banquet, and drank very deep,
while his guests, contrary to their custom, shunned immoderate tippling. So, while all the others were sleeping
soundly, the Swedes, who had been kept from their ordinary rest by their eagerness on their guilty purpose, began furtively to slip down from their sleeping-rooms.
Straightway uncovering the hidden heap of weapons, each
girded on his arms silently and then went to the palace.
Bursting into its recesses, they drew their swords upon
the sleeping figures. Many awoke; but, invaded as much
by the sudden and dreadful carnage as by the drowsiness
of sleep, they faltered in their resistance; for the night
misled them and made it doubtful whether those they met
were friends or foes. Hjalte, who was foremost in tried
bravery among the nobles of the king, chanced to have
gone out in the dead of that same night into the country
and given himself to the embraces of a harlot. But when
his torpid hearing caught from afar the rising din of
battle, preferring valour to wantonness, he chose rather
to seek the deadly perils of the War-god than to yield to
the soft allurements of Love. What a love for his king,
must we suppose, burned in this warrior! For he might
have excused his absence by feigning not to have known;
but he thought it better to expose his life to manifest
danger than save it for pleasure. As he went away, his
mistress asked him how aged a man she ought to marry
if she were to lose him? Then Hjalte bade her come
closer, as though he would speak to her more privately;

and, resenting that she needed a successor to his love, he cut off her nose and made her unsightly, punishing the utterance of that wanton question with a shameful wound, and thinking that the lecherousness of her soul ought to be cooled by outrage to her face. When he had done this, he said he left her choice free in the matter she had asked about. Then he went qiuckly back to the town and plunged into the densest of the fray, mowing down the opposing ranks as he gave blow for blow. Passing the sleeping-room of Bjarke, who was still slumbering, he bade him wake up, addressing him as follows:

"Let him awake speedily, whoso showeth himself by service or avoweth himself in mere loyalty, a friend of the king! Let the princes shake off slumber, let shameless lethargy begone; let their spirits awake and warm to the work; each man's own right hand shall either give him to glory, or steep him in sluggard shame; and this night shall be either end or vengeance of our woes.

"I do not now bid ye learn the sports of maidens, nor stroke soft cheeks, nor give sweet kisses to the bride and press the slender breasts, nor desire the flowing wine and chafe the soft thigh and cast eyes upon snowy arms. I call you out to the sterner fray of War. We need the battle, and not light love; nerveless languor has no business here: our need calls for battles. Whoso cherishes friendship for the king, let him take up arms. Prowess in war is the readiest appraiser of men's spirits. Therefore let warriors have no fearfulness and the brave no fickleness: let pleasure quit their soul and yield place to arms. Glory is now appointed for wages; each can

be the arbiter of his own renown, and shine by his own right hand. Let nought here be tricked out with wantonness: let all be full of sternness, and learn how to rid them of this calamity. He who covets the honours or prizes of glory must not be faint with craven fear, but go forth to meet the brave, nor whiten at the cold steel."

At this utterance, Bjarke, awakened, roused up his chamber-page Skalk speedily, and addressed him as follows:

"Up, lad, and fan the fire with constant blowing; sweep the hearth clear of wood, and scatter the fine ashes. Strike out sparks from the fire, rouse the fallen embers, draw out the smothered blaze. Force the slackening hearth to yield light by kindling the coals to a red glow with a burning log. It will do me good to stretch out my fingers when the fire is brought nigh. Surely he that takes heed for his friend should have warm hands, and utterly drive away the blue and hurtful chill."

Hjalte said again: "Sweet is it to repay the gifts received from our lord, to grip the swords, and devote the steel to glory. Behold, each man's courage tells him loyally to follow a king of such deserts, and to guard our captain with fitting earnestness. Let the Teuton swords, the helmets, the shining armlets, the mail-coats that reach the heel, which Rolf of old bestowed upon his men, let these sharpen our mindful hearts to the fray. The time requires, and it is just, that in time of war we should earn whatsoever we have gotten in the deep idleness of peace, that we should not think more of joyous courses than of sorrowful fortunes, or always prefer prosperity

to hardship. Being noble, let us with even soul accept either lot, nor let fortune sway our behaviour, for it beseems us to receive equably difficult and delightsome days; let us pass the years of sorrow with the same countenance wherewith we took the years of joy. Let us do with brave hearts all the things that in our cups we boasted with sodden lips; let us keep the vows which we swore by highest Jove and the mighty gods. My master is the greatest of the Danes: let each man, as he is valorous, stand by him; far, far hence be all cowards! We need a brave and steadfast man, not one that turns his back on a dangerous pass, or dreads the grim preparations for battle. Often a general's greatest valour depends on his soldiery, for the chief enters the fray all the more at ease that a better array of nobles throngs him round. Let the thane catch up his arms with fighting fingers, setting his right hand on the hilt and holding fast the shield: let him charge upon the foes, nor pale at any strokes. Let none offer himself to be smitten by the enemy behind, let none receive the swords in his back; let the battling breast ever front the blow. 'Eagles fight brow foremost,' and with swift gaping beaks speed onward in the front: be ye like that bird in mien, shrinking from no stroke, but with body facing the foe.

"See how the enemy, furious and confident overduly, his limbs defended by the steel, and his face with a gilded helmet, charges the thick of the battle-wedges, as though sure of victory, fearless of rout and invincible by any endeavour. Ah, misery! Swedish assurance spurns the Danes. Behold, the Goths with savage eyes and grim

aspect advance with crested helms and clanging spears; wreaking heavy slaughter in our blood, they wield their swords and their battle-axes hone-sharpened.

"Why name thee, Hiartuar, whom Skulde hath filled with guilty purpose, and hath suffered thus to harden in sin? Why sing of thee, villain, who hast caused our peril, betrayer of a noble king? Furious lust of sway hath driven thee to attempt an abomination, and, stung with frenzy, to screen thyself behind thy wife's everlasting guilt. What error hath made thee to hurt the Danes and thy lord, and hurled thee into such foul crime as this? Whence entered thy heart the treason framed with such careful guile?

"Why do I linger? Now we have swallowed our last morsel. Our king perishes, and utter doom overtakes our hapless city. Our last dawn has risen, unless perchance there be one here so soft that he fears to offer himself to the blows, or so unwarlike that he dares not avenge his lord, and disowns all honours worthy of his valour.

"Thou, Ruta, rise and put forth thy snow-white head, come forth from thy hiding into the battle. The carnage that is being done without calls thee. By now the council-chamber is shaken with warfare, and the gates creak with the dreadful fray. Steel rends the mail-coats, the woven mesh is torn apart, and the midriff gives under the rain of spears. By now the huge axes have hacked small the shield of the king; by now the long swords clash, and the battle-axe clatters its blows upon the shoulders of men, and cleaves their breasts. Why are your hearts afraid?

Why is your sword faint and blunted? The gate is
cleared of our people, and is filled with the press of the
strangers."

And when Hjalte had wrought very great carnage and
stained the battle with blood, he stumbled for the third
time on Bjarke's berth, and thinking he desired to keep
quiet because he was afraid, made trial of him with such
taunts at his cowardice as these:

"Bjarke, why art thou absent? doth deep sleep hold
thee? I prithee, what makes thee tarry? Come out, or
the fire will overcome thee. Ho! choose the better way,
charge with me! Bears may be kept off with fire; let us
spread fire in the recesses, and let the blaze attack the
door-posts first. Let the firebrand fall upon the bed-
chamber, let the falling roof offer fuel for the flames and
serve to feed the fire. It is right to scatter conflagration on the doomed gates. But let us who honour our
king with better loyalty form the firm battle-wedges, and,
having measured the phalanx in safe rows, go forth in
the way the king taught us: our king, who laid low
Rorik, the son of Bok the covetous, and wrapped the
coward in death. He was rich in wealth, but in enjoyment poor, stronger in gain than bravery; and thinking
gold better than warfare, he set lucre above all things,
and ingloriously accumulated piles of treasure, scorning
the service of noble friends. And when he was attacked
by the navy of Rolf, he bade his servants take the gold
from the chests and spread it out in front of the city
gates, making ready bribes rather than battle, because he
knew not the soldier, and thought that the foe should

**13** · 167

be attempted with gifts and not with arms: as though he could fight with wealth alone, and prolong the war by using, not men, but wares! So he undid the heavy coffers and the rich chests; he brought forth the polished bracelets and the heavy caskets; they only fed his destruction. Rich in treasure, poor in warriors, he left his foes to take away the prizes which he forebore to give to the friends of his own land. He who once shrank to give little rings of his own will, now unwillingly squandered his masses of wealth, rifling his hoarded heap. But our king in his wisdom spurned him and the gifts he proffered, and took from him life and goods at once; nor was his foe profited by the useless wealth which he had greedily heaped up through long years. But Rolf the righteous assailed him, slew him, and captured his vast wealth, and shared among worthy friends what the hand of avarice had piled up in all those years; and, bursting into the camp which was wealthy but not brave, gave his friends a lordly booty without bloodshed. Nothing was so fair to him that he would not lavish it, or so dear that he would not give it to his friends, for he used treasure like ashes, and measured his years by glory and not by gain. Whence it is plain that the king who hath died nobly lived also most nobly, that the hour of his doom is beautiful, and that he graced the years of his life with manliness. For while he lived his glowing valour prevailed over all things, and he was allotted might worthy of his lofty stature. He was as swift to war as a torrent tearing down to sea, and as speedy to begin battle as a stag is to fly with cleft foot upon his fleet way.

"See now, among the pools dripping with human blood, the teeth struck out of the slain are carried on by the full torrent of gore, and are polished on the rough sands. Dashed on the slime they glitter, and the torrent of blood bears along splintered bones and flows above lopped limbs. The blood of the Danes is wet, and the gory flow stagnates far around, and the stream pressed out of the steaming veins rolls back the scattered bodies. Tirelessly against the Danes advances Hiartuar, lover of battle, and challenges the fighters with outstretched spear. Yet here, amid the dangers and dooms of war, I see Frode's grandson smiling joyously, who once sowed the fields of Fyriswald with gold. Let us also be exalted with an honourable show of joy, following in death the doom of our noble father. Be we therefore cheery in voice and bold in daring; for it is right to spurn all fear with words of courage, and to meet our death in deeds of glory. Let fear quit heart and face; in both let us avow our dauntless endeavours, that no sign anywhere may show us to betray faltering fear. Let our drawn sword measure the weight of our service. Fame follows us in death, and glory shall outlive our crumbling ashes! and that which perfect valour hath achieved during its span shall not fade for ever and ever. What want we with closed doors? Why doth the locked bolt close the folding-gates? For it is now the third cry, Bjarke, that calls thee, and bids thee come forth from the barred room."

Bjarke rejoined: "Warlike Hjalte, why dost thou call me so loud? I am the son-in-law of Rolf. He who boasts loud and with big words challenges other men to battle,

is bound to be venturous and act up to his words, that
his deed may avouch his vaunt. But stay till I am armed
and have girded on the dread attire of war.

"And now I tie my sword to my side, now first I get
my body guarded with mail-coat and headpiece, the helm
keeping my brows and the stout iron shrouding my breast.
None shrinks more than I from being burnt a prisoner
inside, and made a pyre together with my own house:
though an island brought me forth, and though the land
of my birth be bounded, I shall hold it a debt to repay
to the king the twelve kindreds which he added to my
honours. Hearken, warriors! Let none robe in mail his
body that shall perish; let him last of all draw tight the
woven steel; let the shields go behind the back; let us
fight with bared breasts, and load all your arms with gold.
Let your right hands receive the bracelets, that they may
swing their blows the more heavily and plant the grievous
wound. Let none fall back! Let each zealously strive
to meet the swords of the enemy and the threatening
spears, that we may avenge our beloved master. Happy
beyond all things is he who can mete out revenge for
such a crime, and with righteous steel punish the guilt
of treacheries.

"Lo, methinks I surely pierced a wild stag with the
Teutonic sword which is called Snyrtir: from which I
won the name of Warrior, when I felled Agnar, son of
Ingild, and brought the trophy home. He shattered and
broke with the bite the sword Hoding which smote upon
my head, and would have dealt worse wounds if the edge
of his blade had held out better. In return I clove

asunder his left arm and part of his left side and his right foot, and the piercing steel ran down his limbs and smote deep into his ribs. By Hercules! no man ever seemed to me stronger than he. For he sank down half-conscious, and, leaning on his elbow, welcomed death with a smile, and spurned destruction with a laugh, and passed rejoicing in the world of Elysium. Mighty was the man's courage, which knew how with one laugh to cover his death-hour, and with a joyous face to suppress utter anguish of mind and body!

"Now also with the same blade I searched the heart of one sprung from an illustrious line, and plunged the steel deep in his breast. He was a king's son, of illustrious ancestry, of a noble nature, and shone with the brightness of youth. The mailed metal could not avail him, nor his sword, nor the smooth target-boss; so keen was the force of my steel, it knew not how to be stayed by obstacles.

"Where, then, are the captains of the Goths, and the soldiery of Hiartuar? Let them come, and pay for their might with their life-blood. Who can cast, who whirl the lance, save scions of kings? War springs from the nobly born: famous pedigrees are the makers of war. For the perilous deeds which chiefs attempt are not to be done by the ventures of common men. Renowned nobles are passing away. Lo! greatest Rolf, thy great ones have fallen, thy holy line is vanishing. No dim and lowly race, no low-born dead, no base souls are Pluto's prey, but he weaves the dooms of the mighty, and fills Phlegethon with noble shapes.

"I do not remember any combat wherein swords were crossed in turn and blow dealt out for blow more speedily. I take three for each I give; thus do the Goths requite the wounds I deal them, and thus doth the stronger hand of the enemy avenge with heaped interest the punishment that they receive. Yet singly in battle I have given over the bodies of so many men to the pyre of destruction, that a mound like a hill could grow up and be raised out of their lopped limbs, and the piles of carcases would look like a burial-barrow. And now what doeth he, who but now bade me come forth, vaunting himself with mighty praise, and chafing others with his arrogant words, and scattering harsh taunts, as though in his one body he enclosed twelve lives?"

Hjalte answered: "Though I have but scant help, I am not far off. Even here, where I stand, there is need of aid, and nowhere is a force or a chosen band of warriors ready for battle wanted more. Already the hard edges and the spear-points have cleft my shield in splinters, and the ravening steel has rent and devoured its portions bit by bit in the battle. The first of these things testifies to and avows itself. Seeing is better than telling, eyesight faithfuller than hearing. For of the broken shield only the fastenings remain, and the boss, pierced and broken in its circle, is all left me. And now, Bjarke, thou art strong, though thou hast come forth more tardily than was right, and thou retrievest by bravery the loss caused by thy loitering."

But Bjarke said: "Art thou not yet weary of girding at me and goading me with taunts? Many things often

cause delay. The reason why I tarried was the sword in my path, which the Swedish foe whirled against my breast with mighty effort. Nor did the guider of the hilt drive home the sword with little might; for though the body was armed he smote it as far as one may when it is bare or defenceless; he pierced the armour of hard steel like yielding waters; nor could the rough, heavy breastplate give me any help.

"But where now is he that is commonly called Odin, the mighty in battle, content ever with a single eye? If thou see him anywhere, Rute, tell me."

Rute replied: "Bring thine eye closer and look under my arm akimbo: thou must first hallow thine eyes with the victorious sign, if thou wilt safely know the War-god face to face."

Then said Bjarke: "If I may look on the awful husband of Frigg, howsoever he be covered with his white shield, and guide his tall steed, he shall in no wise go safe out of Leire; it is lawful to lay low in war the war-waging god. Let a noble death come to those that fall before the eyes of their king. While life lasts, let us strive for the power to die honourably and to reap a noble end by our deeds. I will die overpowered near the head of my slain captain, and at his feet thou also shalt slip on thy face in death, so that whoso scans the piled corpses may see in what wise we rate the gold our lord gave us. We shall be the prey of ravens and a morsel for hungry eagles, and the ravening bird shall feast on the banquet of our body. Thus should fall princes dauntless in war, clasping their famous king in a common death."

173

I have composed this particular series of harangues in metrical shape, because the gist of the same thoughts is found arranged in a short form in a certain ancient Danish song, which is repeated by heart by many conversant with antiquity.

Now, it came to pass that the Goths gained the victory and all the array of Rolf fell, no man save Wigg remaining out of all those warriors. For the soldiers of the king paid this homage to his noble virtues in that battle, that his slaying inspired in all the longing to meet their end, and union with him in death was accounted sweeter than life.

HIARTUAR rejoiced, and had the tables spread for feasting, bidding the banquet come after the battle, and fain to honour his triumph with a carouse. And when he was well filled therewith, he said that it was a matter of great marvel to him, that out of all the army of Rolf no man had been found to take thought for his life by flight or fraud. Hence, he said, it had been manifest with what zealous loyalty they had kept their love for their king, because they had not endured to survive him. He also blamed his ill fortune, because it had not suffered the homage of a single one of them to be left for himself: protesting that he would very willingly accept the service of such men. Then Wigg came forth, and Hiartuar, as though he were congratulating him on the gift, asked him if he were willing to fight for him. Wigg assenting, he drew and proferred him a sword. But Wigg refused the point, and asked for the hilt, saying first that this had been Rolf's custom when he handed forth a sword to

his soldiers. For in old time those who were about to put themselves in dependence on the king used to promise fealty by touching the hilt of the sword. And in this wise Wigg clasped the hilt, and then drove the point through Hiartuar; thus gaining the vengeance which he had promised Rolf to accomplish for him. When he had done this, and the soldiers of Hiartuar rushed at him, he exposed his body to them eagerly and exultantly, shouting that he felt more joy in the slaughter of the tyrant than bitterness at his own. Thus the feast was turned into a funeral, and the wailing of burial followed the joy of victory. Glorious, ever memorable hero, who valiantly kept his vow, and voluntarily courted death, staining with blood by his service the tables of the despot! For the lively valour of his spirit feared not the hands of the slaughterers, when he had once beheld the place where Rolf had been wont to live bespattered with the blood of his slayer. Thus the royalty of Hiartuar was won and ended on the same day. For whatsoever is gotten with guile melts away in like fashion as it is sought, and no fruits are long-lasting that have been won by treachery and crime. Hence it came to pass that the Swedes, who had a little before been the possessors of Denmark, came to lose even their own liberty. For they were straightway cut off by the Zealanders, and paid righteous atonement to the injured shades of Rolf. In this way does stern fortune commonly avenge the works of craft and cunning.

# BOOK THREE.

AFTER Hiartuar, HOTHER, whom I mentioned above, the brother of Athisl, and also the fosterling of King Gewar, became sovereign of both realms. It will be easier to relate his times if I begin with the beginning of his life. For if the earlier years of his career are not doomed to silence, the latter ones can be more fully and fairly narrated.

When Helgi had slain Hodbrodd, his son Hother passed the length of his boyhood under the tutelage of King Gewar. While a stripling, he excelled in strength of body all his foster-brethren and compeers. Moreover, he was gifted with many accomplishments of mind. He was very skilled in swimming and archery, and also with the gloves; and further was as nimble as such a youth could be, his training being equal to his strength. Though his years were unripe, his richly-dowered spirit surpassed them. None was more skilful on lyre or harp; and he was cunning on the timbrel, on the lute, and in every modulation of string instruments. With his changing measures he could sway the feelings of men to what passions he would; he knew how to fill human hearts with joy or sadness, with pity or with hatred, and used to enwrap the soul with the delight or terror of the ear. All these accomplishments of the youth pleased Nanna, the

daughter of Gewar, mightily, and she began to seek his embraces. For the valour of a youth will often kindle a maid, and the courage of those whose looks are not so winning is often acceptable. For love hath many avenues; the path of pleasure is opened to some by grace, to others by bravery of soul, and to some by skill in accomplishments. Courtesy brings to some stores of Love, while most are commended by brightness of beauty. Nor do the brave inflict a shallower wound on maidens than the comely.

Now it befell that Balder the son of Odin was troubled at the sight of Nanna bathing, and was seized with boundless love. He was kindled by her fair and lustrous body, and his heart was set on fire by her manifest beauty; for nothing exciteth passion like comeliness. Therefore he resolved to slay with the sword Hother, who, he feared, was likeliest to baulk his wishes; so that his love, which brooked no postponement, might not be delayed in the enjoyment of its desire by any obstacle.

About this time Hother chanced, while hunting, to be led astray by a mist, and he came on a certain lodge in which were wood-maidens; and when they greeted him by his own name, he asked who they were. They declared that it was their guidance and government that mainly determined the fortunes of war. For they often invisibly took part in battles, and by their secret assistance won for their friends the coveted victories. They averred, indeed, that they could win triumphs and inflict defeats as they would; and further told him how Balder had seen his foster-sister Nanna while she bathed, and

178

BOOK THREE

been kindled with passion for her; but counselled Hother not to attack him in war, worthy as he was of his deadliest hate, for they declared that Balder was a demigod, sprung secretly from celestial seed. When Hother had heard this, the place melted away and left him shelterless, and he found himself standing in the open and out in the midst of the fields, without a vestige of shade. Most of all he marvelled at the swift flight of the maidens, the shifting of the place, and the delusive semblance of the building. For he knew not that all that had passed around him had been a mere mockery and an unreal trick of the arts of magic.

Returning thence, he related to Gewar the mystification that had followed on his straying, and straightway asked him for his daughter. Gewar answered that he would most gladly favour him, but that he feared if he rejected Balder he would incur his wrath; for Balder, he said, had proffered him a like request. For he said that the sacred strength of Balder's body was proof even against steel; adding, however, that he knew of a sword which could deal him his death, which was fastened up in the closest bonds; this was in the keeping of Miming, the Satyr of the woods, who also had a bracelet of a secret and marvellous virtue, that used to increase the wealth of the owner. Moreover, the way to these regions was impassable and filled with obstacles, and therefore hard for mortal men to travel. For the greater part of the road was perpetually beset with extraordinary cold. So he advised him to harness a car with reindeer, by means of whose great speed he could cross the hard-

frozen ridges. And when he had got to the place, he should set up his tent away from the sun in such wise that it should catch the shadow of the cave where Miming was wont to be; while he should not in return cast a shade upon Miming, so that no unaccustomed darkness might be thrown and prevent the Satyr from going out. Thus both the bracelet and the sword would be ready to his hand, one being attended by fortune in wealth and the other by fortune in war, and each of them thus bringing a great prize to the owner. Thus much said Gewar; and Hother was not slow to carry out his instructions. Planting his tent in the manner aforesaid, he passed the nights in anxieties and the days in hunting. But through either season he remained very wakeful and sleepless, allotting the divisions of night and day so as to devote the one to reflection on events, and to spend the other in providing food for his body. Once as he watched all night, his spirit was drooping and dazed with anxiety, when the Satyr cast a shadow on his tent. Aiming a spear at him, he brought him down with the blow, stopped him, and bound him, while he could not make his escape. Then in the most dreadful words he threatened him with the worst, and demanded the sword and bracelets. The Satyr was not slow to tender him the ransom of his life for which he was asked. So surely do all prize life beyond wealth; for nothing is ever cherished more among mortals than the breath of their own life. Hother, exulting in the treasure he had gained, went home enriched with trophies which, though few, were noble.

When Gelder, the King of Saxony, heard that Hother had gained these things, he kept constantly urging his soldiers to go and carry off such glorious booty; and the warriors speedily equipped a fleet in obedience to their king. Gewar, being very learned in divining and an expert in the knowledge of omens, foresaw this; and summoning Hother, told him, when Gelder should join battle with him, to receive his spears with patience, and not let his own fly until he saw the enemy's missiles exhausted; and further, to bring up the curved scythes wherewith the vessels could be rent and the helmets and shields plucked from the soldiers. Hother followed his advice and found its result fortunate. For he bade his men, when Gelder began to charge, to stand their ground and defend their bodies with their shields, affirming that the victory in that battle must be won by patience. But the enemy nowhere kept back their missiles, spending them all in their extreme eagerness to fight; and the more patiently they found Hother bear himself in his reception of their spears and lances, the more furiously they began to hurl them. Some of these stuck in the shields and some in the ships, and few were the wounds they inflicted; many of them were seen to be shaken off idly and to do no hurt. For the soldiers of Hother performed the bidding of their king, and kept off the attack of the spears by a penthouse of interlocked shields; while not a few of the spears smote lightly on the bosses and fell into the waves. When Gelder was emptied of all his store, and saw the enemy picking it up, and swiftly hurling it back at him, he covered the summit

of the mast with a crimson shield, as a signal of peace, and surrendered to save his life. Hother received him with the friendliest face and the kindliest words, and conquered him as much by his gentleness as he had by his skill.

At this time Helgi, King of Halogaland, was sending frequent embassies to press his suit for Thora, daughter of Kuse, sovereign of the Finns and Perms. Thus is weakness ever known by its wanting help from others. For while all other young men of that time used to sue in marriage with their own lips, this man was afflicted with so faulty an utterance that he was ashamed to be heard not only by strangers, but by those of his own house. So much doth calamity shun all witnesses; for natural defects are the more vexing the more manifest they are. Kuse despised his embassy, answering that that man did not deserve a wife who trusted too little to his own manhood, and borrowed by entreaty the aid of others in order to gain his suit. When Helgi heard this, be besought Hother, whom he knew to be an accomplished pleader, to favour his desires, promising that he would promptly perform whatsoever he should command him. The earnest entreaties of the youth prevailed on Hother, and he went to Norway with an armed fleet, intending to achieve by arms the end which he could not by words. And when he had pleaded for Helgi with the most dulcet eloquence, Kuse rejoined that his daughter's wish must be consulted, in order that no paternal strictness might forestall anything against her will. He called her in and asked her whether she felt a

liking for her wooer; and when she assented he promised
Helgi her hand. In this way Hother, by the sweet
sounds of his fluent and well-turned oratory, opened the
ears of Kuse, which were before deaf to the suit he urged.

While this was passing in Halogaland, Balder entered
the country of Gewar armed, in order to sue for Nanna.
Gewar bade him learn Nanna's own mind; so he
approached the maiden with the most choice and cajoling
words; and when he could win no hearing for his prayers,
he persisted in asking the reason of his refusal. She
replied, that a god could not wed with a mortal, because
the vast difference of their natures prevented any bond of
intercourse. Also the gods sometimes used to break
their pledges; and the bond contracted between unequals
was apt to snap suddenly. There was no firm tie between
those of differing estate; for beside the great, the fortunes
of the lowly were always dimmed. Also lack and plenty
dwelt in diverse tents, nor was there any fast bond of
intercourse between gorgeous wealth and obscure poverty.
In fine, the things of earth would not mate with those of
heaven, being sundered by a great original gulf through
a difference in nature; inasmuch as mortal man was
infinitely far from the glory of the divine majesty. With
this shuffling answer she eluded the suit of Balder, and
shrewdly wove excuses to refuse his hand.

When Hother heard this from Gewar, he complained
long to Helgi of Balder's insolence. Both were in doubt
as to what should be done, and beat their brains over
divers plans; for converse with a friend in the day of
trouble, though it removeth not the peril, yet maketh the

heart less sick. Amid all the desires of their souls the passion of valour prevailed, and a naval battle was fought with Balder. One would have thought it a contest of men against gods, for Odin and Thor and the holy array of the gods fought for Balder. There one could have beheld a war in which divine and human might were mingled. But Hother was clad in his steel-defying tunic, and charged the closest bands of the gods, assailing them as vehemently as a son of earth could assail the powers above. However, Thor was swinging his club with marvellous might, and shattered all interposing shields, calling as loudly on his foes to attack him as upon his friends to back him up. No kind of armour withstood his onset, no man could receive his stroke and live. Whatsoever his blow fended off it crushed; neither shield nor helm endured the weight of its dint; no greatness of body or of strength could serve. Thus the victory would have passed to the gods, but that Hother, though his line had already fallen back, darted up, hewed off the club at the haft, and made it useless. And the gods, when they had lost this weapon, fled incontinently. But that antiquity vouches for it, it were quite against common belief to think that men prevailed against gods. (We call them gods in a supposititious rather than in a real sense; for to such we give the title of deity by the custom of nations, not because of their nature.)

As for Balder, he took to flight and was saved. The conquerors either hacked his ships with their swords or sunk them in the sea; not content to have defeated gods, they pursued the wrecks of the fleet with such rage, as

... ... ... Amid all the desires of their souls the ... of valour prevailed, and a naval battle was ... ... ... One would have thought it a ... ... against gods, for Odin and Thor and the holy ... of the gods fought for Balder. There one could ... ... a war in which divine and human might ... ... But Hother was clad in his steel-defying ... and charged the closest bands of the gods, assailing ... as vehemently as a son of earth could assail the ... ... However, Thor was swinging his club ... marvellous might, and shattered all interposing ... calling as loudly on his foes to attack him as upon ...

*[illegible lines]*

... He ... had already fallen back, darted up, hewed off ... club at the haft, and made it useless. And the ... when they had lost this weapon, fled incontinently ... that ... ... ... searches for it, it were quite against ... ... ... ... to think that men prevailed against ... ... all their gods in a supposititious rather than in a ... ... for to such we give the title of deity by ... ... not because of their nature.)

... But Hother, he took to flight and was saved. The ... either hacked his ships with their swords ... ... in the sea, not content to have defeated ... ... the ... of the fleet with such rage, ...

184

if they would destroy them to satiate their deadly passion
for war. Thus doth prosperity commonly whet the edge
of licence. The haven, recalling by its name Balder's
flight, bears witness to the war. Gelder, the King of
Saxony, who met his end in the same war, was set by
Hother upon the corpses of his oarsmen, and then laid
on a pyre built of vessels, and magnificently honoured in
his funeral by Hother, who not only put his ashes in a
noble barrow, treating them as the remains of a king,
but also graced them with most reverent obsequies.
Then, to prevent any more troublesome business delay-
ing his hopes of marriage, he went back to Gewar and
enjoyed the coveted embraces of Nanna. Next, having
treated Helgi and Thora very generously, he brought
his new queen back to Sweden, being as much honoured
by all for his victory as Balder was laughed at for his
flight.

At this time the nobles of the Swedes repaired to
Denmark to pay their tribute; but Hother, who had been
honoured as a king by his countrymen for the splendid
deeds of his father, experienced what a lying pander
Fortune is. For he was conquered in the field by Balder,
whom a little before he had crushed, and was forced to
flee to Gewar, thus losing while a king that victory
which he had won as a common man. The conquering
Balder, in order to slake his soldiers, who were parched
with thirst, with the blessing of a timely draught, pierced
the earth deep and disclosed a fresh spring. The thirsty
ranks made with gaping lips for the water that gushed
forth everywhere. The traces of these springs,

eternised by the name, are thought not quite to have dried up yet, though they have ceased to well so freely as of old. Balder was continually harassed by night phantoms feigning the likeness of Nanna, and fell into such ill health that he could not so much as walk, and began the habit of going his journeys in a two-horse car or a four-wheeled carriage. So great was the love that had steeped his heart and now had brought him down almost to the extremity of decline. For he thought that his victory had brought him nothing if Nanna was not his prize. Also Frey, the regent of the gods, took his abode not far from Upsala, where he exchanged for a ghastly and infamous sin-offering the old custom of prayer by sacrifice, which had been used by so many ages and generations. For he paid to the gods abominable offerings, by beginning to slaughter human victims.

Meantime Hother* learned that Denmark lacked leaders, and that Hiartuar had swiftly expiated the death of Rolf; and he used to say that chance had thrown into his hands that to which he could scarce have aspired. For first, Rolf, whom he ought to have killed, since he remembered that Rolf's father had slain his own, had been punished by the help of another; and also, by the unexpected bounty of events, a chance had been opened to him of winning Denmark. In truth, if the pedigree of his forefathers were rightly traced, that realm was his by ancestral right! Thereupon he took possession, with a very great fleet, of Isefjord, a haven of Zealand, so

---

*Meantime Hother] Saxo now goes back to the history of Denmark. All the events hitherto related in Bk. III, after the first paragraph, are a digression in retrospect.

as to make use of his impending fortune. There the
people of the Danes met him and appointed him king;
and a little after, on hearing of the death of his brother
Athisl, whom he had bidden rule the Swedes, he joined
the Swedish empire to that of Denmark. But Athisl
was cut off by an ignominious death. For whilst, in
great jubilation of spirit, he was honouring the funeral
rites of Rolf with a feast, he drank too greedily, and
paid for his filthy intemperance by his sudden end.
And so, while he was celebrating the death of another
with immoderate joviality, he forced on his own
apace.

While Hother was in Sweden, Balder also came to
Zealand with a fleet; and since he was thought to be rich
in arms and of singular majesty, the Danes accorded
him with the readiest of voices whatever he asked
concerning the supreme power. With such wavering
judgment was the opinion of our forefathers divided.
Hother returned from Sweden and attacked him. They
both coveted sway, and the keenest contest for the
sovereignty began between them; but it was cut short by
the flight of Hother. He retired to Jutland, and caused
to be named after him the village in which he was wont
to stay. Here he passed the winter season, and then
went back to Sweden alone and unattended. There he
summoned the grandees, and told them that he was
weary of the light of life because of the misfortunes
wherewith Balder had twice victoriously stricken him.
Then he took farewell of all, and went by a circuitous
path to a place that was hard of access, traversing forests

uncivilised. For it oft happens that those upon whom
has come some inconsolable trouble of spirit seek, as
though it were a medicine to drive away their sadness,
far and sequestered retreats, and cannot bear the greatness of their grief amid the fellowship of men; so dear,
for the most part, is solitude to sickness. For filthiness
and grime are chiefly pleasing to those who have been
stricken with ailments of the soul. Now he had been
wont to give out from the top of a hill decrees to the
people when they came to consult him; and hence when
they came they upbraided the sloth of the king for hiding
himself, and his absence was railed at by all with the
bitterest complaints.

But Hother, when he had wandered through remotest
byways and crossed an uninhabited forest, chanced to
come upon a cave where dwelt some maidens whom he
knew not; but they proved to be the same who had once
given him the invulnerable coat. Asked by them wherefore he had come thither, he related the disastrous issue
of the war. So he began to bewail the ill luck of his
failures and his dismal misfortunes, condemning their
breach of faith, and lamenting that it had not turned out
for him as they had promised him. But the maidens
said, that though he had seldom come off victorious, he
had nevertheless inflicted as much defeat on the enemy
as they on him, and had dealt as much carnage as he had
shared in. Moreover, the favour of victory would be
speedily his, if he could first lay hands upon a food of
extraordinary delightsomeness which had been devised
to increase the strength of Balder. For nothing would

be difficult if he could only get hold of the dainty which was meant to enhance the vigour of his foe.

Hard as it sounded for earthborn endeavours to make armed assault upon the gods, the words of the maidens inspired Hother's mind with instant confidence to fight with Balder. Also some of his own people said that he could not safely contend with those above; but all regard for their majesty was expelled by the boundless fire of his spirit. For in brave souls vehemence is not always sapped by reason, nor doth counsel defeat rashness. Or perchance it was that Hother remembered how the might of the lordliest oft proveth unstable, and how a little clod can batter down great chariots.

On the other side, Balder mustered the Danes to arms and met Hother in the field. Both sides made a great slaughter; the carnage of the opposing parties was nearly equal, and night stayed the battle. About the third watch, Hother, unknown to any man, went out to spy upon the enemy, anxiety about the impending peril having banished sleep. This strong excitement favours not bodily rest, and inward disquiet suffers not outward repose. So, when he came to the camp of the enemy he heard that three maidens had gone out carrying the secret feast of Balder. He ran after them (for their footsteps in the dew betrayed their flight), and at last entered their accustomed dwelling. When they asked him who he was, he answered, a lutanist, nor did the trial belie his profession. For when the lyre was offered him, he tuned its strings, ordered and governed the chords with his quill, and with ready modulation poured forth a

melody pleasant to the ear. Now they had three snakes, of whose venom they were wont to mix a strengthening compound for the food of Balder, and even now a flood of slaver was dripping on the food from the open mouths of the serpents. And some of the maidens would, for kindness sake, have given Hother a share of the dish, had not eldest of the three forbidden them, declaring that Balder would be cheated if they increased the bodily powers of his enemy. He had said, not that he was Hother, but that he was one of his company. Now the same nymphs, in their gracious kindliness, bestowed on him a belt of perfect sheen and a girdle which assured victory.

Retracing the path by which he had come, he went back on the same road, and meeting Balder plunged his sword into his side, and laid him low half dead. When the news was told to the soldiers, a cheery shout of triumph rose from all the camp of Hother, while the Danes held a public mourning for the fate of Balder. He, feeling no doubt of his impending death, and stung by the anguish of his wound, renewed the battle on the morrow; and, when it raged hotly, bade that he should be borne on a litter into the fray, that he might not seem to die ignobly within his tent. On the night following, Proserpine was seen to stand by him in a vision, and to promise that on the morrow he should have her embrace. The boding of the dream was not idle; for when three days had passed, Balder perished from the excessive torture of his wound; and his body given a royal funeral, the army causing it to be buried in a barrow which they had made,

## BOOK THREE

Certain men of our day, chief among whom was Harald,* since the story of the ancient burial-place still survived, made a raid on it by night in the hope of finding money, but abandoned their attempt in sudden panic. For the hill split, and from its crest a sudden and mighty torrent of loud-roaring waters seemed to burst; so that its flying mass, shooting furiously down, poured over the fields below, and enveloped whatsoever it struck upon. And at its onset the delvers were dislodged, flung down their mattocks, and fled divers ways; thinking that if they strove any longer to carry through their enterprise they would be caught in the eddies of the water that was rushing down. Thus the guardian gods of that spot smote fear suddenly into the minds of the youths, taking them away from covetousness, and turning them to see to their safety; teaching them to neglect their greedy purpose and be careful of their lives. Now it is certain that this apparent flood was not real but phantasmal; not born in the bowels of the earth (since Nature suffereth not liquid springs to gush forth in a dry place), but produced by some magic agency. All men afterwards, to whom the story of that breaking in had come down, left this hill undisturbed. Wherefore it has never been made sure whether it really contains any wealth; for the dread of peril has daunted anyone since Harald from probing its dark foundations.

But Odin, though he was accounted the chief of the gods, began to inquire of the prophets and diviners

---

*Harald] M. conjectures that this was a certain Harald, the bastard son of Erik the Good, and a wild and dissolute man, who died in 1135, not long before the probable date of Saxo's birth,

concerning the way to acomplish vengeance for his son, as
well as all others whom he had heard were skilled in the
most recondite arts of soothsaying. For godhead that
is incomplete is oft in want of the help of man. Rostioph
(Hrossthiof), the Finn, foretold to him that another son
must be born to him by Rinda (Wrinda), daughter of
the King of the Ruthenians; this son was destined to
exact punishment for the slaying of his brother. For
the gods had appointed to the brother that was yet to be
born the task of avenging his kinsman. Odin, when he
heard this, muffled his face with a cap, that his garb
might not betray him, and entered the service of the said
king as a soldier; and being made by him captain of the
soldiers, and given an army, won a splendid victory
over the enemy. And for his stout achievement in this
battle the king admitted him into the chief place in his
friendship, distinguishing him as generously with gifts
as with honours. A very little while afterwards Odin
routed the enemy single-handed, and returned, at once the
messenger and the doer of the deed. All marvelled that
the strength of one man could deal such slaughter upon a
countless host. Trusting in these services, he privily let
the king into the secret of his love, and was refreshed by
his most gracious favour; but when he sought a kiss from
the maiden, he received a cuff. But he was not driven
from his purpose either by anger at the slight or by the
odiousness of the insult.

Next year, loth to quit ignobly the quest he had taken
up so eagerly, he put on the dress of a foreigner and went
back to dwell with the king. It was hard for those who

met him to recognise him; for his assumed filth obliterated
his true features, and new grime hid his ancient aspect.
He said that his name was Roster (Hrosstheow), and
that he was skilled in smithcraft. And his handiwork did
honour to his professions: for he portrayed in bronze
many and many a shape most beautifully, so that he
received a great mass of gold from the king, and was
ordered to hammer out the ornaments of the matrons.
So, after having wrought many adornments for women's
wearing, he at last offered to the maiden a bracelet which
he had polished more laboriously than the rest and several
rings which were adorned with equal care. But no
services could assuage the wrath of Rinda; when he was
fain to kiss her she cuffed him; for gifts offered by one
we hate are unacceptable, while those tendered by a
friend are far more grateful: so much doth the value of
the offering oft turn on the offerer. For this stubborn-
hearted maiden never doubted that the crafty old man was
feigning generosity in order to seize an opening to work
his lust. His temper, moreover, was keen and indomi-
table; for she knew that his homage covered guile, and
that under the devotion of his gifts there lay a desire
for crime. Her father fell to upbraiding her heavily for
refusing the match; but she loathed to wed an old man,
and the plea of her tender years lent her some support
in her scorning of his hand; for she said that a young
girl ought not to marry prematurely.

But Odin, who had found that nothing served the
wishes of lovers more than tough persistency, though he
was stung with the shame of his double rebuff, neverthe-

less, effacing the form he had worn before, went to the king for the third time, professing the completest skill in soldiership. He was led to take this pains not only by pleasure but by the wish to wipe out his disgrace. For of old those who were skilled in magic gained this power of instantly changing their aspect and exhibiting the most different shapes. Indeed, they were clever at imitating any age, not only in its natural bodily appearance, but also in its stature; and so the old man, in order to exhibit his calling agreeably, used to ride proudly up and down among the briskest of them. But not even such a tribute could move the rigour of the maiden; for it is hard for the mind to come back to a genuine liking for one against whom it has once borne heavy dislike. When he tried to kiss her at his departure, she repulsed him so that he tottered and smote his chin upon the ground. Straightway he touched her with a piece of bark whereon spells were written, and made her like unto one in frenzy: which was a gentle revenge to take for all the insults he had received.

But still he did not falter in the fulfilment of his purpose; for trust in his divine majesty buoyed him up with confidence; so, assuming the garb of a maiden, this indefatigable journeyer repaired for the fourth time to the king, and, on being received by him, showed himself assiduous and even forward. Most people believed him to be a woman, as he was dressed almost in female attire. Also he declared that his name was Wecha, and his calling that of a physician: and this assertion he confirmed by the readiest services. At last he was taken

into the household of the queen, and played the part of
a waiting-woman to the princess, and even used to wash
the soil off her feet at eventide; and as he was applying
the water he was suffered to touch her calves and the upper
part of the thighs. But fortune goes with mutable steps,
and thus chance put into his hand what his address had
never won. For it happened that the girl fell sick, and looked
around for a cure; and she summoned to protect her
health those very hands which aforetime she had rejected,
and appealed for preservation to him whom she had
ever held in loathing. He examined narrowly all the
symptoms of the trouble, and declared that, in order to
check the disease as soon as possible, it was needful to
use a certain drugged draught; but that it was so bitterly
compounded, that the girl could never endure so violent
a cure unless she submitted to be bound; since the stuff
of the malady must be ejected from the very innermost
tissues. When her father heard this he did not hesitate
to bind his daughter; and laying her on the bed, he bade
her endure patiently all the applications of the doctor.
For the king was tricked by the sight of the female dress,
which the old man was using to disguise his persistent
guile; and thus the seeming remedy became an opportunity of outrage. For the physician seized the chance
of love, and, abandoning his business of healing, sped
to the work, not of expelling the fever, but of working
his lust; making use of the sickness of the princess, whom
in sound health he had found adverse to him. It will
not be wearisome if I subjoin another version of this
affair. For there are certain who say that the king,

when he saw the physician groaning with love, but despite all his expense of mind and body accomplishing nothing, did not wish to rob of his due reward one who had so well earned it, and allowed him to lie privily with his daughter. So doth the wickedness of the father sometimes assail the child, when vehement passion perverts natural mildness. But his fault was soon followed by a remorse that was full of shame, when his daughter bore a child.

But the gods, whose chief seat was then at Byzantium, (Asgard), seeing that Odin had tarnished the fair name of godhead by divers injuries to its majesty, thought that he ought to be removed from their society. And they had him not only ousted from the headship, but outlawed and stripped of all worship and honour at home; thinking it better that the power of their infamous president should be overthrown than that public religion should be profaned; and fearing that they might themselves be involved in the sin of another, and though guiltless be punished for the crime of the guilty. For they saw that, now the derision of their great god was brought to light, those whom they had lured to proffer them divine honours were exchanging obeisance for scorn and worship for shame; that holy rites were being accounted sacrilege, and fixed and regular ceremonies deemed so much childish raving. Fear was in their souls, death before their eyes, and one would have supposed that the fault of one was visited upon the heads of all. So, not wishing Odin to drive public religion into exile, they exiled him and put one Oller (Wulder?) in his place,

to bear the symbols not only of royalty but also of godhead, as though it had been as easy a task to create a god as a king. And though they had appointed him priest for form's sake, they endowed him actually with full distinction, that he might be seen to be the lawful heir to the dignity, and no mere deputy doing another's work. Also, to omit no circumstance of greatness, they further gave his the name of Odin, trying by the prestige of that title to be rid of the obloquy of innovation. For nearly ten years Oller held the presidency of the divine senate; but at last the gods pitied the horrible exile of Odin, and thought that he had now been punished heavily enough; so˙ he exchanged his foul and unsightly estate for his ancient splendour; for the lapse of time had now wiped out the brand of his earlier disgrace. Yet some were to be found who judged that he was not worthy to approach and resume his rank, because by his stage-tricks and his assumption of a woman's work he had brought the foulest scandal on the name of the gods. Some declare that he bought back the fortune of his lost divinity with money; flattering some of the gods and mollifying some with bribes; and that at the cost of a vast sum he contrived to get back to the distinction which he had long quitted. If you ask how much he paid for them, inquire of those who have found out what is the price of a godhead. I own that to me it is but little worth.

Thus Oller was driven out from Byzantium by Odin and retired into Sweden. Here, while he was trying, as if in a new world, to repair the records of his glory,

the Danes slew him. The story goes that he was such a cunning wizard that he used a certain bone, which he had marked with awful spells, wherewith to cross the seas, instead of a vessel; and that by this bone he passed over the waters that barred his way as quickly as by rowing.

But Odin, now that he had regained the emblems of godhead, shone over all parts of the world with such a lustre of renown that all nations welcomed him as though he were light restored to the universe; nor was any spot to be found on the earth which did not homage to his might. Then finding that Boe, his son by Rinda, was enamoured of the hardships of war, he called him, and bade him bear in mind the slaying of his brother: saying that it would be better for him to take vengeance on the murderers of Balder than to overcome the innocent in battle; for warfare was most fitting and wholesome when a holy occasion for waging it was furnished by a righteous opening for vengeance.

News came meantime that Gewar had been slain by the guile of his own satrap (jarl), Gunne. Hother determined to visit his murder with the strongest and sharpest revenge. So he surprised Gunne, cast him on a blazing pyre, and burnt him; for Gunne had himself treacherously waylaid Gewar, and burnt him alive in the night. This was his offering of vengeance to the shade of his foster-father; and then he made his sons, Herlek and Gerit, rulers of Norway.

Then he summoned the elders to assembly, and told them that he would perish in the war wherein he was

bound to meet Boe, and said that he knew this by no doubtful guesswork, but by sure prophecies of seers. So he besought them to make his son RORIK king, so that the judgment of wicked men should not transfer the royalty to strange and unknown houses; averring that he would reap more joy from the succession of his son than bitterness from his own impending death. This request was speedily granted. Then he met Boe in battle and was killed; but small joy the victory gave Boe. Indeed, he left the battle so sore stricken that he was lifted on his shield and carried home by his foot-soldiers supporting him in turn, to perish next day of the pain of his wounds. The Ruthenian army gave his body a gorgeous funeral and buried it in a splendid howe, which it piled in his name, to save the record of so mighty a warrior from slipping out of the recollection of after ages.

So the Kurlanders and the Swedes, as though the death of Hother set them free from the burden of their subjection, resolved to attack Denmark, to which they were accustomed to do homage with a yearly tax. By this the Slavs also were emboldened to revolt, and a number of others were turned from subjects into foes. Rorik, in order to check this wrongdoing, summoned his country to arms, recounted the deeds of his forefathers, and urged them in a passionate harangue unto valorous deeds. But the barbarians, loth to engage without a general, and seeing that they needed a head, appointed a king over them; and, displaying all the rest of their military force, hid two companies of armed men in a dark spot. But Rorik saw the trap; and perceiving that his fleet was

wedged in a certain narrow creek among the shoal water, took it out from the sands where it was lying, and brought it forth to sea; lest it should strike on the oozy swamps, and be attacked by the foe on different sides. Also, he resolved that his men should go into hiding during the day, where they could stay and suddenly fall on the invaders of his ships. He said that perchance the guile might in the end recoil on the heads of its devisers. And in fact the barbarians who had been appointed to the ambuscade knew nothing of the wariness of the Danes, and sallying against them rashly, were all destroyed. The remaining force of the Slavs, knowing nothing of the slaughter of their friends, hung in doubt wondering over the reason of Rorik's tarrying. And after waiting long for him as the months wearily rolled by, and finding delay every day more burdensome, they at last thought they should attack him with their fleet.

Now among them there was a man of remarkable stature, a wizard by calling. He, when he beheld the squadrons of the Danes, said: "Suffer a private combat to forestall a public slaughter, so that the danger of many may be bought off at the cost of a few. And if any of you shall take heart to fight it out with me, I'will not flinch from these terms of conflict. But first of all I demand that you accept the terms I prescribe, the form whereof I have devised as follows: If I conquer, let freedom be granted us from taxes; if I am conquered, let the tribute be paid you as of old: For to-day I will either free my country from the yoke of slavery by my victory or bind her under it by my defeat. Accept me as the

surety and the pledge for either issue." One of the Danes, whose spirit was stouter than his strength, heard this, and proceeded to ask Rorik, what would be the reward for the man who met the challenger in combat? Rorik chanced to have six bracelets, which were so intertwined that they could not be parted from one another, the chain of knots being inextricably laced; and he promised them as a reward for the man who would venture on the combat. But the youth, who doubted his fortune, said: "Rorik, if I prove successful, let thy generosity award the prize of the conqueror, do thou decide and allot the palm; but if my enterprise go little to my liking, what prize canst thou owe to the beaten, who will be wrapped either in cruel death or in bitter shame? These things commonly go with feebleness, these are the wages of the defeated, for whom naught remains but utter infamy. What guerdon must be paid, what thanks offered, to him who lacks the prize of courage? Who has ever garlanded with ivy the weakling in War, or decked him with a conqueror's wage? Valour wins the prize, not sloth, and failure lacks renown. For one is followed by triumph and honour, the other by an unsightly life or by a stagnant end. I, who know not which way the issue of this duel inclines, dare not boldly anticipate that as a reward, of which I know not whether it be rightly mine. For one whose victory is doubtful may not seize the assured reward of the victor. I forbear, while I am not sure of the day, to claim firmly the title to the wreath. I refuse the gain, which may be the wages of my death as much as of my life. It is folly to lay hands on the fruit

before it is ripe, and to be fain to pluck that which one is not yet sure is one's due. This hand shall win me the prize, or death." Having thus spoken, he smote the barbarian with his sword; but his fortune was tardier than his spirit; for the other smote him back, and he fell dead under the force of the first blow. Thus he was a sorry sight unto the Danes, but the Slavs granted their triumphant comrade a great procession, and received him with splendid dances. On the morrow the same man, whether he was elated with the good fortune of his late victory, or was fired with the wish to win another, came close to the enemy, and set to girding at them in the words of his former challenge. For, supposing that he had laid low the bravest of the Danes, he did not think that any of them would have any heart left to fight further with him upon his challenge. Also, trusting that, now one champion had fallen, he had shattered the strength of the whole army, he thought that naught would be hard to achieve upon which his later endeavours were bent. For nothing pampers arrogance more than success, or prompts to pride more surely than prosperity.

So Rorik was vexed that the general courage should be sapped by the impudence of one man; and that the Danes, with their roll of victories, should be met presumptuously by those whom they had beaten of old; nay, should be ignominiously spurned; further, that in all that host not one man should be found so quick of spirit or so vigorous of arm, that he longed to sacrifice his life for his country. It was the high-hearted Ubbe who first wiped off this infamous reproach upon the hesitating Danes. For he

was of great bodily strength and powerful in incantations. He also purposely asked the prize of the combat, and the king promised him the bracelets. Then said he: "How can I trust the promise when thou keepest the pledge in thine own hands, and dost not deposit the gift in the charge of another? Let there be some one to whom thou canst entrust the pledge, that thou mayst not be able to take thy promise back. For the courage of the champion is kindled by the irrevocable certainty of the prize." Of course it was plain that he had said this in jest; sheer courage had armed him to repel the insult to his country. But Rorik thought he was tempted by avarice, and was loth to seem as if, contrary to royal fashion, he meant to take back the gift or revoke his promise; so, being stationed on his vessel, he resolved to shake off the bracelets, and with a mighty swing send them to the asker. But his attempt was baulked by the width of the gap between them; for the bracelets fell short of the intended spot, the impulse being too faint and slack, and were reft away by the waters. For this nickname of Slyngebond, (swing-bracelet) clung to Rorik. But this event testified much to the valour of Ubbe. For the loss of his drowned prize never turned his mind from his bold venture; he would not seem to let his courage be tempted by the wages of covetousness. So he eagerly went to fight, showing that he was a seeker of honour and not the slave of lucre, and that he set bravery before lust of pelf; and intent to prove that his confidence was based not on hire, but on his own great soul. Not a moment is lost; a ring is made; the course is thronged

with soldiers; the champions engage; a din arises; the crowd of onlookers shouts in discord, each backing his own.  And so the valour of the champions blazes to white-heat; falling dead under the wounds dealt by one another, they end together the combat and their lives.  I think that it was a provision of fortune that neither of them should reap joy and honour by the other's death. This event won back to Rorik the hearts of the insurgents and regained him the tribute.

At this time Horwendil and Feng, whose father Ger-wendil had been governor of the Jutes, were appointed in his place by Rorik to defend Jutland.  But Horwendil held the monarchy for three years, and then, to win the height of glory, devoted himself to roving.  Then Koller, King of Norway, in rivalry of his great deeds and renown, deemed it would be a handsome deed if by his greater strength in arms he could bedim the far-famed glory of the rover; and cruising about the sea, he watched for Horwendil's fleet and came up with it.  There was an island lying in the middle of the sea, which each of the rovers, bringing his ships up on either side, was holding.  The captains were tempted by the pleasant look of the beach, and the comeliness of the shores led them to look through the interior of the springtide woods, to go through the glades, and roam over the sequestered forests.  It was here that the advance of Koller and Horwendil brought them face to face without any witness.  Then Horwendil endeavoured to address the king first, asking him in what way it was his pleasure to fight, and declaring that one best which needed the

courage of as few as possible. For, said he, the duel was the surest of all modes of combat for winning the meed of bravery, because it relied only upon native courage, and excluded all help from the hand of another. Koller marvelled at so brave a judgment in a youth, and said: "Since thou hast granted me the choice of battle, I think it is best to employ that kind which needs only the endeavours of two, and is free from all the tumult. Certainly it is more venturesome, and allows of a speedier award of the victory. This thought we share, in this opinion we agree of our own accord. But since the issue remains doubtful, we must pay some regard to gentle dealing, and must not give way so far to our inclinations as to leave the last offices undone. Hatred is in our hearts; yet let piety be there also, which in its due time may take the place of rigour. For the rights of nature reconcile us, though we are parted by differences of purpose; they link us together, howsoever rancour estrange our spirit. Let us, therefore, have this pious stipulation, that the conqueror shall give funeral rites to the conquered. For all allow that these are the last duties of human kind, from which no righteous man shrinks. Let each army lay aside its sternness and perform this function in harmony. Let jealousy depart at death, let the feud be buried in the tomb. Let us not show such an example of cruelty as to persecute one another's dust, though hatred has come between us in our lives. It will be a boast for the victor if he has borne his beaten foe in a lordly funeral. For the man who pays the rightful dues over his dead enemy wins the

goodwill of the survivor; and whoso devotes gentle dealing to him who is no more, conquers the living by his kindness. Also there is another disaster, not less lamentable, which sometimes befalls the living—the loss of some part of their body; and I think that succor is due to this just as much as to the worst hap that may befall. For often those who fight keep their lives safe, but suffer maiming; and this lot is commonly thought more dismal than any death; for death cuts off memory of all things, while the living cannot forget the devastation of his own body. Therefore this mischief also must be helped somehow; so let it be agreed, that the injury of either of us by the other shall be made good with ten talents (marks) of gold. For if it be righteous to have compassion on the calamities of another, how much more is it to pity one's own? No man but obeys nature's prompting; and he who slights it is a self-murderer."

After mutually pledging their faiths to these terms, they began the battle. Nor was their strangeness in meeting one another, nor the sweetness of that spring-green spot, so heeded as to prevent them from the fray. Horwendil, in his too great ardour, became keener to attack his enemy than to defend his own body; and, heedless of his shield, had grasped his sword with both hands; and his boldness did not fail. For by his rain of blows he destroyed Koller's shield and deprived him of it, and at last hewed off his foot and drove him lifeless to the ground. Then, not to fail of his compact, he buried him royally, gave him a howe of lordly make and pompous obsequies. Then he pursued and slew Koller's

sister Sela, who was a skilled warrior and experienced in roving.

He had now passed three years in valiant deeds of war; and, in order to win higher rank in Rorik's favour, he assigned to him the best trophies and the pick of the plunder. His friendship with Rorik enabled him to woo and win in marriage his daughter Gerutha, who bore him a son Amleth.

Such great good fortune stung Feng with jealousy, so that he resolved treacherously to waylay his brother, thus showing that goodness is not safe even from those of a man's own house. And behold, when a chance came to murder him, his bloody hand sated the deadly passion of his soul. Then he took the wife of the brother he had butchered, capping unnatural murder with incest. For whoso yields to one iniquity, speedily falls an easier victim to the next, the first being an incentive to the second. Also, the man veiled the monstrosity of his deed with such hardihood of cunning, that he made up a mock pretence of goodwill to excuse his crime, and glossed over fratricide with a show of righteousness. Gerutha, said he, though so gentle that she would do no man the slightest hurt, had been visited with her husband's extremest hate; and it was all to save her that he had slain his brother; for he thought it shameful that a lady so meek and unrancorous should suffer the heavy disdain of her husband. Nor did his smooth words fail in their intent; for at courts, where fools are sometimes favoured and backbiters preferred, a lie lacks not credit. Nor did Feng keep from shameful

embraces the hands that had slain a brother; pursuing with equal guilt both of his wicked and impious deeds.

Amleth beheld all this, but feared lest too shrewd a behaviour might make his uncle suspect him. So he chose to feign dulness, and pretend an utter lack of wits. This cunning course not only concealed his intelligence but ensured his safety. Every day he remained in his mother's house utterly listless and unclean, flinging himself on the ground and bespattering his person with foul and filthy dirt. His discoloured face and visage smutched with slime denoted foolish and grotesque madness. All he said was of a piece with these follies; all he did savoured of utter lethargy. In a word, you would not have thought him a man at all, but some absurd abortion due to a mad fit of destiny. He used at times to sit over the fire, and, raking up the embers with his hands, to fashion wooden crooks, and harden them in the fire, shaping at their tips certain barbs, to make them hold more tightly to their fastenings. When asked what he was about, he said that he was preparing sharp javelins to avenge his father. This answer was not a little scoffed at, all men deriding his idle and ridiculous pursuit; but the thing helped his purpose afterwards. Now it was his craft in this matter that first awakened in the deeper observers a suspicion of his cunning. For his skill in a trifling art betokened the hidden talent of the craftsman; nor could they believe the spirit dull where the hand had acquired so cunning a workmanship. Lastly, he always watched with the most punctual care over his pile of stakes that he had pointed in the fire. Some

people, therefore, declared that his mind was quick
enough, and fancied that he only played the simpleton in
order to hide his understanding, and veiled some deep
purpose under a cunning feint. His wiliness (said these)
would be most readily detected, if a fair woman were put
in his way in some secluded place, who should provoke
his mind to the temptations of love; all men's natural
temper being too blindly amorous to be artfully dissembled, and this passion being also too impetuous to be
checked by cunning. Therefore, if his lethargy were
feigned, he would seize the opportunity, and yield straightway to violent delights. So men were commissioned to
draw the young man in his rides into a remote part of
the forest, and there assail him with a temptation of this
nature. Among these chanced to be a foster-brother of
Amleth, who had not ceased to have regard to their
common nurture; and who esteemed his present orders
less than the memory of their past fellowship. He
attended Amleth among his appointed train, being
anxious not to entrap, but to warn him; and was per-
suaded that he would suffer the worst if he showed the
slightest glimpse of sound reason, and above all if he did
the act of love openly. This was also plain enough to
Amleth himself. For when he was bidden mount his
horse, he deliberately set himself in such a fashion that he
turned his back to the neck and faced about, fronting the
tail; which he proceeded to encompass with the reins, just
as if on that side he would check the horse in its furious
pace. By this cunning thought he eluded the trick, and
overcame the treachery of his uncle. The reinless steed

galloping on, with rider directing its tail, was ludicrous enough to behold.

Amleth went on, and a wolf crossed his path amid the thicket. When his companions told him that a young colt had met him, he retorted, that in Feng's stud there were too few of that kind fighting. This was a gentle but witty fashion of invoking a curse upon his uncle's riches. When they averred that he had given a cunning answer, he answered that he had spoken deliberately; for he was loth to be thought prone to lying about any matter, and wished to be held a stranger to falsehood; and accordingly he mingled craft and candour in such wise that, though his words did lack truth, yet there was nothing to betoken the truth and betray how far his keenness went.

Again, as he passed along the beach, his companions found the rudder of a ship which had been wrecked, and said they had discovered a huge knife. "This," said he, "was the right thing to carve such a huge ham;" by which he really meant the sea, to whose infinitude, he thought, this enormous rudder matched. Also, as they passed the sandhills, and bade him look at the meal, meaning the sand, he replied that it had been ground small by the hoary tempests of the ocean. His companions praising his answer, he said that he had spoken it wittingly. Then they purposely left him, that he might pluck up more courage to practise wantonness. The woman whom his uncle had dispatched met him in a dark spot, as though she had crossed him by chance; and he took her and would have ravished her, had not his foster-

brother, by a secret device, given him an inkling of the
trap. For this man, while pondering the fittest way to
play privily the prompter's part, and forestall the young
man's hazardous lewdness, found a straw on the ground
and fastened it underneath the tail of a gadfly that was
flying past; which he then drove towards the particular
quarter where he knew Amleth to be: an act which
served the unwary prince exceedingly well. The token was
interpreted as shrewdly as it had been sent. For Amleth
saw the gadfly, espied with curiosity the straw which it
wore embedded in its tail, and perceived that it was a
secret warning to beware of treachery. Alarmed,
scenting a trap, and fain to possess his desire in greater
safety, he caught up the woman in his arms and dragged
her off to a distant and impenetrable fen. Moreover,
when they had lain together, he conjured her earnestly to
disclose the matter to none, and the promise of silence was
accorded as heartily as it was asked. For both of them
had been under the same fostering in their childhood; and
this early rearing in common had brought Amleth and
the girl into great intimacy.

So, when he had returned home, they all jeeringly
asked him whether he had given way to love, and he
avowed that he had ravished the maid. When he was
next asked where he did it, and what had been his pillow,
he said that he had rested upon the hoof of a beast of
burden, upon a cockscomb, and also upon a ceiling. For,
when he was starting into temptation, he had gathered
fragments of all these things, in order to avoid lying.
And though his jest did not take aught of the truth out

of the story, the answer was greeted with shouts of merriment from the bystanders. The maiden, too, when questioned on the matter, declared that he had done no such thing; and her denial was the more readily credited when it was found that the escort had not witnessed the deed. Then he who had marked the gadfly in order to give a hint, wishing to show Amleth that to his trick he owed his salvation, observed that latterly he had been singly devoted to Amleth. The young man's reply was apt. Not to seem forgetful of his informant's service, he said that he had seen a certain thing bearing a straw flit by suddenly, wearing a stalk of chaff fixed in its hinder parts. The cleverness of this speech, which made the rest split with laughter, rejoiced the heart of Amleth's friend.

Thus all were worsted, and none could open the secret lock of the young man's wisdom. But a friend of Feng, gifted more with assurance than judgment, declared that the unfathomable cunning of such a mind could not be detected by any vulgar plot, for the man's obstinacy was so great that it ought not to be assailed with any mild measures; there were many sides to his wiliness, and it ought not to be entrapped by any one method. Accordingly, said he, his own profounder acuteness had hit on a more delicate way, which was well fitted to be put in practice, and would effectually discover what they desired to know. Feng was purposely to absent himself, pretending affairs of great import. Amleth should be closeted alone with his mother in her chamber; but a man should first be commissioned to place himself in a concealed part

of the room and listen heedfully to what they talked about. For if the son had any wits at all he would not hesitate to speak out in the hearing of his mother, or fear to trust himself to the fidelity of her who bore him. The speaker, loth to seem readier to devise than to carry out the plot, zealously proffered himself as the agent of the eavesdropping. Feng rejoiced at the scheme, and departed on pretence of a long journey. Now he who had given this counsel repaired privily to the room where Amleth was shut up with his mother, and lay down skulking in the straw. But Amleth had his antidote for the treachery. Afraid of being overheard by some eavesdropper, he at first resorted to his usual imbecile ways, and crowed like a noisy cock, beating his arms together to mimic the flapping of wings. Then he mounted the straw and began to swing his body and jump again and again, wishing to try if aught lurked there in hiding. Feeling a lump beneath his feet, he drove his sword into the spot, and impaled him who lay hid. Then he dragged him from his concealment and slew him. Then, cutting his body into morsels, he seethed it in boiling water, and flung it through the mouth of an open sewer for the swine to eat, bestrewing the stinking mire with his hapless limbs. Having in this wise eluded the snare, he went back to the room. Then his mother set up a great wailing, and began to lament her son's folly to his face; but he said: "Most infamous of women; dost thou seek with such lying lamentations to hide thy most heavy guilt? Wantoning like a harlot, thou hast entered a wicked and abominable state of wed-

213

lock, embracing with incestuous bosom thy husband'
slayer, and wheedling with filthy lures of blandishmen
him who had slain the father of thy son. This, forsooth
is the way that the mares couple with the vanquisher
of their mates; for brute beasts are naturally incited t
pair indiscriminately; and it would seem that thou, lik
them, hast clean forgot thy first husband. As for me
not idly do I wear the mask of folly; for I doubt no
that he who destroyed his brother will riot as ruthlessl
in the blood of his kindred. Therefore it is better t
choose the garb of dulness than that of sense, and t
borrow some protection from a show of utter frenzy
Yet the passion to avenge my father still burns in m
heart; but I am watching the chances, I await the fittin
hour. There is a place for all things; against so merciles
and dark spirit must be used the deeper devices of th
mind. And thou, who hadst been better employed i
lamenting thine own disgrace, know it is superfluity t
bewail my witlessness; thou shouldst weep for the blemis
in thine own mind, not for that in another's. On th
rest see thou keep silence." With such reproaches h
rent the heart of his mother and redeemed her to walk i
the ways of virtue; teaching her to set the fires of the pas
above the seductions of the present.

When Feng returned, nowhere could he find the ma
who had suggested the treacherous espial; he searche
for him long and carefully, but none said they had see
him anywhere. Amleth, among others, was asked i
jest if he had come on any trace of him, and replied tha
the man had gone to the sewer, but had fallen throug

its bottom and been stifled by the floods of filth, and that he had then been devoured by the swine that came up all about that place. This speech was flouted by those who heard; for it seemed senseless, though really it expressly avowed the truth.

Feng now suspected that his stepson was certainly full of guile, and desired to make away with him, but durst not do the deed for fear of the displeasure, not only of Amleth's grandsire Rorik, but also of his own wife. So he thought that the King of Britain should be employed to slay him, so that another could do the deed, and he be able to feign innocence. Thus, desirous to hide his cruelty, he chose rather to besmirch his friend than to bring disgrace on his own head. Amleth, on departing, gave secret orders to his mother to hang the hall with woven knots, and to perform pretended obsequies for him a year thence; promising that he would then return. Two retainers of Feng then accompanied him, bearing a letter graven on wood—a kind of writing material frequent in old times; this letter enjoined the king of the Britons to put to death the youth who was sent over to him. While they were reposing, Amleth seached their coffers, found the letter, and read the instructions therein. Whereupon he erased all the writing on the surface, substituted fresh characters, and so, changing the purport of the instructions, shifted his own doom upon his companions. Nor was he satisfied with removing from himself the sentence of death and passing the peril on to others, but added an entreaty that the King of Britain would grant his daughter in marriage to a youth of great

judgment whom he was sending to him. Under this was falsely marked the signature of Feng.

Now when they had reached Britain, the envoys went to the king, and proffered him the letter which they supposed was an implement of destruction to another, but which really betokened death to themselves. The king dissembled the truth, and entreated them hospitably and kindly. Then Amleth scouted all the splendour of the royal banquet like vulgar viands, and abstaining very strangely, rejected that plenteous feast, refraining from the drink even as from the banquet. All marvelled that a youth and a foreigner should disdain the carefully-cooked dainties of the royal board and the luxurious banquet provided, as if it were some peasant's relish. So, when the revel broke up, and the king was dismissing his friends to rest, he had a man sent into the sleeping-room to listen secretly, in order that he might hear the midnight conversation of his guests. Now, when Amleth's companions asked him why he had refrained from the feast of yestereve, as if it were poison, he answered that the bread was flecked with blood and tainted; that there was a tang of iron in the liquor; while the meats of the feast reeked of the stench of a human carcase, and were infected by a kind of smack of the odour of the charnel. He further said that the king had the eyes of a slave, and that the queen had in three ways shown the behaviour of a bondmaid. Thus he reviled with insulting invective not so much the feast as its givers. And presently his companions, taunting him with his old defect of wits, began to flout him with many saucy jeers, because he

blamed and cavilled at seemly and worthy things, and because he attacked thus ignobly an illustrous king and a lady of so refined a behaviour, bespattering with the shamefullest abuse those who merited all praise.

All this the king heard from his retainer; and declared that he who could say such things had either more than mortal wisdom or more than mortal folly; in these few words fathoming the full depth of Amleth's penetration. Then he summoned his steward and asked him whence he had procured the bread. The steward declared that it had been made by the king's own baker. The king asked where the corn had grown of which it was made, and whether any sign was to be found there of human carnage? The other answered, that not far off was a field, covered with the ancient bones of slaughtered men, and still bearing plainly all the signs of ancient carnage; and that he had himself planted this field with grain in springtide, thinking it more fruitful than the rest, and hoping for plenteous abundance; and so, for aught he knew, the bread had caught some evil savour from this bloodshed. The king, on hearing this, surmised that Amleth had spoken truly, and took the pains to learn also what had been the source of the lard. The other declared that his hogs had, through negligence, strayed from keeping, and battened on the the rotten carcase of a robber, and that perchance their pork had thus come to have something of a corrupt smack. The king, finding that Amleth's judgment was right in this thing also, asked of what liquor the steward had mixed the drink? Hearing that it had been brewed of water and meal, he had the

217

spot of the spring pointed out to him, and set to digging deep down; and there he found, rusted away, several swords, the tang whereof it was thought had tainted the waters. Others relate that Amleth blamed the drink because, while quaffing it, he had detected some bees that had fed in the paunch of a dead man; and that the taint, which had formerly been imparted to the combs, had reappeared in the taste. The king, seeing that Amleth had rightly given the causes of the taste he had found so faulty, and learning that the ignoble eyes wherewith Amleth had reproached him concerned some stain upon his birth, had a secret interview with his mother, and asked her who his father had really been. She said she had submitted to no man but the king. But when he threatened that he would have the truth out of her by a trial, he was told that he was the offspring of a slave. By the evidence of the avowal thus extorted he understood the whole mystery of the reproach upon his origin. Abashed as he was with shame for his low estate, he was so ravished with the young man's cleverness, that he asked him why he had aspersed the queen with the reproach that she had demeaned herself like a slave? But while resenting that the courtliness of his wife had been accused in the midnight gossip of a guest, he found that her mother had been a bondmaid. For Amleth said he had noted in her three blemishes showing the demeanor of a slave; first, she had muffled her head in her mantle as bondmaids do; next, that she had gathered up her gown for walking; and thirdly, that she had first picked out with a splinter, and then chewed up, the

218

remnant of food that stuck in the crevices between her teeth. Further, he mentioned that the king's mother had been brought into slavery from captivity, lest she should seem servile only in her habits, yet not in her birth.

Then the king adored the wisdom of Amleth as though it were inspired, and gave him his daughter to wife; accepting his bare word as though it were a witness from the skies. Moreover, in order to fulfil the bidding of his friend, he hanged Amleth's companions on the morrow. Amleth, feigning offence, treated this piece of kindness as a grievance, and received from the king, as compensation, some gold, which he afterwards melted in the fire, and secretly caused to be poured into some hollowed sticks.

When he had passed a whole year with the king he obtained leave to make a journey, and returned to his own land, carrying away of all his princely wealth and state only the sticks which held the gold. On reaching Jutland, he exchanged his present attire for his ancient demeanour, which he had adopted for righteous ends, purposely assuming an aspect of absurdity. Covered with filth, he entered the banquet-room where his own obsequies were being held, and struck all men utterly aghast, rumour having falsely noised abroad his death. At last terror melted into mirth, and the guests jeered and taunted one another, that he whose last rites they were celebrating as though he were dead, should appear in the flesh. When he was asked concerning his comrades, he pointed to the sticks he was carrying, and said, "Here is both the one and the other." This he observed with equal truth and pleasantry; for his speech, though most thought it idle, yet

departed not from the truth; for it pointed at the weregild of the slain as though it were themselves. Thereon, wishing to bring the company into a gayer mood, he joined the cupbearers, and diligently did the office of plying the drink. Then, to prevent his loose dress hampering his walk, he girdled his sword upon his side, and purposely drawing it several times, pricked his fingers with its point. The bystanders accordingly had both sword and scabbard riveted across with an iron nail. Then, to smooth the way more safely to his plot, he went to the lords and plied them heavily with draught upon draught, and drenched them all so deep in wine, that their feet were made feeble with drunkenness, and they turned to rest within the palace, making their bed where they had revelled. Then he saw they were in a fit state for his plots, and thought that here was a chance offered to do his purpose. So he took out of his bosom the stakes he had long ago prepared, and went into the building, where the ground lay covered with the bodies of the nobles wheezing off their sleep and their debauch. Then, cutting away its support, he brought down the hanging his mother had knitted, which covered the inner as well as the outer walls of the hall. This he flung upon the snorers, and then applying the crooked stakes, he knotted and bound them up in such insoluble intricacy, that not one of the men beneath, however hard he might struggle, could contrive to rise. After this he set fire to the palace. The flames spread, scattering the conflagration far and wide. It enveloped the whole dwelling, destroyed the palace, and burnt them all while they were either buried

in deep sleep or vainly striving to arise. Then he went
to the chamber of Feng, who had before this been conducted by his train into his pavilion; plucked up a sword
that chanced to be hanging to the bed, and planted his
own in its place. Then, awakening his uncle, he told
him that his nobles were perishing in the flames, and that
Amleth was here, armed with his crooks to help him,
and thirsting to exact the vengeance, now long overdue,
for his father's murder. Feng, on hearing this, leapt from
his couch, but was cut down while deprived of his own
sword, and as he strove in vain to draw the strange one.
O valiant Amleth, and worthy of immortal fame, who
being shrewdly armed with a feint of folly, covered a
wisdom too high for human wit under a marvellous
disguise of silliness! and not only found in his subtlety
means to protect his own safety, but also by its guidance
found opportunity to avenge his father. By this skilful
defence of himself, and strenuous revenge for his parent,
he has left it doubtful whether we are to think more of
his wit or his bravery.*

---

*Shakespere's tragedy, "Hamlet," is derived from this story.

# BOOK FOUR.

AMLETH, when he had accomplished the slaughter of
his stepfather, feared to expose his deed to the fickle
judgment of his countrymen, and thought it well to lie in
hiding till he had learnt what way the mob of the uncouth
populace was tending. So the whole neighbourhood,
who had watched the blaze during the night, and in the
morning desired to know the cause of the fire they had
seen, perceived the royal palace fallen in ashes; and, on
searching through its ruins, which were yet warm, found
only some shapeless remains of burnt corpses. For the
devouring flame had consumed everything so utterly that
not a single token was left to inform them of the cause of
such a disaster. Also they saw the body of Feng lying
pierced by the sword, amid his blood-stained raiment.
Some were seized with open anger, others with grief, and
some with secret delight. One party bewailed the death
of their leader, the other gave thanks that the tyranny of
the fratricide was now laid at rest. Thus the occurrence of the king's slaughter was greeted by the beholders
with diverse minds.

Amleth, finding the people so quiet, made bold to leave
his hiding. Summoning those in whom he knew the
memory of his father to be fast-rooted, he went to the
assembly and there made a speech after this manner;

"Nobles! Let not any who are troubled by the piteous end of Horwendil be worried by the sight of this disaster before you; be not ye, I say, distressed, who have remained loyal to your king and duteous to your father. Behold the corpse, not of a prince, but of a fratricide. Indeed, it was a sorrier sight when ye saw our prince lying lamentably butchered by a most infamous fratricide—brother, let me not call him. With your own compassionating eyes ye have beheld the mangled limbs of Horwendil; they have seen his body done to death with many wounds. Surely that most abominable butcher only deprived his king of life that he might despoil his country of freedom! The hand that slew him made you slaves. Who then so mad as to choose Feng the cruel before Horwendil the righteous? Remember how benignantly Horwendil fostered you, how justly he dealt with you, how kindly he loved you. Remember how you lost the mildest of princes and the justest of fathers, while in his place was put a tyrant and an assassin set up; how your rights were confiscated; how everything was plague-stricken; how the country was stained with infamies; how the yoke was planted on your necks, and how your free will was forfeited! And now all this is over; for ye see the criminal stifled in his own crimes, the slayer of his kin punished for his misdoings. What man of but ordinary wit, beholding it, would account this kindness a wrong? What sane man could be sorry that the crime has recoiled upon the culprit? Who could lament the killing of a most savage executioner? or bewail the righteous death of a most cruel despot? Ye

behold the doer of the deed; he is before you. Yea, I own
that I have taken vengeance for my country and my
father. Your hands were equally bound to the task
which mine fulfilled. What it would have beseemed
you to accomplish with me, I achieved alone. Nor had I
any partner in so glorious a deed, or the service of any
man to help me. Not that I forget that you would have
helped this work, had I asked you; for doubtless you have
remained loyal to your king and loving to your prince.
But I chose that the wicked should be punished without
imperilling you; I thought that others need not set their
shoulders to the burden when I deemed mine strong
enough to bear it. Therefore I consumed all the others
to ashes, and left only the trunk of Feng for your hands
to burn, so that on this at least you may wreak all your
longing for a righteous vengeance. Now haste up
speedily, heap the pyre, burn up the body of the wicked,
consume away his guilty limbs, scatter his sinful ashes,
strew broadcast his ruthless dust; let no urn or barrow
enclose the abominable remnants of his bones. Let no
trace of his fratricide remain; let there be no spot in his
own land for his tainted limbs; let no neighbourhood
suck infection from him; let not sea nor soil be defiled by
harbouring his accursed carcase. I have done the rest;
this one loyal duty is left for you. These must be the
tyrant's obsequies, this the funeral procession of the
fratricide. It is not seemly that he who stripped his
country of her freedom should have his ashes covered by
his country's earth.

"Besides, why tell again my own sorrows? Why count

over my troubles? Why weave the thread of my miseries
anew? Ye know them more fully than I myself. I,
pursued to the death by my stepfather, scorned by my
mother, spat upon by friends, have passed my years in
pitiable wise, and my days in adversity; and my insecure
life has teemed with fear and perils. In fine, I passed
every season of my age wretchedly and in extreme
calamity. Often in your secret murmurings together you
have sighed over my lack of wits; there was none (you
said) to avenge the father, none to punish the fratricide.
And in this I found a secret testimony of your love; for
I saw that the memory of the King's murder had not yet
faded from your minds.

"Whose breast is so hard that it can be softened by no
fellow-feeling for what I have felt? Who is so stiff and
stony, that he is swayed by no compassion for my griefs?
Ye whose hands are clean of the blood of Horwendil, pity
your fosterling, be moved by my calamities. Pity also
my stricken mother, and rejoice with me that the infamy
of her who was once your queen is quenched. For this
weak woman had to bear a twofold weight of ignominy,
embracing one who was her husband's brother and
murderer. Therefore, to hide my purpose of revenge
and to veil my wit, I counterfeited a listless bearing;
I feigned dulness; I planned a stratagem; and now you
can see with your own eyes whether it has succeeded,
whether it has achieved its purpose to the full; I am
content to leave you to judge so great a matter. It is
your turn; trample under foot the ashes of the murderer!
Disdain the dust of him who slew his brother, and defiled

226

his brother's queen with infamous desecration, who outraged his sovereign and treasonably assailed his majesty,
who brought the sharpest tyranny upon you, stole your
freedom, and crowned fratricide with incest.  I have been
the agent of this just vengeance; I have burned for this
righteous retribution; uphold me with a high-born spirit;
pay me the homage that you owe; warm me with your
kindly looks.  It is I who have wiped off my country's
shame; I who have quenched my mother's dishonour;
I who have beaten back oppression; I who have put to
death the murderer; I who have baffled the artful hand
of my uncle with retorted arts.  Were he living, each
new day would have multiplied his crimes.  I resented
the wrong done to father and to fatherland: I slew him
who was governing you outrageously and more hardly
than it beseemed men.  Acknowledge my service, honour
my wit, give me the throne if I have earned it; for you
have in me one who has done you a mighty service, and
who is no degenerate heir to his father's power; no
fratricide, but the lawful successor to the throne; and a
dutiful avenger of the crime of murder.  It is I who have
stripped you of slavery, and clothed you with freedom;
I have restored your height of fortune, and given you
your glory back; I have deposed the despot and triumphed
over the butcher.  In your hands is the reward; you
know what I have done for you, and from your righteousness I ask my wage."

Every heart had been moved while the young man thus
spoke; he affected some to compassion, and some even to
tears.  When the lamentation ceased, he was appointed

king by prompt and general acclaim. For one and all rested their greatest hopes on his wisdom, since he had devised the whole of such an achievement with the deepest cunning, and accomplished it with the most astonishing contrivance. Many could have been seen marvelling how he had concealed so subtle a plan over so long a space of time.

After these deeds in Denmark, Amleth equipped three vessels, and went back to Britain to see his wife and her father. He had also enrolled in his service the flower of the warriors, and arrayed them very choicely, wishing to have everything now magnificently appointed, even as of old he had always worn contemptible gear, and to change all his old devotion to poverty for outlay on luxury. He also had a shield made for him, whereon the whole series of his exploits, beginning with his earliest youth, was painted in exquisite designs. This he bore as a record of his deeds of prowess, and gained great increase of fame thereby. Here were to be seen depicted the slaying of Horwendil; the fratricide and incest of Feng; the infamous uncle, the whimsical nephew; the shapes of the hooked stakes; the stepfather suspecting, the stepson dissembling; the various temptations offered, and the woman brought to beguile him; the gaping wolf; the finding of the rudder; the passing of the sand; the entering of the wood; the putting of the straw through the gadfly; the warning of the youth by the tokens; and the privy dealings with the maiden after the escort was eluded. And likewise could be seen the picture of the palace; the queen there with her son; the slaying of the eavesdropper;

and how, after being killed, he was boiled down, and so dropped into the sewer, and so thrown out to the swine; how his limbs were strewn in the mud, and so left for the beasts to finish. Also it could be seen how Amleth surprised the secret of his sleeping attendants, how he erased the letters, and put new characters in their places; how he disdained the banquet and scorned the drink; how he condemned the face of the king and taxed the queen with faulty behaviour. There was also represented the hanging of the envoys, and the young man's wedding; then the voyage back to Denmark; the festive celebration of the funeral rites; Amleth, in answer to questions, pointing to the sticks in place of his attendants, acting as cup-bearer, and purposely drawing his sword and pricking his fingers; the sword riveted through, the swelling cheers of the banquet, the dance growing fast and furious; the hangings flung upon the sleepers, then fastened with the interlacing crooks, and wrapped tightly round them as they slumbered; the brand set to the mansion, the burning of the guests, the royal palace consumed with fire and tottering down; the visit to the sleeping-room of Feng, the theft of his sword, the useless one set in its place; and the king slain with his own sword's point by his stepson's hand. All this was there, painted upon Amleth's battle-shield by a careful craftsman in the choicest of handiwork; he copied truth in his figures, and embodied real deeds in his outlines. Moreover, Amleth's followers, to increase the splendour of their presence, wore shields which were gilt over.

The King of Britain received them very graciously, and

treated them with costly and royal pomp. During the
feast he asked anxiously whether Feng was alive and
prosperous. His son-in-law told him that the man of
whose welfare he was vainly inquiring had perished by
the sword. With a flood of questions he tried to find out
who had slain Feng, and learnt that the messenger of his
death was likewise its author. And when the king heard
this, he was secretly aghast, because he found that an old
promise to avenge Feng now devolved upon himself.
For Feng and he had determined of old, by a mutual
compact, that one of them should act as avenger of the
other. Thus the king was drawn one way by his love for
his daughter and his affection for his son-in-law; another
way by his regard for his friend, and moreover by his
strict oath and the sanctity of their mutual declarations,
which it was impious to violate. At last he slighted the
ties of kinship, and sworn faith prevailed. His heart
turned to vengeance, and he put the sanctity of his oath
before family bonds. But since it was thought sin to
wrong the holy ties of hospitality, he preferred to execute
his revenge by the hand of another, wishing to mask
his secret crime with a show of innocence. So he veiled
his treachery with attentions, and hid his intent to harm
under a show of zealous goodwill. His queen having
lately died of illness, he requested Amleth to undertake
the mission of making him a fresh match, saying that he
was highly delighted with his extraordinary shrewdness.
He declared that there was a certain queen reigning in
Scotland, whom he vehemently desired to marry. Now
he knew that she was not only unwedded by reason of

230

her chastity, but that in the cruelty of her arrogance she had always loathed her wooers, and had inflicted on her lovers the uttermost punishment, so that not one out of all the multitude was to be found who had not paid for his insolence with his life.

Perilous as this commission was Amleth started, never shrinking to obey the duty imposed upon him, but trusting partly in his own servants, and partly in the attendants of the king. He entered Scotland, and, when quite close to the abode of the queen, he went into a meadow by the wayside to rest his horses. Pleased by the look of the spot, he thought of resting—the pleasant prattle of the stream exciting a desire to sleep—and posted men to keep watch some way off. The queen on hearing of this, sent out ten warriors to spy on the approach of the foreigners and their equipment. One of these, being quick-witted, slipped past the sentries, pertinaciously made his way up, and took away the shield, which Amleth had chanced to set at his head before he slept, so gently that he did not ruffle his slumbers, though he was lying upon it, nor awaken one man of all that troop; for he wished to assure his mistress not only by report but by some token. With equal address he filched the letter entrusted to Amleth from the coffer in which it was kept. When these things were brought to the queen, she scanned the shield narrowly, and from the notes appended made out the whole argument. Then she knew that here was the man who, trusting in his own nicely-calculated scheme, had avenged on his uncle the murder of his father. She also looked at the letter containing the

suit for her hand, and rubbed out all the writing; for wedlock with the old she utterly abhorred, and desired the embraces of young men. But she wrote in its place a commission purporting to be sent from the King of Britain to herself, signed like the other with his name and title, wherein she pretended that she was asked to marry the bearer. Moreover, she included an account of the deeds of which she had learnt from Amleth's shield, so that one would have thought the shield confirmed the letter, while the letter explained the shield. Then she told the same spies whom she had employed before to take the shield back, and put the letter in its place again; playing the very trick on Amleth which, as she had learnt, he had himself used in outwitting his companions.

Amleth, meanwhile, who found that his shield had been filched from under his head, deliberately shut his eyes and cunningly feigned sleep, hoping to regain by pretended what he had lost by real slumbers. For he thought that the success of his one attempt would incline the spy to deceive him a second time. And he was not mistaken. For as the spy came up stealthily, and wanted to put back the shield and the writing in their old place, Amleth leapt up, seized him, and detained him in bonds. Then he roused his retinue, and went to the abode of the queen. As representing his father-in-law, he greeted her, and handed her the writing, sealed with the king's seal. The queen, who was named Hermutrude, took and read it, and spoke most warmly of Amleth's diligence and shrewdness, saying, that Feng had deserved his punishment, and that the unfathomable wit of Amleth had accomplished a deed

past all human estimation; seeing that not only had his impenetrable depth devised a mode of revenging his father's death and his mother's adultery, but it had further, by his notable deeds of prowess, seized the kingdom of the man whom he had found constantly plotting against him. She marvelled therefore that a man of such instructed mind could have made the one slip of a mistaken marriage; for though his renown almost rose above mortality, he seemed to have stumbled into an obscure and ignoble match. For the parents of his wife had been slaves, though good luck had graced them with the honours of royalty. Now (said she), when looking for a wife a wise man must reckon the lustre of her birth and not of her beauty. Therefore, if he were to seek a match in a proper spirit, he should weigh the ancestry, and not be smitten by the looks; for though looks were a lure to temptation, yet their empty bedizenment had tarnished the white simplicity of many a man. Now there was a woman, as nobly born as himself, whom he could take. She herself, whose means were not poor nor her birth lowly, was worthy his embraces, since he did not surpass her in royal wealth nor outshine her in the honour of his ancestors. Indeed she was a queen, and but that her sex gainsaid it, might be deemed a king; nay (and this is yet truer), whomsoever she thought worthy of her bed was at once a king, and she yielded her kingdom with herself. Thus her sceptre and her hand went together. It was no mean favour for such a woman to offer her love, who in the case of other men had always followed her refusal with the sword. Therefore she pressed him to

233

transfer his wooing, to make over to her his marriage vows, and to learn to prefer birth to beauty. So saying, she fell upon him with a close embrace.

Amleth was overjoyed at the gracious speech of the maiden, fell to kissing back, and returned her close embrace, protesting that the maiden's wish was his own. Then a banquet was held, friends bidden, the nobles gathered, and the marriage rites performed. When they were accomplished, he went back to Britain with his bride, a strong band of Scots being told to follow close behind, that he might have its help against the diverse treacheries in his path. As he was returning, the daughter of the King of Britain, to whom he was still married, met him. Though she complained that she was slighted by the wrong of having a paramour put over her, yet, she said, it would be unworthy for her to hate him as an adulterer more than she loved him as a husband: nor would she so far shrink from her lord as to bring herself to hide in silence the guile which she knew was intended against him. For she had a son as a pledge of their marriage, and regard for him, if nothing else, must have inclined his mother to the affection of a wife. "He," she said, "may hate the supplanter of his mother, I will love her; no disaster shall put out my flame for thee; no ill-will shall quench it, or prevent me from exposing the malignant designs against thee, or from revealing the snares I have detected. Bethink thee, then, that thou must beware of thy father-in-law, for thou hast thyself reaped the harvest of thy mission, foiled the wishes of him who sent thee, and with wilful trespass seized over all the fruit

234

for thyself." By this speech she showed herself more inclined to love her husband than her father.

While she thus spoke, the King of Britain came up and embraced his son-in-law closely, but with little love, and welcomed him with a banquet, to hide his intended guile under a show of generosity. But Amleth, having learnt the deceit, dissembled his fear, took a retinue of two hundred horsemen, put on an under-shirt (of mail), and complied with the invitation, preferring the peril of falling in with the king's deceit to the shame of hanging back. So much heed for honour did he think that he must take in all things. As he rode up close, the king attacked him just under the porch of the folding doors, and would have thrust him through with his javelin, but that the hard shirt of mail threw off the blade. Amleth received a slight wound, and went to the spot where he had bidden the Scottish warriors wait on duty. He then sent back to the king his new wife's spy, whom he had captured. This man was to bear witness that he had secretly taken from the coffer where it was kept the letter which was meant for his mistress, and thus was to make the whole blame recoil on Hermutrude, by this studied excuse absolving Amleth from the charge of treachery. The king without tarrying pursued Amleth hotly as he fled, and deprived him of most of his forces. So Amleth, on the morrow, wishing to fight for dear life, and utterly despairing of his powers of resistance, tried to increase his apparent numbers. He put stakes under some of the dead bodies of his comrades to prop them up, set others on horseback like living men, and tied others to neighbouring stones, not

taking off any of their armour, and dressing them in due order of line and wedge, just as if they were about to engage. The wing composed of the dead was as thick as the troop of the living. It was an amazing spectacle this, of dead men dragged out to battle, and corpses mustered to fight. The plan served him well, for the very figures of the dead men showed like a vast array as the sunbeams struck them. For those dead and senseless shapes restored the original number of the army so well, that the mass might have been unthinned by the slaughter of yesterday. The Britons, terrified at the spectacle, fled before fighting, conquered by the dead men whom they had overcome in life. I cannot tell whether to think more of the cunning or of the good fortune of this victory. The Danes came down on the king as he was tardily making off, and killed him. Amleth, triumphant, made a great plundering, seized the spoils of Britain, and went back with his wives to his own land.

Meanwhile Rorik had died, and Wiglek, who had come to the throne, had harassed Amleth's mother with all manner of insolence and stripped her of her royal wealth, complaining that her son had usurped the kingdom of Jutland and defrauded the King of Leire, who had the sole privilege of giving and taking away the rights of high offices. This treatment Amleth took with such forbearance as apparently to return kindness for slander, for he presented Wiglek with the richest of his spoils. But afterwards he seized a chance of taking vengeance, attacked him, subdued him, and from a covert became an open foe. Fialler, the governor of Skaane, he drove into

236

exile; and the tale is that Fialler retired to a spot called Undensakre, which is unknown to our peoples. After this, Wiglek, recruited with the forces of Skaane and Zealand, sent envoys to challenge Amleth to a war. Amleth, with his marvellous shrewdness, saw that he was tossed between two difficulties, one of which involved disgrace and the other danger. For he knew that if he took up the challenge he was threatened with peril of his life, while to shrink from it would disgrace his reputation as a soldier. Yet in that spirit ever fixed on deeds of prowess the desire to save his honour won the day. Dread of disaster was blunted by more vehement thirst for glory; he would not tarnish the unblemished lustre of his fame by timidly skulking from his fate. Also he saw that there is almost as wide a gap between a mean life and a noble death as that which is acknowledged between honour and disgrace themselves.

Yet Amleth was enchained by such great love for Hermutrude, that he was more deeply concerned in his mind about her future widowhood than about his own death, and cast about very zealously how he could decide on some second husband for her before the opening of the war. Hermutrude, therefore, declared that she had the courage of a man, and promised that she would not forsake him even on the field, saying that the woman who dreaded to be united with her lord in death was abominable. But she kept this rare promise ill; for when Amleth had been slain by Wiglek in battle in Jutland, she yielded herself up unasked to be the conqueror's spoil and bride. Thus all vows of woman are loosed by change of

fortune and melted by the shifting of time; the faith of their soul rests on a slippery foothold, and is weakened by casual chances; glib in promises, and as sluggish in performance, all manner of lustful promptings enslave it, and it bounds away with panting and precipitate desire, forgetful of old things in the ever hot pursuit after something fresh. So ended Amleth. Had fortune been as kind to him as nature, he would have equalled the gods in glory, and surpassed the labours of Hercules by his deeds of prowess. A plain in Jutland is to be found, famous for his name and burial-place. Wiglek's administration of the kingdom was long and peaceful, and he died of disease.

WERMUND, his son, succeeded him. The long and leisurely tranquillity of a most prosperous and quiet time flowed by and Wermund in undisturbed security maintained a prolonged and steady peace at home. He had no children during the prime of his life, but in his old age, by a belated gift of fortune, he begat a son, Uffe, though all the years which had glided by had raised him up no offspring. This Uffe surpassed all of his age in stature, but in his early youth was supposed to have so dull and foolish a spirit as to be useless for all affairs public or private. For from his first years he never used to play or make merry, but was so void of all human pleasure that he kept his lips sealed in a perennial silence, and utterly restrained his austere visage from the business of laughter. But though through the years of his youth he was reputed for an utter fool, he afterwards left that despised estate and became famous, turning out as great a pattern of

238

wisdom and hardihood as he had been a picture of stagnation. His father, seeing him such a simpleton, got him for a wife the daughter of Frowin, the governor of the men of Sleswik; thinking that by his alliance with so famous a man Uffe would receive help which would serve him well in administering the realm. Frowin had two sons, Ket and Wig, who were youths of most brilliant parts, and their excellence, not less than that of Frowin, Wermund destined to the future advantage of his son.

At this time the King of Sweden was Athisl, a man of notable fame and energy. After defeating his neighbours far around, he was loth to leave the renown won by his prowess to be tarnished in slothful ease, and by constant and zealous practice brought many novel exercises into vogue. For one thing he had a daily habit of walking alone girt with splendid armour: in part because he knew that nothing was more excellent in warfare than the continual practice of arms; and in part that he might swell his glory by ever following this pursuit. Self-confidence claimed as large a place in this man as thirst for fame. Nothing, he thought, could be so terrible as to make him afraid that it would daunt his stout heart by its opposition. He carried his arms into Denmark, and challenged Frowin to battle near Sleswik. The armies routed one another with vast slaughter, and it happened that the generals came to engage in person, so that they conducted the affair like a duel; and, in addition to the public issues of the war, the fight was like a personal conflict. For both of them longed with equal earnestness for an issue of the combat by which they might exhibit

their valour, not by the help of their respective sides, but
by a trial of personal strength.  The end was that, though
the blows rained thick on either side, Athisl prevailed and
overthrew Frowin, and won a public victory as well as a
duel, breaking up and shattering the Danish ranks in all
directions.  When he returned to Sweden, he not only
counted the slaying of Frowin among the trophies of his
valour, but even bragged of it past measure, so ruining
the glory of the deed by his wantonness of tongue.  For
it is sometimes handsomer for deeds of valour to be
shrouded in the modesty of silence than to be blazoned
in wanton talk.

Wermund raised the sons of Frowin to honours of the
same rank as their father's, a kindness which was only due
to the children of his friend who had died for the country.
This prompted Athisl to carry the war again into Denmark.  Emboldened therefore by his previous battle, he
came back, bringing with him not only no slender and
feeble force, but all the flower of the valour of Sweden,
thinking he would seize the supremacy of all Denmark.
Ket, the son of Frowin, sent Folk, his chief officer, to
take this news to Wermund, who then chanced to be in
his house Jellinge.* Folk found the king feasting with his
friends, and did his errand, admonishing him that here
was the long-wished-for chance of war at hand, and
pressing itself upon the wishes of Wermund, to whom
was given an immediate chance of victory and the free
choice of a speedy and honourable triumph.  Great and
unexpected were the sweets of good fortune, so long

*Jellinge] Lat. *Ialunga,* Icel. *Jalángr.*

sighed for, and now granted to him by this lucky event.
For Athisl had come encompassed with countless forces of
the Swedes, just as though in his firm assurance he had
made sure of victory; and since the enemy who was
going to fight would doubtless prefer death to flight, this
chance of war gave them a fortunate opportunity to take
vengeance for their late disaster.

Wermund, declaring that he had performed his mission
nobly and bravely, ordered that he should take some little
refreshment of the banquet, since "far-faring ever hurt
fasters." When Folk said that he had no kind of leisure
to take food, he begged him to take a draught to quench
his thirst. This was given him; and Wermund also
bade him keep the cup, which was of gold, saying that
men who were weary with the heat of wayfaring found it
handier to take up the water in a goblet than in the palms,
and that it was better to use a cup for drinking than the
hand. When the king accompanied his great gift with
such gracious words, the young man, overjoyed at both,
promised that, before the king should see him turn and
flee, he would take a draught of his own blood to the
full measure of the liquor he had drunk.

With this doughty vow Wermund accounted himself
well repaid, and got somewhat more joy from giving the
boon than the soldier had from gaining it. Nor did he
find that Folk's talk was braver than his fighting.

For, when battle had begun, it came to pass that amidst
divers charges of the troops Folk and Athisl met and
fought a long while together; and that the host of the
Swedes, following the fate of their captain, took to flight,

and Athisl also was wounded and fled from the battle to
his ships. And when Folk, dazed with wounds and toils,
and moreover steeped alike in heat and toil and thirst, had
ceased to follow the rout of the enemy, then, in order to
refresh himself, he caught his own blood in his helmet,
. and put it to his lips to drain: by which deed he gloriously
requited the king's gift of the cup. Wermund, who
chanced to see this, praised him warmly for fulfilling his
vow. Folk answered, that a noble vow ought to be
strictly performed to the end: a speech wherein he showed
no less approval of his own deed than Wermund.

Now, while the conquerors had laid down their arms,
and, as is usual after battle, were exchanging diverse talk
with one another, Ket, the governor of the men of
Sleswik, declared that it was a matter of great marvel to
him how it was that Athisl, though difficulties strewed his
path, had contrived an opportunity to escape, especially
as he had been the first and foremost in the battle, but
last of all in the retreat; and though there had not been
one of the enemy whose fall was so vehemently desired by
the Danes. Wermund rejoined that he should know that
there were four kinds of warrior to be distinguished in
every army. The fighters of the first order were those
who, tempering valour with forbearance, were keen to
slay those who resisted, but were ashamed to bear hard
on fugitives. For these were the men who had won
undoubted proofs of prowess by veteran experience in
arms, and who found their glory not in the flight of the
conquered, but in overcoming those whom they had to
conquer. Then there was a second kind of warriors, who

242

were endowed with stout frame and spirit, but with no jot
of compassion, and who raged with savage and indiscriminate carnage against the backs as well as the breasts
of their foes.  Now of this sort were the men carried
away by hot and youthful blood, and striving to grace
their first campaign with good auguries of warfare.
They burned as hotly with the glow of youth as with the
glow for glory, and thus rushed headlong into right or
wrong with equal recklessness.  There was also the
third kind, who, wavering betwixt shame and fear, could
not go forward for terror, while shame barred retreat.
Of distinguished blood, but only notable for their useless
stature, they crowded the ranks with numbers and not
with strength, smote the foe more with their shadows
than with their arms, and were only counted among the
throng of warriors as so many bodies to be seen.  These
men were lords of great riches, but excelled more in birth
than bravery; hungry for life because owning great
possessions, they were forced to yield to the sway of
cowardice rather than nobleness.  There were others,
again, who brought show to the war, and not substance,
and who, foisting themselves into the rear of their comrades, were the first to fly and the last to fight.  One sure
token of fear betrayed their feebleness; for they always
deliberately sought excuses to shirk, and followed with
timid and sluggish advance in the rear of the fighters.
It must be supposed, therefore, that these were the reasons
why the king had escaped safely; for when he fled he was
not pursued pertinaciously by the men of the front rank;
since these made it their business to preserve the victory,

243

not to arrest the conquered, and massed their wedges, in order that the fresh-won victory might be duly and sufficiently guarded, and attain the fulness of triumph.

Now the second class of fighters, whose desire was to cut down everything in their way, had left Athisl unscathed, from lack not of will but of opportunity; for they had lacked the chance to hurt him rather than the daring. Moreover, though the men of the third kind, who frittered away the very hour of battle by wandering about in a flurried fashion, and also hampered the success of their own side, had had their chance of harming the king, they yet lacked courage to assail him. In this way Wermund satisfied the dull amazement of Ket, and declared that he had set forth and expounded the true reasons of the king's safe escape.

After this Athisl fled back to Sweden, still wantonly bragging of the slaughter of Frowin, and constantly boasting the memory of his exploit with prolix recital of his deeds; not that he bore calmly the shame of his defeat, but that he might salve the wound of his recent flight by the honours of his ancient victory. This naturally much angered Ket and Wig, and they swore a vow to unite in avenging their father. Thinking that they could hardly accomplish this in open war, they took an equipment of lighter armament, and went to Sweden alone. Then, entering a wood in which they had learnt by report that the king used to take his walks unaccompanied, they hid their weapons. Then they talked long with Athisl, giving themselves out as deserters; and when he asked them what was their native country, they said they were

men of Sleswik, and had left their land "for manslaughter." The king thought that this statement
referred not to their vow to commit the crime, but to the
guilt of some crime already committed. For they desired
by this deceit to foil his inquisitiveness, so that the truth-
fulness of the statement might baffle the wit of the
questioner, and their true answer, being covertly shadowed
forth in a fiction, might inspire in him a belief that it was
false. For famous men of old thought lying a most
shameful thing. Then Athisl said he would like to
know whom the Danes believed to be the slayer of
Frowin. Ket replied that there was a doubt as to who
ought to claim so illustrious a deed, especially as the
general testimony was that he had perished on the field of
battle. Athisl answered that it was idle to credit others
with the death of Frowin, which he, and he alone, had
accomplished in mutual combat. Soon he asked whether
Frowin had left any children. Ket answering that two
sons of his were alive, said that he would be very glad
to learn their age and stature. Ket replied that they
were almost of the same size as themselves in body, alike
in years, and much resembling them in tallness. Then
Athisl said: "If the mind and the valour of their sire
were theirs, a bitter tempest would break upon me."
Then he asked whether those men constantly spoke of the
slaying of their father. Ket rejoined that it was idle to
go on talking and talking about a thing that could not be
softened by any remedy, and declared that it was no good
to harp with constant vexation on an inexpiable ill. By
saying this he showed that threats ought not to anticipate
vengeance.

245

When Ket saw that the king regularly walked apart alone in order to train his strength, he took up his arms, and with his brother followed the king as he walked in front of them. Athisl, when he saw them, stood his ground on the sand, thinking it shameful to avoid threateners. Then they said that they would take vengeance for his slaying of Frowin, especially as he avowed with so many arrogant vaunts that he alone was his slayer. But he told them to take heed lest while they sought to compass their revenge, they should be so foolhardy as to engage him with their feeble and powerless hand, and while desiring the destruction of another, should find they had fallen themselves. Thus they would cut off their goodly promise of overhasty thirst for glory. Let them then save their youth and spare their promise; let them not be seized so lightly with a desire to perish. Therefore, let them suffer him to requite with money the trespass done them in their father's death, and account it great honour that they would be credited with forcing so mighty a chief to pay a fine, and in a manner with shaking him with overmastering fear. Yet he said he advised them thus, not because he was really terrified, but because he was moved with compassion for their youth. Ket replied that it was idle to waste time in beating so much about the bush, and trying to sap their righteous longing for revenge by an offer of pelf. So he bade him come forward and make trial with him in single combat of whatever strength he had. He himself would do without the aid of his brother, and would fight with his own strength, lest it should appear a shameful and unequal combat, for

246

the ancients held it to be unfair, and also infamous, for
two men to fight against one; and a victory gained by this
kind of fighting they did not account honourable, but
more like a disgrace than a glory. Indeed, it was
considered not only a poor, but a most shameful exploit
for two men to overpower one.

But Athisl was filled with such assurance that he bade
them both assail him at once, declaring that if he could
not cure them of the desire to fight, he would at least give
them the chance of fighting more safely. But Ket shrank
so much from this favour that he swore he would accept
death sooner: for he thought that the terms of battle
thus offered would be turned into a reproach to himself.
So he engaged hotly with Athisl, who desirous to fight
him in a forbearing fashion, merely thrust lightly with
his blade and struck upon his shield; thus guarding his
own safety with more hardihood than success. When he
had done this some while, he advised him to take his
brother to share in his enterprise, and not be ashamed to
ask for the help of another hand, since his unaided efforts
were useless. If he refused, said Athisl, he should not
be spared; then making good his threats, he assailed him
with all his might. But Ket received him with so sturdy
a stroke of his sword, that it split the helmet and forced
its way down upon the head. Stung by the wound (for a
stream of blood flowed from his poll), he attacked Ket
with a shower of nimble blows, and drove him to his
knees. Wig, leaning more to personal love than to general usage,* could not bear the sight, but made affection

*General usage] *publicae consuetudini*: namely, the rule of combat that
two should not fight against one.

conquer shame, and attacking Athisl, chose rather to defend the weakness of his brother than to look on at it. But he won more infamy than glory by the deed. In helping his brother he had violated the appointed conditions of the duel; and the help that he gave him was thought more useful than honourable. For on the one scale he inclined to the side of disgrace, and on the other to that of affection. Thereupon they perceived themselves that their killing of Athisl had been more swift than glorious. Yet, not to hide the deed from the common people, they cut off his head, slung his body on a horse, took it out of the wood, and handed it over to the dwellers in a village near, announcing that the sons of Frowin had taken vengeance upon Athisl, King of the Swedes, for the slaying of their father. Boasting of such a victory as this, they were received by Wermund with the highest honours; for he thought they had done a most useful deed, and he preferred to regard the glory of being rid of a rival with more attention than the infamy of committing an outrage. Nor did he judge that the killing of a tyrant was in any wise akin to shame. It passed into a proverb among foreigners, that the death of the king had broken down the ancient principle of combat.

When Wermund was losing his sight by infirmity of age, the King of Saxony, thinking that Denmark lacked a leader, sent envoys ordering him to surrender to his charge the kingdom which he held beyond the due term of life; lest, if he thirsted to hold sway too long, he should strip his country of laws and defence. For how could he be reckoned a king, whose spirit was darkened

with age, and his eyes with blindness not less black and
awful? If he refused, but yet had a son who would dare
to accept a challenge and fight with his son, let him agree
that the victor should possess the realm. But if he
approved neither offer, let him learn that he must be dealt
with by weapons and not by warnings; and in the end he
must unwillingly surrender what he was too proud at
first to yield uncompelled. Wermund, shaken by deep
sighs, answered that it was too insolent to sting him with
these taunts upon his years; for he had passed no timorous
youth, nor shrunk from battle, that age should bring him
to this extreme misery. It was equally unfitting to cast
in his teeth the infirmity of his blindness: for it was
common for a loss of this kind to accompany such a time
of life as his, and it seemed a calamity fitter for sympathy
than for taunts. It were juster to fix the blame on the
impatience of the King of Saxony, whom it would have
beseemed to wait for the old man's death, and not demand
his throne; for it was somewhat better to succeed to the
dead than to rob the living. Yet, that he might not be
thought to make over the honours of his ancient freedom,
like a madman, to the possession of another, he would
accept the challenge with his own hand. The envoys
answered that they knew that their king would shrink
from the mockery of fighting a blind man, for such an
absurd mode of combat was thought more shameful than
honourable. It would surely be better to settle the affair by
means of their offspring on either side. The Danes were
in consternation, and at a sudden loss for a reply: but
Uffe, who happened to be there with the rest, craved his

249

father's leave to answer; and suddenly the dumb as it were
spake. When Wermund asked who had thus begged leave
to speak, and the attendants said that it was Uffe, he declared that it was enough that the insolent foreigner should
jeer at the pangs of his misery, without those of his own
household vexing him with the same wanton effrontery.
But the courtiers persistently averred that this man was
Uffe; and the king said: "He is free, whosoever he be, to
say out what he thinks." Then said Uffe, "that it was
idle for their king to covet a realm which could rely not
only on the service of its own ruler, but also on the arms
and wisdom of most valiant nobles. Moreover, the king
did not lack a son nor the kingdom an heir; and they were
to know that he had made up his mind to fight not only
the son of their king, but also, at the same time, whatsoever man the prince should elect as his comrade out of
the bravest of their nation."

The envoys laughed when they heard this, thinking it
idle lip-courage. Instantly the ground for the battle was
agreed on, and a fixed time appointed. But the bystanders
were so amazed by the strangeness of Uffe's speaking·and
challenging, that one can scarce say if they were more
astonished at his words or at his assurance.

But on the departure of the envoys Wermund praised
him who had made the answer, because he had proved his
confidence in his own valour by challenging not one only,
but two; and said that he would sooner quit his kingdom
for him, whoever he was, than for an insolent foe. But
when one and all testified that he who with lofty self-
confidence had spurned the arrogance of the envoys was

his own son, he bade him come nearer to him, wishing to test with his hands what he could not with his eyes. Then he carefully felt his body, and found by the size of his limbs and by his features that he was his son; and then began to believe their assertions, and to ask him why he had taken pains to hide so sweet an eloquence with such careful dissembling, and had borne to live through so long a span of life without utterance or any intercourse of talk, so as to let men think him utterly incapable of speech, and a born mute. He replied that he had been hitherto satisfied with the protection of his father, that he had not needed the use of his own voice, until he saw the wisdom of his own land hard pressed by the glibness of a for- eigner. The king. also asked him why he had chosen to challenge two rather than one. He said he had desired this mode of combat in order that the death of King Athisl, which, having been caused by two men, was a standing reproach to the Danes, might be balanced by the exploit of one, and that a new ensample of valour might erase the ancient record of their disgrace. Fresh honour, he said, would thus obliterate the guilt of their old dishonour.

Wermund said that his son had judged all things rightly, and bade him first learn the use of arms, since he had been little accustomed to them. When they were offered to Uffe, he split the narrow links of the mail-coats by the mighty girth of his chest, nor could any be found large enough to hold him properly. For he was too hugely built to be able to use the arms of any other man. At last, when he was bursting even his father's coat of mail

251

by the violent compression of his body, Wermund ordered
it to be cut away on the left side and patched with a
buckle; thinking it mattered little if the side guarded by
the shield were exposed to the sword.  He also told him
to be most careful in fixing on a sword which he could use
safely.  Several were offered him; but Uffe, grasping
the hilt, shattered them one after the other into flinders
by shaking them, and not a single blade was of so hard a
temper but at the first blow he broke it into many pieces.
But the king had a sword of extraordinary sharpness,
called "Skrep," which at a single blow of the smiter
struck straight through and cleft asunder any obstacle
whatsoever; nor would aught be hard enough to check its
edge when driven home.  The king, loth to leave this for
the benefit of posterity, and greatly grudging others the
use of it, had buried it deep in the earth, meaning, since
he had no hopes of his son's improvement, to debar everyone else from using it.  But when he was now asked
whether he had a sword worthy of the strength of Uffe,
he said that he had  one which, if he could recognize the
lie of the ground and find what he had consigned long
ago to earth, he could offer him as worthy of his bodily
strength.  Then he bade them lead him into a field, and
kept questioning his companions over all the ground.  At
last he recognised the tokens, found the spot where he had
buried the sword, drew it out of its hole, and handed it
to his son.  Uffe saw it was frail with great age and
rusted away; and, not daring to strike with it, asked if
he must prove this one also like the rest, declaring that
he must try its temper before the battle ought to be

252

fought. Wermund replied that if this sword were shattered by mere brandishing, there was nothing left which
could serve for such strength as his. He must, therefore, forbear from the act, whose issue remained so
doubtful.

So they repaired to the field of battle as agreed. It is
fast encompassed by the waters of the river Eider, which
roll between, and forbid any approach save by ship.
Hither Uffe went unattended, while the Prince of Saxony
was followed by a champion famous for his strength.
Dense crowds on either side, eager to see, thronged each
winding bank, and all bent their eyes upon this scene.
Wermund planted himself on the end of the bridge, determined to perish in the waters if defeat were the lot of
his son: he would rather share the fall of his own flesh
and blood than behold, with heart full of anguish, the
destruction of his own country. Both the warriors
assaulted Uffe; but, distrusting his sword, he parried the
blows of both with his shield, being determined to wait
patiently and see which of the two he must beware of
most heedfully, so that he might reach that one at all
events with a single stroke of his blade. Wermund,
thinking that his feebleness was at fault, that he took
the blows so patiently, dragged himself little by little, in
his longing for death, forward to the western edge of
the bridge, meaning to fling himself down and perish,
should all be over with his son.

Fortune shielded the old father, for Uffe told the prince
to engage with him more briskly, and to do some deed of
prowess worthy of his famous race; lest the lowborn

SAXO GRAMMATICUS

squire should seem braver than the prince. Then,
order to try the bravery of the champion, he bade hi
not skulk timorously at his master's heels, but requite 1
noble deeds of combat the trust placed in him by 1
prince, who had chosen him to be his single partner
the battle. The other complied, and when shame dro
him to fight at close quarters, Uffe clove him throu
with the first stroke of his blade. The sound reviv
Wermund, who said that he heard the sword of his so
and asked "on what particular part he had dealt t
blow?" Then the retainers answered that it had go
through no one limb, but the man's whole frame; where
Wermund drew back from the precipice and came on 1
bridge, longing now as passionately to live as he had j
wished to die. Then Uffe, wishing to destroy his 1
maining foe after the fashion of the first, incited t
prince with vehement words to offer some sacrifice
way of requital to the shade of the servant slain in 1
cause. Drawing him by those appeals, and warily noti
the right spot to plant his blow, he turned the other ed
of his sword to the front, fearing that the thin side
his blade was too frail for his strength, and smote wi
a piercing stroke through the prince's body. When W
mund heard it, he said that the sound of his swo
"Skrep" had reached his ear for the second time. Th
when the judges announced that his son had killed b
enemies, he burst into tears from excess of joy. Th
gladness bedewed the cheeks which sorrow could 1
moisten. So while the Saxons, sad and shamefaced, b
their champions to burial with bitter shame, the Da

254

welcomed Uffe and bounded for joy. Then no more was
heard of the disgrace of the murder of Athisl, and there
was an end of the taunts of the Saxons.

Thus the realm of Saxony was transferred to the
Danes, and UFFE, after his father, undertook its government; and he, who had not been thought equal to administering a single kingdom properly, was now appointed
to manage both. Most men have called him Olaf, and
he has won the name of "the Gentle" for his forbearing
spirit. His later deeds, lost in antiquity, have lacked
formal record. But it may well be supposed that when
their beginnings were so notable, their sequel was glorious. I am so brief in considering his doings, because
the lustre of the famous men of our nation has been
lost to memory and praise by the lack of writings. But
if by good luck our land had in old time been endowed
with the Latin tongue, there would have been countless
volumes to read of the exploits of the Danes.

Uffe was succeeded by his son DAN, who carried his
arms against foreigners, and increased his sovereignty
with many a trophy; but he tarnished the brightness of
the glory he had won by foul and abominable presump-
tion; falling so far away from the honour of his famous
father, who surpassed all others in modesty, that he contrariwise was puffed up and proudly exalted in spirit,
so that he scorned all other men. He also squandered
the goods of his father on infamies, as well as his own
winnings from the spoils of foreign nations; and he devoured in expenditure on luxuries the wealth which
should have ministered to his royal estate. Thus do

sons sometimes, like monstrous births, degenerate from their ancestors.

After this HUGLEIK was king, who is said to have defeated in battle at sea Homod and Hogrim, the despots of Sweden.

To him succeeded FRODE, surnamed the Vigorous, who bore out his name by the strength of his body and mind. He destroyed in war ten captains of Norway, and finally approached the island which afterwards had its name from him, meaning to attack the king himself last of all. This king, Froger, was in two ways very distinguished, being notable in arms no less than in wealth; and graced his sovereignty with the deeds of a champion, being as rich in prizes for bodily feats as in the honours of rank. According to some, he was the son of Odin, and when he begged the immortal gods to grant him a boon, received the privilege that no man should conquer him, save he who at the time of the conflict could catch up in his hand the dust lying beneath Froger's feet. When Frode found that Heaven had endowed this king with such might, he challenged him to a duel, meaning to try to outwit the favour of the gods. So at first, feigning inexperience, he besought the king for a lesson in fighting, knowing (he said) his skill and experience in the same. The other, rejoicing that his enemy not only yielded to his pretensions, but even made him a request, said that he was wise to submit his youthful mind to an old man's wisdom; for his unscarred face and his brow, ploughed by no marks of battle, showed that his knowledge of such matters was

but slender. So he marked off on the ground two square spaces with sides an ell long, opposite one another, meaning to begin by instructing him about the use of these plots. When they had been marked off, each took the side assigned to him. Then Frode asked Froger to exchange arms and ground with him, and the request was readily granted. For Froger was excited with the flashing of his enemy's arms, because Frode wore a gold-hilted sword, a breastplate equally bright, and a headpiece most brilliantly adorned in the same manner. So Frode caught up some dust from the ground whence Froger had gone, and thought that he had been granted an omen of victory. Nor was he deceived in his presage; for he straightway slew Froger, and by this petty trick won the greatest name for bravery; for he gained by craft what had been permitted to no man's strength before.

After him DAN came to the throne. When he was in the twelfth year of his age, he was wearied by the insolence of the embassies, which commanded him either to fight the Saxons or to pay them tribute. Ashamed, he preferred fighting to payment and was moved to die stoutly rather than live a coward. So he elected to fight; and the warriors of the Danes filled the Elbe with such a throng of vessels, that the decks of the ships lashed together made it quite easy to cross, as though along a continuous bridge. The end was that the King of Saxony had to accept the very terms he was demanding from the Danes.

After Dan, FRIDLEIF, surnamed the Swift, assumed

the sovereignty. During his reign, Huyrwil, the lord of Oland, made a league with the Danes and attacked Norway. No small fame was added to his deeds by the defeat of the amazon Rusila, who aspired with military ardour to prowess in battle: but he gained manly glory over a female foe. Also he took into his alliance, on account of their deeds of prowess, her five partners, the children of Finn, named Brodd, Bild, Bug, Fanning, and Gunholm. Their confederacy emboldened him to break the treaty which he made with the Danes; and the treachery of the violation made it all the more injurious, for the Danes could not believe that he could turn so suddenly from a friend into an enemy; so easily can some veer from goodwill into hate. I suppose that this man inaugurated the morals of our own day, for we do not account lying and treachery as sinful and sordid. When Huyrwil attacked the southern side of Zealand, Fridleif assailed him in the harbour which was afterwards called by Huyrwil's name. In this battle the soldiers, in their rivalry for glory, engaged with such bravery that very few fled to escape peril, and both armies were utterly destroyed; nor did the victory fall to either side, where both were enveloped in an equal ruin. So much more desirous were they all of glory than of life. So the survivors of Huyrwil's army, in order to keep united, had the remnants of their fleet lashed together at night. But, in the same night, Bild and Brodd cut the cables with which the ships were joined, and stealthily severed their own vessels from the rest, thus yielding to their own terrors by deserting their brethren, and obey-

ing the impulses of fear rather than fraternal love. When daylight returned, Fridleif, finding that after the great massacre of their friends only Huyrwil, Gunholm, Bug, and Fanning were left, determined to fight them all single-handed, so that the mangled relics of his fleet might not again have to be imperilled. Besides his innate courage, a shirt of steel-defying mail gave him confidence; a garb which he used to wear in all public battles and in duels, as a preservative of his life. He accomplished his end with as much fortune as courage, and ended the battle successfully. For, after slaying Huyrwil, Bug, and Fanning, he killed Gunholm, who was accustomed to blunt the blade of an enemy with spells, by a shower of blows from his hilt. But while he gripped the blade too eagerly, the sinews, being cut and disabled, contracted the fingers upon the palm, and cramped them with life-long curvature.

While Fridleif was besieging Dublin, a town in Ireland, and saw from the strength of the walls that there was no chance of storming them, he imitated the shrewd wit of Hadding, and ordered fire to be shut up in wicks and fastened to the wings of swallows. When the birds got back in their own nesting-place, the dwellings suddenly flared up; and while the citizens all ran up to quench them, and paid more heed to abating the fire than to looking after the enemy, Fridleif took Dublin. After this he lost his soldiers in Britain, and, thinking that he would find it hard to get back to the coast, he set up the corpses of the slain (Amleth's device) and stationed them in line, thus producing so nearly the look of

his original host that its great reverse seemed not to have lessened the show of it a whit. By this deed he not only took out of the enemy all heart for fighting, but inspired them with the desire to make their escape.

.

# BOOK FIVE.

AFTER the death of Fridleif, his son FRODE, aged seven, was elected in his stead by the unanimous decision of the Danes. But they held an assembly first, and judged that the minority of the king should be taken in charge by guardians, lest the sovereignty should pass away owing to the boyishness of the ruler. For one and all paid such respect to the name and memory of Fridleif, that the royalty was bestowed on his son despite his tender years. So a selection was made, and the brothers Westmar and Koll were summoned to the charge of bringing up the king. Isulf, also, and Agg and eight other men of mark were not only entrusted with the guardianship of the king, but also granted authority to administer the realm under him. These men were rich in strength and courage, and endowed with ample gifts of mind as well as of body. Thus the state of the Danes was governed with the aid of regents until the time when the king should be a man.

The wife of Koll was Gotwar, who used to paralyse the most eloquent and fluent men by her glib and extraordinary insolence; for she was potent in wrangling, and full of resource in all kinds of disputation. Words were her weapons; and she not only trusted in questions, but was armed with stubborn answers. No man could sub-

due this woman, who could not fight, but who found
darts in her tongue instead. Some she would argue down
with a flood of impudent words, while others she seemed
to entangle in the meshes of her quibbles, and strangle
in the noose of her sophistries; so nimble a wit had the
woman. Moreover, she was very strong, either in making or cancelling a bargain, and the sting of her tongue
was the secret of her power in both. She was clever
both at making and at breaking leagues; thus she had
two sides to her tongue, and used it for either purpose.

Westmar had twelve sons, three of whom had the
same name—Grep—in common. These three men were
conceived at once and delivered at one birth, and their
common name declared their simultaneous origin. They
were exceedingly skillful swordsmen and boxers. Frode
had also given the supremacy of the sea to Odd; who was
very closely related to the king. Koll rejoiced in an
offspring of three sons. At this time a certain son of
Frode's brother held the chief command of naval affairs
for the protection of the country? Now the king had a
sister, Gunwar, surnamed the Fair because of her surpassing beauty. The sons of Westmar and Koll, being
ungrown in years and bold in spirit, let their courage
become recklessness and devoted their guilt-stained minds
to foul and degraded orgies.

Their behaviour was so outrageous and uncontrollable
that they ravished other men's brides and daughters, and
seemed to have outlawed chastity and banished it to the
stews. Nay, they defiled the couches of matrons, and did
not even refrain from the bed of virgins. A man's own

chamber was no safety to him: there was scarce a spot
in the land but bore traces of their lust. Husbands were
vexed with fear, and wives with insult to their persons:
and to these wrongs folk bowed. No ties were respected,
and forced embraces became a common thing. Love was
prostituted, all reverence for marriage ties died out, and
lust was greedily run after. And the reason of all this
was the peace; for men's bodies lacked exercise and were
enervated in the ease so propitious to vices. At last the
eldest of those who shared the name of Grep, wishing to
regulate and steady his promiscuous wantonness, ventured to seek a haven for his vagrant amours in the love
of the king's sister. Yet he did amiss. For though it
was right that his vagabond and straying delights should
be bridled by modesty, yet it was audacious for a man
of the people to covet the child of a king. She, much
fearing the impudence of her wooer, and wishing to be
safer from outrage, went into a fortified building. Thirty
attendants were given to her, to keep guard and constant
watch over her person.

Now the comrades of Frode, sadly lacking the help of
women in the matter of the wear of their garments, inasmuch as they had no means of patching or of repairing
rents, advised and urged the king to marry. At first he
alleged his tender years as an excuse, but in the end
yielded to the persistent requests of his people. And
when he carefully inquired of his advisers who would be
a fit wife for him, they all praised the daughter of the
King of the Huns beyond the rest. When the question
was pushed, what reason Frode had for objecting to her,

he replied that he had heard from his father that it was not expedient for kings to seek alliance far afield, or to demand love save from neighbours. When Gotwar heard this she knew that the king's resistance to his friends was wily. Wishing to establish his wavering spirit, and strengthen the courage of his weakling soul, she said: "Bridals are for young men, but the tomb awaits the old. The steps of youth go forward in desires and in fortune; but old age declines helpless to the sepulchre. Hope attends youth; age is bowed with hopeless decay. The fortune of young men increases; it will never leave unfinished what it begins." Respecting her words, he begged her to undertake the management of the suit. But she refused, pleading her age as her pretext, and declaring herself too stricken in years to bear so difficult a commission. The king saw that a bribe was wanted, and, proffering a golden necklace, promised it as the reward of her embassy. For the necklace had links consisting of studs, and figures of kings interspersed in bas-relief, which could be now separated and now drawn together by pulling a thread inside; a gewgaw devised more for luxury than use. Frode also ordered that Westmar and Koll, with their sons, should be summoned to go on the same embassy, thinking that their cunning would avoid the shame of a rebuff.

They went with Gotwar, and were entertained by the King of the Huns at a three days' banquet, ere they uttered the purpose of their embassy. For it was customary of old thus to welcome guests. When the feast had been prolonged three days, the princess came forth

to make herself pleasant to the envoys with a most courteous address, and her blithe presence added not a little
to the festal delights of the banqueters. And as the drink
went faster Westmar revealed his purpose in due course,
in a very merry declaration, wishing to sound the mind
of the maiden in talk of a friendly sort. And, in order
not to inflict on himself a rebuff, he spoke in a mirthful
vein, and broke the ground of his mission, by venturing
to make up a sportive speech amid the applause of the
revellers. The princess said that she disdained Frode
because he lacked honour and glory. For in days of old
no men were thought fit for the hand of high-born women
but those who had won some great prize of glory by the
lustre of their admirable deeds. Sloth was the worst of
vices in a suitor, and nothing was more of a reproach in
one who sought marriage than the lack of fame. A harvest of glory, and that alone, could bring wealth in
everything else. Maidens admired in their wooers not
so much good looks as deeds nobly done. So the envoys,
flagging and despairing of their wish, left the further conduct of the affair to the wisdom of Gotwar, who tried to
subdue the maiden not only with words but with love-
philtres, and began to declare that Frode used his left
hand as well as his right, and was a quick and skillful
swimmer and fighter. Also by the drink which she gave
she changed the strictness of the maiden to desire, and
replaced her vanished anger with love and delight. Then
she bade Westmar, Koll, and their sons go to the king
and urge their mission afresh; and finally, should they
find him froward, to anticipate a rebuff by a challenge
to fight.      265

So Westmar entered the palace with his men-at-arms, and said: "Now thou must needs either consent to our entreaties, or meet in battle us who entreat thee. We would rather die nobly than go back with our mission unperformed; lest, foully repulsed and foiled of our purpose, we should take home disgrace where we hoped to win honour. If thou refuse thy daughter, consent to fight: thou must needs grant one thing or the other. We wish either to die or to have our prayers heard. Something —sorrow if not joy—we will get from thee. Frode will be better pleased to hear of our slaughter than of our repulse." Without another word, he threatened to aim a blow at the king's throat with his sword. The king replied that it was unseemly for the royal majesty to meet an inferior in rank in level combat, and unfit that those of unequal station should fight as equals. But when Westmar persisted in urging him to fight, he at last bade him find out what the real mind of the maiden was; for in old time men gave women who were to marry, free choice of a husband. For the king was embarrassed, and hung vacillating betwixt shame and fear of battle. Thus Westmar, having been referred to the thoughts of the girl's heart, and knowing that every woman is as changeable in purpose as she is fickle in soul, proceeded to fulfil his task all the more confidently because he knew how mutable the wishes of maidens were. His confidence in his charge was increased and his zeal encouraged, because she had both a maiden's simplicity, which was left to its own counsels, and a woman's freedom of choice, which must be wheedled with the most delicate and mollifying

flatteries; and thus she would be not only easy to lead away, but even hasty in compliance. But her father went after the envoys, that he might see more surely into his daughter's mind. She had already been drawn by the stealthy working of the draught to love her suitor, and answered that the promise of Frode, rather than his present renown, had made her expect much of his nature: since he was sprung from so famous a father, and every nature commonly answered to its origin. The youth therefore had pleased her by her regard of his future, rather than his present, glory. These words amazed the father; but neither could he bear to revoke the freedom he had granted her, and he promised her in marriage to Frode. Then, having laid in ample stores, he took her away with the most splendid pomp, and, followed by the envoys, hastened to Denmark, knowing that a father was the best person to give away a daughter in marriage. Frode welcomed his bride most joyfully, and also bestowed the highest honours upon his future royal father-in-law; and when the marriage rites were over, dismissed him with a large gift of gold and silver.

And so with Hanund, the daughter of the King of the Huns, for his wife, he passed three years in the most prosperous peace. But idleness brought wantonness among his courtiers, and peace begot lewdness, which they displayed in the most abominable crimes. For they would draw some men up in the air on ropes, and torment them, pushing their bodies as they hung, like a ball that is tossed; or they would put a kid's hide under the feet of others as they walked, and, by stealthily pulling a rope,

trip their unwary steps on the slippery skin in their path; others they would strip of their clothes, and lash with sundry tortures of stripes; others they fastened to pegs, as with a noose, and punished with mock-hanging. They scorched off the beard and hair with tapers; of others they burned the hair of the groin with a brand. Only those maidens might marry whose chastity they had first deflowered. Strangers they battered with bones; others they compelled to drunkenness with immoderate draughts, and made them burst. No man might give his daughter to wife unless he had first bought their favour and goodwill. None might contract any marriage without first purchasing their consent with a bribe. Moreover, they extended their abominable and abandoned lust not only to virgins, but to the multitude of matrons indiscriminately. Thus a twofold madness incited this mixture of wantonness and frenzy. Guests and strangers were proffered not shelter but revilings. All these maddening mockeries did this insolent and wanton crew devise, and thus under a boy-king freedom fostered licence. For nothing prolongs reckless sin like the procrastination of punishment and vengeance. This unbridled impudence of the soldiers ended by making the king detested, not only by foreigners, but even by his own people, for the Danes resented such an arrogant and cruel rule. But Grep was contented with no humble loves; he broke out so outrageously that he was guilty of intercourse with the queen, and proved as false to the king as he was violent to all other men. Then by degrees the scandal grew, and the suspicion of his guilt crept on with silent step. The

common people found it out before the king. For Grep, by always punishing all who alluded in the least to this circumstance, had made it dangerous to accuse him. But the rumour of his crime, which at first was kept alive in whispers, was next passed on in public reports; for it is hard for men to hide another's guilt if they are aware of it. Gunwar had many suitors; and accordingly Grep, trying to take revenge for his rebuff by stealthy wiles, demanded the right of judging the suitors, declaring that the princess ought to make the choicest match. But he disguised his anger, lest he should seem to have sought the office from hatred of the maiden. At his request the king granted him leave to examine the merits of the young men. So he first gathered all the wooers of Gunwar together on the pretence of a banquet, and then lined the customary room of the princess with their heads— a gruesome spectacle for all the rest. Yet he forfeited none of his favour with Frode, nor abated his old intimacy with him. For he decided that any opportunity of an interview with the king must be paid for, and gave out that no one should have any conversation with him who brought no present. Access, he announced, to so great a general must be gained by no stale or usual method, but by making interest most zealously. He wished to lighten the scandal of his cruelty by the pretence of affection to his king. The people, thus tormented, vented their complaint of their trouble in silent groans. None had the spirit to lift up his voice in public against this season of misery. No one had become so bold as to complain openly of the affliction that was fall-

ing upon them. Inward resentment vexed the hearts of men, secretly indeed, but all the more bitterly.

When Gotar, the King of Norway, heard this, he assembled his soldiers, and said that the Danes were disgusted with their own king, and longed for another if they could get the opportunity; that he had himself resolved to lead an army thither, and that Denmark would be easy to seize if attacked. Frode's government of his country was as covetous as it was cruel. Then Erik rose up and gainsaid the project with contrary reasons. "We remember," he said, "how often coveters of other men's goods lose their own. He who snatches at both has oft lost both. It must be a very strong bird that can wrest the prey from the claws of another. It is idle for thee to be encouraged by the internal jealousies of the country, for these are oft blown away by the approach of an enemy. For though the Danes now seem divided in counsel, yet they will soon be of one mind to meet the foe. The wolves have often made peace between the quarrelling swine. Every man prefers a leader of his own land to a foreigner, and every province is warmer in loyalty to a native than to a stranger king. For Frode will not await thee at home, but will intercept thee abroad as thou comest. Eagles claw each other with their talons, and fowls fight fronting. Thou thyself knowest that the keen sight of the wise man must leave no cause for repentance. Thou hast an ample guard of nobles. Keep thou quiet as thou art; indeed thou wilt almost be able to find out by means of others what are thy resources for war. Let the soldiers first try the fortunes of their

king. Provide in peace for thine own safety, and risk others if thou dost undertake the enterprise: better that the slave should perish than the master. Let thy servant do for thee what the tongs do for the smith, who by the aid of his iron tool guards his hand from scorching, and saves his fingers from burning. Learn thou also, by using thy men, to spare and take thought for thyself."

So spake Erik, and Gotar, who had hitherto held him a man of no parts, now marvelled that he had graced his answer with sentences so choice and weighty, and gave him the name of Shrewd-spoken, thinking that his admirable wisdom deserved some title. For the young man's reputation had been kept in the shade by the exceeding brilliancy of his brother Roller. Erik begged that some substantial gift should be added to the name, declaring that the bestowal of the title ought to be graced by a present besides. The king gave him a ship, and the oarsmen called it "Skroter." Now Erik and Roller were the sons of Ragnar, the champion, and children of one father by different mothers; Roller's mother and Erik's stepmother was named Kraka.

And so, by leave of Gotar, the task of making a raid on the Danes fell to one Hrafn. He was encountered by Odd, who had at that time the greatest prestige among the Danes as a rover, for he was such a skilled magician that he could range over the sea without a ship, and could often raise tempests by his spells, and wreck the vessels of the enemy. Accordingly, that he might not have to condescend to pit his sea-forces against the rovers, he

271

used to ruffle the waters by enchantment, and cause them to shipwreck his foes. To traders this man was ruthless, but to tillers of the soil he was merciful, for he thought less of merchandise than of the plough-handle, but rated the clean business of the country higher than the toil for filthy lucre. When he began to fight with the Northmen he so dulled the sight of the enemy by the power of his spells that they thought the drawn swords of the Danes cast their beams from afar off, and sparkled as if aflame. Moreover, their vision was so blunted that they could not so much as look upon the sword when it was drawn from the sheath: the dazzle was too much for their eyesight, which could not endure the glittering mirage. So Hrafn and many of his men were slain, and only six vessels slipped back to Norway to teach the king that it was not so easy to crush the Danes. The survivors also spread the news that Frode trusted only in the help of his champions, and reigned against the will of his people, for his rule had become a tyranny.

In order to examine this rumour, Roller, who was a great traveller abroad, and eager to visit unknown parts, made a vow that he would get into the company of Frode. But Erik declared that, splendid as were his bodily parts, he had been rash in pronouncing the vow. At last, seeing him persisting stubbornly in his purpose, Erik bound himself under a similar vow; and the king promised them that he would give them for companions whomsoever they approved by their choice. The brethren, therefore, first resolved to visit their father and beg for the stores and the necessaries that were wanted for so long a journey.

272

He welcomed them paternally, and on the morrow took
them to the forest to inspect the herd, for the old man
was wealthy in cattle. Also he revealed to them treasures which had long lain hid in caverns of the earth;
and they were suffered to gather up whatsoever of these
they would. The boon was accepted as heartily as it was
offered: so they took the riches out of the ground, and
bore away what pleased them.

Their rowers meanwhile were either refreshing themselves or exercising their skill with casting weights.
Some sped leaping, some running; others tried their
strength by sturdily hurling stones; others tested their
archery by drawing the bow. Thus they essayed to
strengthen themselves with divers exercises. Some again
tried to drink themselves into a drowse. Roller was sent
by his father to find out what had passed at home in the
meanwhile. And when he saw smoke coming from his
mother's hut he went up outside, and, stealthily applying his eye, saw through the little chink and into the
house, where he perceived his mother stirring a cooked
mess in an ugly-looking pot. Also he looked up at three
snakes hanging from above by a thin cord, from whose
mouths flowed a slaver which dribbled drops of moisture
on the meal. Now two of these were pitchy of hue, while
the third seemed to have whitish scales, and was hung
somewhat higher than the others. This last had a fastening on its tail, while the others were held by a cord round
their bellies. Roller thought the affair looked like magic,
but was silent on what he had seen, that he might not
be thought to charge his mother with sorcery. For he did

not know that the snakes were naturally harmless, or how much strength was being brewed for that meal. Then Ragnar and Erik came up, and, when they saw the smoke issuing from the cottage, entered and went to sit at meat. When they were at table, and Kraka's son and stepson were about to eat together, she put before them a small dish containing a piebald mess, part looking pitchy, but spotted with specks of yellow, while part was whitish: the pottage having taken a different hue answering to the different appearance of the snakes. And when each had tasted a single morsel, Erik, judging the feast not by the colours but by the inward strengthening effected, turned the dish around very quickly, and transferred to himself the part which was black but compounded of stronger juices; and, putting over to Roller the whitish part which had first been set before himself, throve more on his supper. And, to avoid showing that the exchange was made on purpose, he said, "Thus does prow become stern when the sea boils up." The man had no little shrewdness, thus to use the ways of a ship to dissemble his cunning act.

So Erik, now refreshed by this lucky meal, attained by its inward working to the highest pitch of human wisdom. For the potency of the meal bred in him the fulness of all kinds of knowledge to an incredible degree, so that he had cunning to interpret even the utterances of wild beasts and cattle. For he was not only well versed in all the affairs of men, but he could interpret the particular feelings which brutes experienced from the sounds which expressed them. He was also gifted

274

with an eloquence so courteous and graceful, that he adorned whatsoever he desired to expound with a flow of witty adages. But when Kraka came up, and found that the dish had been turned round, and that Erik had eaten the stronger share of the meal, she lamented that the good luck she had bred for her son should have passed to her stepson. Soon she began to sigh, and entreat Erik that he should never fail to help his brother, whose mother had heaped on him fortune so rich and strange: for by tasting a single savoury meal he had clearly attained sovereign wit and eloquence, besides the promise of success in combat. She added also, that Roller was almost as capable of good counsel, and that he should not utterly miss the dainty that had been intended for him. She also told him that in case of extreme and violent need, he could find speedy help by calling on her name; declaring that she trusted partially in her divine attributes, and that, consorting as she did in a manner with the gods, she wielded an innate and heavenly power. Erik said that he was naturally drawn to stand by his brother, and that the bird was infamous which fouled its own nest. But Kraka was more vexed by her own carelessness than weighed down by her son's ill-fortune: for in old time it made a craftsman bitterly ashamed to be outwitted by his own cleverness.

Then Kraka, accompanied by her husband, took away the brothers on their journey to the sea. They embarked in a single ship, but soon attached two others. They had already reached the coast of Denmark, when, reconnoitering, they learned that seven ships had come up at

no great distance. Then Erik bade two men who could speak the Danish tongue well, to go to them unclothed, and, in order to spy better, to complain to Odd of their nakedness, as if Erik had caused it, and to report when they had made careful scrutiny. These men were received as friends by Odd, and hunted for every plan of the general with their sharp ears. He had determined to attack the enemy unawares at daybreak, that he might massacre them the more speedily while they were swathed in their night garments: for he said that men's bodies were wont to be most dull and heavy at that hour of dawn. He also told them, thereby hastening what was to prove his own destruction, that his ships were laden with stones fit for throwing. The spies slipped off in the first sleep of the night, reported that Odd had filled all his vessels with pebbles, and also told everything else they had heard. Erik now quite understood the case, and, when he considered the smallness of his own fleet, thought that he must call the waters to destroy the enemy, and win their aid for himself.

So he got into a boat and rowed, pulling silently, close up to the keels of the enemy; and gradually, by screwing in an auger, he bored the planks (a device practiced by Hadding and also by Frode), nearest to the water, and soon made good his return, the oar-beat being scarce audible. Now he bore himself so warily, that not one of the watchers noted his approach or departure. As he rowed off, the water got in through the chinks of Odd's vessels, and sank them, so that they were seen disappearing in the deep, as the water flooded them more

and more within. The weight of the stones inside helped
them mightily to sink. The billows were washing away
the thwarts, and the sea was flush with the decks, when
Odd, seeing the vessels almost on a level with the waves,
ordered the heavy seas that had been shipped to be baled
out with pitchers. And so, while the crews were toiling
on to protect the sinking parts of the vessels from the
flood of waters, the enemy hove close up. Thus, as they
fell to their arms, the flood came upon them harder, and
as they prepared to fight, they found they must swim
for it. Waves, not weapons, fought for Erik, and the
sea, which he had himself enabled to approach and do
harm, battled for him. Thus Erik made better use of
the billow than of the steel, and by the effectual aid of
the waters seemed to fight in his own absence, the ocean
lending him defence. The victory was given to his craft;
for a flooded ship could not endure a battle. Thus was
Odd slain with all his crew; the look-outs were captured,
and it was found that no man escaped to tell the tale
of the disaster.

Erik, when the massacre was accomplished, made a
rapid retreat, and put in at the isle Lessö. Finding
nothing there to appease his hunger, he sent the spoil
homeward on two ships, which were to bring back supplies for another year. He tried to go by himself to the
king in a single ship. So he put in to Zealand, and the
sailors ran about over the shore, and began to cut down
the cattle: for they must either ease their hunger or
perish of famine. So they killed the herd, skinned the
carcases, and cast them on board. When the owners of

the cattle found this out, they hastily pursued the free-booters with a fleet. And when Erik found that he was being attacked by the owners of the cattle, he took care that the carcases of the slaughtered cows should be tied with marked ropes and hidden under water. Then, when the Zealanders came up, he gave them leave to look about and see if any of the carcases they were seeking were in his hands; saying that a ship's corners were too narrow to hide things. Unable to find a carcase anywhere, they turned their suspicions on others, and thought the real criminals were guiltless of the plunder. Since no traces of freebooting were to be seen, they fancied that others had injured them, and pardoned the culprits. As they sailed off, Erik lifted the carcase out of the water and took it in.

Meantime Frode learnt that Odd and his men had gone down. For a widespread rumour of the massacre had got wind, though the author of the deed was unknown. There were men, however, who told how they had seen three sails putting in to shore, and departing again northwards. Then Erik went to the harbour, not far from which Frode was tarrying, and, the moment that he stepped out of the ship, tripped inadvertently, and came tumbling to the ground. He found in the slip a presage of a lucky issue, and forecast better results from this mean beginning. When Grep heard of his coming, he hastened down to the sea, intending to assail with chosen and pointed phrases the man whom he had heard was better-spoken than all other folk. Grep's eloquence was not so much excellent as impudent, for he surpassed all

278

in stubbornness of speech. So he began the dispute with reviling, and assailed Erik as follows:

*Grep.* "Fool, who art thou? What idle quest is thine? Tell me, whence or whither dost thou journey? What is thy road? What thy desire? Who thy father? What thy lineage? Those have strength beyond others who have never left their own homes, and the Luck of kings is their houseluck. For the doings of a vile man are acceptable unto few, and seldom are the deeds of the hated pleasing."

*Erik.* "Ragnar is my father; eloquence clothes my tongue; I have ever loved virtue only. Wisdom hath been my one desire; I have travelled many ways over the world, and seen the different manners of men. The mind of the fool can keep no bounds in aught: it is base and cannot control its feelings. The use of sails is better than being drawn by the oar; the gale troubles the waters, a drearier gust the land. For rowing goes through the seas and lying the lands; and it is certain that the lands are ruled with the lips, but the seas with the hand."

*Grep.* "Thou art thought to be as full of quibbling as a cock of dirt. Thou stinkest heavy with filth, and reekest of nought but sin. There is no need to lengthen the plea against a buffoon, whose strength is in an empty and voluble tongue."

*Erik.* "By Hercules, if I mistake not, the coward word is wont to come back to the utterer. The gods with righteous endeavour bring home to the speaker words cast forth without knowledge. As soon as we espy the

20          279

sinister ears of the wolf, we believe that the wolf himself is near. Men think no credit due to him that hath no credit, whom report accuses of treachery."

*Grep.* "Shameless boy, owl astray from the path, night-owl in the darkness, thou shalt pay for thy reckless words. Thou shalt be sorry for the words thou now belchest forth madly, and shalt pay with thy death for thy unhallowed speech. Lifeless thou shalt pasture crows on thy bloodless corpse, to be a morsel for beasts, a prey to the ravenous bird."

*Erik.* "The boding of the coward, and the will that is trained to evil, have never kept themselves within due measure. He who betrays his lord, he who conceives foul devices, will be as great a snare to himself as to his friends. Whoso fosters a wolf in his house is thought to feed a thief and a pest for his own hearth."

*Grep.* "I did not, as thou thinkest, beguile the queen, but I was the guardian of her tender estate. She increased my fortunes, and her favour first brought me gifts and strength, and wealth and counsel."

*Erik.* "Lo, thy guilty disquiet lies heavy on thee; that man's freedom is safest whose mind remains untainted. Whoso asks a slave to be a friend, is deceived; often the henchman hurts his master."

At this Grep, shorn of his glibness of rejoinder, set spurs to his horse and rode away. Now when he reached home, he filled the palace with uproarious and vehement clamour; and shouting that he had been worsted in words, roused all his soldiers to fight, as though he would avenge by main force his luckless warfare of tongues.

For he swore that he would lay the host of the foreigners under the claws of eagles. But the king warned him that he should give his frenzy pause for counsel, that blind plans were commonly hurtful; that nothing could be done both cautiously and quickly at once; that headstrong efforts were the worst obstacle; and lastly, that it was unseemly to attack a handful with a host. Also, said he, the sagacious man was he who could bridle a raging spirit, and stop his frantic empetuosity in time. Thus the king forced the headlong rage of the young man to yield to reflection. But he could not wholly recall to self-control the frenzy of his heated mind, or prevent the champion of wrangles, abashed by his hapless debate, and finding armed vengeance refused him, from asking leave at least to try his sorceries by way of revenge. He gained his request, and prepared to go back to the shore with a chosen troop of wizards. So he first put on a pole the severed head of a horse that had been sacrificed to the gods, and setting sticks beneath displayed the jaws grinning agape; hoping that he would foil the first efforts of Erik by the horror of this wild spectacle. For he supposed that the silly souls of the barbarians would give away at the bogey of a protruding neck.

Erik was already on his road to meet them, and saw the head from afar off, and, understanding the whole foul contrivance, he bade his men keep silent and behave warily; no man was to be rash or hasty of speech, lest by some careless outburst they might give some opening to the sorceries; adding that if talking happened to be needed, he would speak for all. And they were now parted by

a river; when the wizards, in order to dislodge Erik from the approach to the bridge, set up close to the river, on their own side, the pole on which they had fixed the horse's head. Nevertheless Erik made dauntlessly for the bridge, and said: "On the bearer fall the ill-luck of what he bears! May a better issue attend our steps! Evil befall the evil-workers! Let the weight of the ominous burden crush the carrier! Let the better auguries bring us safety!" And it happened according to his prayer. For straightway the head was shaken off, the stick fell and crushed the bearer. And so all that array of sorceries was baffled at the bidding of a single curse, and extinguished.

Then, as Erik advanced a little, it came into his mind that strangers ought to fix on gifts for the king. So he carefully wrapped up in his robe a piece of ice which he happened to find, and managed to take it to the king 'by way of a present. But when they reached the palace he sought entrance first, and bade his brother follow close behind. Already the slaves of the king, in order to receive him with mockery as he entered, had laid a slippery hide on the threshold; and when Erik stepped upon it, they suddenly jerked it away by dragging a rope, and would have tripped him as he stood upon it, had not Roller, following behind, caught his brother on his breast as he tottered. So Erik, having half fallen, said that "bare was the back of the brotherless." And when Gunwar said that such a trick ought not to be permitted by a king, the king condemned the folly of the messenger who took no heed against treachery. And thus

he excused his flout by the heedlessness of the man he flouted.

Within the palace was blazing a fire, which the aspect of the season required: for it was now gone midwinter. By it, in different groups, sat the king on one side and the champions on the other. These latter, when Erik joined them, uttered gruesome sounds like things howling. The king stopped the clamour, telling them that the noises of wild beasts ought not to be in the breasts of men. Erik added, that it was the way of dogs, for all the others to set up barking when one started it; for all folk by their bearing betrayed their birth and revealed their race. But when Koll, who was the keeper of the gifts offered to the king, asked him whether he had brought any presents with him, he produced the ice which he had hidden in his breast. And when he had handed it to Koll across the hearth, he purposely let it go into the fire, as though it had slipped from the hand of the receiver. All present saw the shining fragment, and it seemed as though molten metal had fallen into the fire. Erik, maintaining that it had been jerked away by the carelessness of him who took it, asked what punishment was due to the loser of the gift.

The king consulted the opinion of the queen, who advised him not to relax the statute of the law which he had passed, whereby he gave warning that all who lost presents that were transmitted to him should be punished with death. Everyone else also said that the penalty by law appointed ought not to be remitted. And so the king, being counselled to allow the pun-

ishment as inevitable, gave leave for Koll to be hanged.

Then Frode began to accost Erik thus: "O thou, wantoning in insolent phrase, in boastful and bedizened speech, whence dost thou say that thou hast come hither, and why?"

Erik answered: "I came from Rennes Isle, and I took my seat by a stone."

Frode rejoined: "I ask, whither thou wentest next?"

Erik answered. "I went off from the stone riding on a beam, and often again took station by a stone."

Frode replied: "I ask thee whither thou next didst bend thy course, or where the evening found thee?"

Then said Erik: "Leaving a crag, I came to a rock, and likewise lay by a stone."

Frode said: "The boulders lay thick in those parts."

Erik answered: "Yet thicker lies the sand, plain to see."

Frode said: "Tell what thy business was, and whither thou struckest off thence."

Then said Erik: "Leaving the rock, as my ship ran on, I found a dolphin."

Frode said: "Now thou hast said something fresh, though both these things are common in the sea: but I would know what path took thee after that?"

Erik answered: "After a dolphin I went to a dolphin."

Frode said: "The herd of dolphins is somewhat common."

Then said Erik: "It does swim somewhat commonly on the waters."

Frode said: "I would fain know whither thou wert borne on thy toilsome journey after leaving the dolphins?"

Erik answered: "I soon came upon the trunk of a tree."

Frode rejoined: "Whither didst thou next pass on thy journey?"

Then said Erik: "From a trunk I passed on to a log."

Frode said: "That spot must be thick with trees, since thou art always calling the abodes of thy hosts by the name of trunks."

Erik replied: "There is a thicker place in the woods."

Frode went on: "Relate whither thou next didst bear thy steps."

Erik answered: "Oft again I made my way to the lopped timbers of the woods; but, as I rested there, wolves that were sated on human carcases licked the points of the spears. There a lance-head was shaken from the shaft of the king, and it was the grandson of Fridleif."

Frode said: "I am bewildered, and know not what to think about the dispute: for thou hast beguiled my mind with very dark riddling."

Erik answered: "Thou owest me the prize for this contest that is finished: for under a veil I have declared to thee certain things thou hast ill understood. For under the name I gave before of 'spear-point' I signified Odd, whom my hand had slain."

And when the queen also had awarded him the palm of eloquence and the prize for flow of speech, the king

straightway took a bracelet from his arm, and gave it to him as the appointed reward, adding: "I would fain learn from thyself thy debate with Grep, wherein he was not ashamed openly to avow himself vanquished."

Then said Erik: "He was smitten with shame for the adultery wherewith he was taxed; for since he could bring no defence, he confessed that he had committed it with thy wife."

The king turned to Hanund and asked her in what spirit she received the charge; and she not only confessed her guilt by a cry, but also put forth in her face a blushing signal of her sin, and gave manifest token of her fault. The king, observing not only her words, but also the signs of her countenance, but doubting with what sentence he should punish the criminal, let the queen settle by her own choice the punishment which her crime deserved. When she learnt that the sentence committed to her concerned her own guilt, she wavered awhile as she pondered how to appraise her transgression; but Grep sprang up and ran forward to tranfix Erik with a spear, wishing to buy off his own death by slaying the accuser. But Roller fell on him with drawn sword, and dealt him first the doom he had himself purposed.

Erik said: "The service of kin is best for the helpless."

And Roller said: "In sore needs good men should be dutifully summoned."

Then Frode said: "I think it will happen to you according to the common saying, 'that the striker sometimes has short joy of his stroke', and 'that the hand is seldom long glad of the smiting'."

Erik answered: "The man must not be impeached whose deed justice excuses. For my work is as far as from that of Grep, as an act of self-defence is from an attack upon another."

Then the brethren of Grep began to spring up and clamour and swear that they would either bring avengers upon the whole fleet of Erik, or would fight him and ten champions with him.

Erik said to them: "Sick men have to devise by craft some provision for their journey. He whose sword-point is dull should only probe things that are soft and tender. He who has a blunt knife must search out the ways to cut joint by joint. Since, therefore, it is best for a man in distress to delay the evil, and nothing is more fortunate in trouble than to stave off hard necessity, I ask three days' space to get ready, provided that I may obtain from the king the skin of a freshly slain ox."

Frode answered: "He who fell on a hide deserves a hide"; thus openly taunting the asker with his previous fall. But Erik, when the hide was given him, made some sandals, which he smeared with a mixture of tar and sand, in order to plant his steps the more firmly, and fitted them on to the feet of himself and his people. At last, having meditated what spot he should choose for the fight—for he said that he was unskilled in combat by land and in all warfare—he demanded it should be on the frozen sea. To this both sides agreed. The king granted a truce for preparations, and bade the sons of Westmar withdraw, saying that it was amiss that a guest, even if he had deserved ill should be driven from his lodging.

Then he went back to examine into the manner of the punishment, which he had left to the queen's own choice to exact. For she forebore to give judgment, and begged pardon for her slip. Erik added, that woman's errors must often be forgiven, and that punishment ought not to be inflicted, unless amendment were unable to get rid of her fault. So the king pardoned Hanund. As twilight drew near, Erik said: "With Gotar, not only are rooms provided when the soldiers are coming to feast at the banquet, but each is appointed a separate place and seat where he is to lie." Then the king gave up for their occupation the places where his own champions had sat; and next the servants brought the banquet. But Erik, knowing well the courtesy of the king, which made him forbid them to use up any of the meal that was left, cast away the piece of which he had tasted very little, calling whole portions broken bits of food. And so, as the dishes dwindled, the servants brought up fresh ones to the lacking and shamefaced guests, thus spending on a little supper what might have served for a great banquet.

So the king said: "Are the soldiers of Gotar wont to squander the meat after once touching it, as if it were so many pared-off crusts? And to spurn the first dishes as if they were the last morsels?"

Erik said: "Uncouthness claims no place in the manners of Gotar, neither does any disorderly habit feign there."

But Frode said: "Then thy manners are not those of thy lord, and thou hast proved that thou hast not taken all wisdom to heart. For he who goes against the exam-

288

ple of his elders shows himself a deserter and a rene-
gade."

Then said Erik: "The wise man must be taught by
the wiser. For knowledge grows by learning, and instruction is advanced by doctrine."

Frode rejoined: "This affectation of thine of super-
fluous words, what exemplary lesson will it teach me?"

Erik said: "A loyal few are a safer defence for a king
than many traitors."

Frode said to him: "Wilt thou then show us closer
allegiance than the rest?"

Erik answered: "No man ties the unborn (horse) to
the crib, or the unbegotten to the stall. For thou hast not
yet experienced all things. Besides, with Gotar there is
always a mixture of drinking with feasting; liquor, over
and above, and as well as meat, is the joy of the revel-
ler."

Frode said: "Never have I found a more shameless
beggar of meat and drink."

Erik replied: "Few reckon the need of the silent, or
measure the wants of him who holds his peace."

Then the king bade his sister bring forth the drink in
a great goblet. Erik caught hold of her right hand and
of the goblet she offered at the same time, and said:
"Noblest of kings, hath thy benignity granted me this
present? Dost thou assure me that what I hold shall
be mine as an irrevocable gift?"

The king, thinking that he was only asking for the
cup, declared it was a gift. But Erik drew the maiden
to him, as if she was given with the cup. When the

king saw it, he said: "A fool is shown by his deed; with us freedom of maidens is ever held inviolate."

Then Erik, feigning that he would cut off the girl's hand with his sword, as though it had been granted under the name of the cup, said: "If I have taken more than thou gavest, or if I am rash to keep the whole, let me at least get some." The king saw his mistake in his promise, and gave him the maiden, being loth to undo his heedlessness by fickleness, and that the weight of his pledge might seem the greater; though it is held an act more of ripe judgment than of unsteadfastness to take back a foolish promise.

Then, taking from Erik security that he would return, he sent him to the ships; for the time appointed for the battle was at hand. Erik and his men went on to the sea, then covered near with ice; and, thanks to the stability of their sandals, felled the enemy, whose footing was slippery and unsteady. For Frode had decreed that no man should help either side if it wavered or were distressed. Then he went back in triumph to the king. So Gotwar, sorrowing at the destruction of her children who had miserably perished, and eager to avenge them, announced that it would please her to have a flyting with Erik, on condition that she should gage a heavy necklace and he his life; so that if he conquered he should win gold, but if he gave in, death. Erik agreed to the contest, and the gage was deposited with Gunwar.

So Gotwar began thus:

"Quando tuam limas admissa cote bipennem,
Nonne terit tremulas mentula quassa nates?"

290

Erik rejoined:

"Ut cuivis natura pilos in corpore sevit,
    Omnis nempe suo barba ferenda loco est.
Re Veneris homines artus agitare necesse est;
    Motus quippe suos nam labor omnis habet.
Cum natis excipitur nate, vel cum subdita penem
    Vulva capit, quid ad haec addere mas renuit?"

Powerless to answer this, Gotwar had to give the gold to the man whom she had meant to kill, and thus wasted a lordly gift instead of punishing the slayer of her son. For her ill fate was crowned, instead of her ill-will being avenged. First bereaved, and then silenced by furious words, she lost at once her wealth and all reward of her eloquence. She made the man blest who had taken away her children, and enriched her bereaver with a present: and took away nothing to make up the slaughter of her sons save the reproach of ignorance and the loss of goods. Westmar, when he saw this, determined to attack the man by force, since he was the stronger of tongue, and laid down the condition that the reward of the conqueror should be the death of the conquered, so that the life of both parties was plainly at stake. Erik, unwilling to be thought quicker of tongue than of hand, did not refuse the terms.

Now the manner of combat was as follows. A ring, plaited of withy or rope, used to be offered to the combatants for them to drag away by wrenching it with a great effort of foot and hand; and the prize went to the stronger, for if either of the combatants could wrench it from the other, he was awarded the victory. Erik strug-

291

gled in this manner, and, grasping the rope sharply, wrested it out of the hands of his opponent. When Frode saw this, he said: "I think it is hard to tug at a rope with a strong man."

And Erik said: "Hard, at any rate, when a tumour is in the body or a hunch sits on the back."

And straightway, thrusting his foot forth, he broke the infirm neck and back of the old man, and crushed him. And so Westmar failed to compass his revenge: zealous to retaliate, he fell into the portion of those who need revenging; being smitten down even as those whose slaughter he had desired to punish.

Now Frode intended to pierce Erik by throwing a dagger at him. But Gunwar knew her brother's purpose, and said, in order to warn her betrothed of his peril, that no man could be wise who took no forethought for himself. This speech warned Erik to ward off the treachery, and he shrewdly understood the counsel of caution. For at once he sprang up and said that the glory of the wise man would be victorious, but that guile was its own punishment; thus censuring his treacherous intent in very gentle terms. But the king suddenly flung his knife at him, yet was too late to hit him; for he sprang aside, and the steel missed its mark and ran into the wall opposite. Then said Erik: "Gifts should be handed to friends, and not thrown; thou hadst made the present acceptable if thou hadst given the sheath to keep the blade company."

On this request the king at once took the sheath from his girdle and gave it to him, being forced to abate his hatred by the self-control of his foe. Thus he was molli-

fied by the prudent feigning of the other, and with goodwill gave him for his own the weapon which he had cast
with ill will. And thus Erik, by taking the wrong done
him in a dissembling manner, turned it into a favour,
accepting as a splendid gift the steel which had been
meant to slay him. For he put a generous complexion
on what Frode had done with intent to harm. Then they
gave themselves up to rest. In the night Gunwar awoke
Erik silently, and pointed out to him that they ought
to fly, saying that it was very expedient to return with
safe chariot ere harm was done. He went with her to
the shore, where he happened to find the king's fleet
beached: so, cutting away part of the sides, he made it
unseaworthy, and by again replacing some laths he
patched it so that the damage might be unnoticed by
those who looked at it. Then he caused the vessel whither
he and his company had retired to put off a little from
the shore.

*Continuation of Book V. in Vol. II.*